ACCOUNTING
The Language of Business

EIGHTH EDITION

Roman L. Weil, Ph.D., CPA, CMA
University of Chicago

Clyde P. Stickney, D.B.A., CPA
Dartmouth College

Sidney Davidson, Ph.D., CPA
University of Chicago

THOMAS HORTON AND DAUGHTERS
26662 S. New Town Drive • Sun Lakes, Arizona 85248

For Our Children

ISBN 0-913878-47-2

Library of Congress Cataloging in Publication Data

Weil, Roman L. 1940-
   Accounting: the language of business, eighth edition

1. Accounting-Terminology.   2. Accounting.

I. Stickney, Clyde P., 1944-   joint author.

II. Davidson, Sidney, 1919-   joint author.

III. Title.

   HF5621.D28   657.03   90-5974

Typography by Publication Services
Printed by Bookcrafters, Inc.

Preface

Business increases in importance. Accounting is the language of business. Understanding accounting, therefore, increases in importance. We hope this book will assist the student in becoming familiar with the language required to understand business communications. The first edition appeared in 1974. Since that time feedback from readers about the contents of the book has enabled us to refine the presentation—adding here, deleting there—to suit the wishes of teacher and students as well as those earning a living in business. Although some of the material here will seem too advanced for the beginner, we think the book has something cost-effective for all interested in business.

WE ARE PROFIT-ORIENTED and are eager to learn from you how we can make the book more successful. We will pay the first person who makes a given suggestion incorporated in subsequent editions. Such suggestions might include typographical errors ($1), additional cross references ($1), errors of fact or substance ($5), and additional terms with their explanation ($5).
This edition contains the following sections.

Glossary. Accounting's vocabulary comprises many words that have other meanings in ordinary usage. Understanding the concepts and using accounting reports require that the reader know how to interpret the words used and their special meaning. Students of accounting and readers of accounting reports will find the tasks easier the sooner they learn, for example, the difference between the meanings of *revenue* and *receipt*, between *fund* and *reserve*. The Glossary defines these and some 1,400 other terms. A glossary is not a dictionary, so that we have given definitions of terms only as accounting uses them.

Students and readers of financial reports will not encounter all the terms in the Glossary. We have tried to include, however, the terms found in textbooks, problems, financial reports, financial periodicals, and newspapers.

The Glossary defines many words and phrases in terms of other entries in the Glossary. Terms in a given definition themselves explained elsewhere are *italicized*. Many of the entries in the Glossary are multiple-word phrases because much of the specialized terminology of accounting depends upon such phrases. We have tried to anticipate the most likely phrase that will occur to the reader and have used that phrase in the Glossary. Nevertheless, we probably have failed in some cases to put the explanation by the word or phrase that occurs to you. As Jim Schindler (our co-author before his death) used to say, "if you can't find what you're looking for under one listing, keep looking under others."

Words and phrases are alphabetized using the word-by-word principle. Thus, the following terms appear in the order shown: *account, account form, account payable, accountancy, accounting, accounting standards, accounts receivable turnover.*

A few words in accounting, for example *cost* and *expense*, mean different things to different people. We believe that the more precise the meaning of the words used, the easier is the understanding of accounting. Consequently, we give the restricted definition, for example, of cost that we think enhances the user's ability to understand. We also give the variants in meaning often used in practice. Further, certain terms used widely in the accounting profession, for example, *prepaid expenses* seem to us to be oxymorons given our preference for restricted and unambiguous definitions.

Penn Central Transportation Company's Balance Sheet Just Before Its Bankruptcy. One of the most widely known bankruptcies, and one of the largest, was that of Penn Central. We reproduce the balance sheet so that the reader can see the limitations of analyzing the stockholders' equity section of the balance sheet in forecasting bankruptcy. The annual report shows retained earnings of almost half a billion dollars and stockholders' equity of almost $2 billion. Yet soon after the report appeared, the company petitioned for bankruptcy because it could not meet its obligations.

General Electric Company's Annual Report. GE's annual report is consistently among the best published. We reproduce GE's annual report issued in 1990 along with our own comments and notes which should help in understanding it, and, we hope, other financial statements as well.

Accounting Magic. This example shows how generally accepted accounting principles allow such a range of accounting treatments that two firms, exactly alike in all respects except for their accounting methods, report drastically different incomes.

Pronouncements Governing Generally Accepted Accounting Principles. We include a list of pronouncements governing generally accepted accounting principles and their dates of issuance.

We gratefully acknowledge the permission of Harcourt, Bruce Jovanovich, Inc to reproduce material from our *Financial Accounting* and *Managerial Accounting* texts they publish. Publication Services, Tempe, AZ, Jennifer Colleton, and Eli Worman designed the book and planned the layout. We thank them for their help.

Table of Contents

Glossary 5

Annual Report of the General Electric Company 98

Balance Sheet for a Company Approaching Bankruptcy 133

Accounting Magic 136

Pronouncements Governing Generally Accepted Accounting Principles 142

Glossary

The definitions of many words and phrases in the Glossary use other words and phrases. We *italicize* terms in a given definition (definiens) that themselves (or variants thereof) appear elsewhere under their own listings (as definienda). The cross references generally take one of two forms:

[1] *Accounting Series Release.* *ASR.* See *SEC.*
[2] **accounting standards.** *Accounting principles.*

Form [1] refers you to another term for discussion of this term (definiendum). Form [2] tells you that this term (definiendum) is synonymous with the italicized term, which you can consult for discussion if necessary.

A

AAA. *American Accounting Association.*

Abacus. A scholarly journal containing articles on theoretical aspects of accounting. Published twice a year by the Sydney University Press, Sydney, Australia.

abatement. A complete or partial cancellation of a levy imposed by a government unit.

ABC. *Activity-based costing.*

abnormal spoilage. Actual spoilage exceeding that expected when operations are normally efficient. Usual practice treats this cost as an *expense* of the period rather than as a *product cost.* Contrast with *normal spoilage.*

aboriginal cost. In public utility accounting, the *acquisition cost* of an *asset* incurred by the first *entity* devoting that asset to public use. Most public utility regulation is based on aboriginal cost. If it were not, then public utilities could exchange assets among themselves at ever-increasing prices in order to raise the rate base and, then, prices based thereon.

absorbed overhead. *Overhead* costs allocated to individual products at some *overhead rate.* Also called *applied overhead.*

absorption costing. See *full absorption costing.*

Accelerated Cost Recovery System. ACRS. A form of *accelerated depreciation* enacted by the Congress in 1981 and amended in 1986. The system provides percentages of the asset's cost to be depreciated each year for tax purposes. *Salvage value* is ignored. These amounts are generally not used for *financial accounting.*

accelerated depreciation. Any method of calculating *depreciation* charges where the charges become progressively smaller each period. Examples are *double-declining-balance* and *sum-of-the-years'-digits* methods.

acceptance. A written promise to pay that is equivalent to a *promissory* note.

account. Any device for accumulating additions and subtractions relating to a single *asset, liability, owners' equity* item, including *revenues* and *expenses.*

account analysis method. A method of separating *fixed* from *variable costs* involving the classification of the various *product cost accounts.* For example, *direct labor* and *direct material* are classified as variable and *depreciation* on the factory building as fixed.

account form. The form of *balance sheet* where *assets* are shown on the left and *equities* are shown on the right. Contrast with *report form.* See also *T-account.*

5

account payable. A *liability* representing an amount owed to a *creditor*, usually arising from purchase of *merchandise* or materials and supplies; not necessarily due or past due. Normally, a *current* liability.

account receivable. A claim against a *debtor* usually arising from sales or services rendered; not necessarily due or past due. Normally, a *current* asset.

accountability center. *Responsibility center.*

accountancy. The British word for *accounting*. In the United States, it means the theory and practice of accounting.

accountant's comments. Canada. A written communication issued by a public accountant at the conclusion of a review engagement. It consists of a description of the work performed and a statement that, under the terms of the engagement, the accountant has not performed an audit and consequently expresses no opinion. (Compare *auditor's report; denial of opinion.*)

Accountants' Index. A publication of the *AICPA* that indexes, in detail, the accounting literature of the period

accountant's opinion. *Auditor's report.*

accountant's report. *Auditor's report.*

accounting. An *information system* conveying information about a specific *entity*. The information is in financial terms and is restricted to information that can be made reasonably precise. The *AICPA* defines accounting as a service activity whose "function is to provide quantitative information, primarily financial in nature, about economic entities that is intended to be useful in making economic decisions."

accounting changes. As defined by *APB Opinion No. 20*, a change in (a) an *accounting principle* (such as a switch from *FIFO* to *LIFO* or from *sum-of-the-years'-digits* to *straight-line depreciation*), (b) an accounting estimate (such as estimated useful lives or salvage value of depreciable assets and estimates of *warranty* costs or *uncollectible accounts*), and (c) the reporting *entity*. Changes of type (a) should be disclosed. The cumulative effect of the change on *retained earnings* at the start of the period during which the change was made should be included in reported earnings for the period of change. Changes of type (b) should be treated as affecting only the period of change and, if necessary, future periods. The reasons for changes of type (c) should be disclosed and, in statements reporting on operations of the period of the change, the effect of the change on all other periods reported on for comparative purposes should also be shown. In some cases (such as a change from *LIFO* to other inventory *flow assumptions* or in the method of accounting for long-term construction contracts), changes of type (a) are treated like changes of type (c). That is, for these changes

all statements shown for prior periods must be restated to show the effect of adopting the change for those periods as well. See *all-inclusive concept* and *accounting errors.*

accounting conventions. Methods or procedures used in accounting. This term tends to be used when the method or procedure has not been given official authoritative sanction by a pronouncement of a group such as the *APB, EITF, FASB,* or *SEC.* Contrast with *accounting principles.*

accounting cycle. The sequence of accounting procedures starting with *journal entries* for various transactions and events and ending with the *financial statements* or, perhaps, the *post-closing trial balance.*

accounting deficiency. Canada. A failure to adhere to generally accepted *accounting principles* or to disclose essential information in *financial statements.*

accounting entity. See *entity.*

accounting equation. *Assets = Equities. Assets = Liabilities + Owners' Equity.*

accounting errors. Arithmetic errors and misapplication of *accounting principles* in previously published financial statements that are corrected in the current period with direct *debits* or *credits* to *retained earnings.* In this regard, they are treated like *prior-period adjustments,* but, technically, they are not classified by *APB Opinion No. 9* as prior-period adjustments. See *accounting changes* and contrast with changes in accounting estimates as described there.

accounting event. Any occurrence that is recorded in the accounting records.

accounting methods. *Accounting principles.* Procedures for carrying out accounting principles.

accounting period. The time period for which *financial statements* that measure *flows,* such as the *income statement* and the *statement of cash flows,* are prepared. Should be clearly identified on the financial statements. See *interim statements.*

accounting policies. *Accounting principles* adopted by a specific *entity.*

accounting principles. The methods or procedures used in accounting for events reported in the *financial statements.* This term tends to be used when the method or procedure has been given official authoritative sanction by a pronouncement of a group such as the *APB, EITF, FASB,* or *SEC.* Contrast with *accounting conventions* and *conceptual framework.*

Accounting Principles Board.   See *APB*.

accounting procedures.   See *accounting principles*; however, this term usually refers to the methods for implementing accounting principles.

accounting rate of return.   Income for a period divided by average investment during the period. Based on income, rather than discounted cash flows and, hence, is a poor decision making aid or tool. See *ratio*.

Accounting Research Bulletin. **ARB.**   The name of the official pronouncements of the former *Committee on Accounting Procedure* of the *AICPA*. Fifty-one bulletins were issued between 1939 and 1959. *ARB No. 43* summarizes the first forty-two bulletins.

Accounting Research Study. **ARS.**   One of a series of studies published by the Director of Accounting Research of the *AICPA* "designed to provide professional accountants and others interested in the development of accounting with a discussion and documentation of accounting problems." Fifteen such studies were published between 1961 and 1974.

The Accounting Review.   Scholarly publication of the *American Accounting Association*.

Accounting Series Release. **ASR.**   See *SEC*.

accounting standards.   *Accounting principles*.

Accounting Standards Executive Committee. AcSEC.   The senior technical committee of the *AICPA* authorized to speak for the AICPA in the areas of *financial accounting* and reporting as well as *cost accounting*.

accounting system.   The procedures for collecting and summarizing financial data in a firm.

Accounting Terminology Bulletin. **ATB.**   One of four releases of the Committee on Terminology of the *AICPA* issued in the period 1953-1957.

Accounting Trends and Techniques.   An annual publication of the *AICPA* that surveys the reporting practices of 600 large corporations. It presents tabulations of specific practices, terminology, and disclosures along with illustrations taken from individual annual reports.

accounts receivable turnover.   Net *sales on account* divided by average *accounts receivable*. See *ratio*.

accretion.   See *amortization*. When a *book value* grows over time, such as a *bond* originally issued at a *discount*, the correct technical term is "accretion," not "amortization." Also, increase in economic worth through physical change,

usually said of a natural resource such as an orchard, caused by natural growth. Contrast with *appreciation*.

accrual.   Recognition of an *expense (or revenue)* and the related *liability (or asset)* that is caused by an *accounting event*, frequently by the passage of time, and that is not signaled by an explicit cash transaction. For example, the recognition of interest expense or revenue (or wages, salaries, or rent) at the end of a period even though no explicit cash transaction is made at that time. Cash flow follows accounting recognition; contrast with *deferral*.

accrual basis of accounting.   The method of recognizing *revenues* as *goods* are sold (or delivered) and as *services* are rendered, independent of the time when cash is received. *Expenses* are recognized in the period when the related revenue is recognized independent of the time when cash is paid out. *SFAC No. 1* says "accrual accounting attempts to record the financial effects on an enterprise of transactions and other events and circumstances that have cash consequences for the enterprise in the periods in which those transactions, events, and circumstances occur rather than only in the periods in which cash is received or paid by the enterprise." Contrast with the *cash basis of accounting*. See *accrual* and *deferral*. The basis would more correctly be called "accrual/deferral" accounting.

accrued.   Said of a *revenue (expense)* that has been earned (recognized) even though the related *receivable (payable)* is not yet due. This adjective should not be used as part of an account title. Thus, we prefer to use Interest Receivable (Payable) as the account title, rather than Accrued Interest Receivable (Payable). See *matching convention*. See *accrual*.

accrued depreciation.   An incorrect term for *accumulated depreciation*. Acquiring an asset with cash, capitalizing it, and then amortizing its cost over periods of use is a process of *deferral* and allocation, not of *accrual*.

accrued payable.   A *payable* usually resulting from the passage of time. For example, *salaries* and *interest* accrue as time passes. See *accrued*.

accrued receivable.   A *receivable* usually resulting from the passage of time. See *accrued*.

accumulated benefit obligation.   See *projected benefit obligation* for definition and contrast.

accumulated depreciation.   A preferred title for the *contra-asset* account that shows the sum of *depreciation* charges on an asset since it was acquired. Other titles used are *allowance* for *depreciation* (acceptable term) and *reserve* for *depreciation* (unacceptable term).

accurate presentation.   The qualitative accounting objective suggesting that information reported in financial statements should correspond as precisely as possible with the economic effects underlying transactions and events. See *fair presentation* and *full disclosure*.

acid test ratio. *Quick ratio.*

acquisition cost. Of an *asset*, the net *invoice* price plus all *expenditures* to place and ready the asset for its intended use. The other expenditures might include legal fees, transportation charges, and installation costs.

ACRS. *Accelerated Cost Recovery System.*

AcSEC. *Accounting Standards Executive Committee* of the *AICPA*.

activity accounting. *Responsibility accounting.*

activity-based costing. ABC. Method of assigning *indirect* costs, including non-manufacturing overhead, to products and services. ABC assumes that almost all overhead costs associate with activities within the firm and vary with respect to the *drivers* of those activities. Some practitioners suggest that one goal of ABC is to find the drivers for all indirect costs; these people note that in the long run, all costs are *variable*, so there need be no *fixed* indirect costs

activity-based depreciation. *Production method of depreciation.*

activity basis. *Costs* are *variable* or *fixed* (*incremental* or *unavoidable*) with respect to some activity, such as production of units (or the undertaking of some new project). This activity is referred to as the "activity basis."

actual cost (basis). *Acquisition* or *historical cost*. Also contrast with *standard cost*.

actual costing (system). Method of allocating costs to products using actual *direct materials*, actual *direct labor*, and actual *factory overhead*. Contrast with *normal costing* and *standard cost system*.

actuarial. Usually said of computations or analyses that involve both *compound interest* and probabilities, such as the computation of the *present value* of a life-contingent *annuity*. Sometimes the term is used if only one of the two is involved.

actuarial accrued liability. A 1981 report of the Joint Committee on Pension Terminology (of various actuarial societies) stated that this term is the preferred one for *prior service cost*.

ad valorem. A method of levying a tax or duty on goods by using their estimated value as the tax base.

additional paid-in capital. An alternative acceptable title for the *capital contributed in excess of par (or stated) value account*.

additional processing cost. *Costs* incurred in processing *joint products* after the *splitoff point*.

adequate disclosure. *Fair presentation* of *financial statements* requires *disclosure* of *material* items. This *auditing standard* does not, however, require publicizing all information detrimental to a company. For example, the company may be threatened with a lawsuit and disclosure might seem to require a *debit* to a *loss* account and a *credit* to an *estimated liability*. But the mere making of this entry might adversely affect the actual outcome of the suit. Such entries need not be made although impending suits should be disclosed.

adjunct account. An *account* that accumulates additions to another account. For example, Premium on Bonds Payable is adjunct to the liability Bonds Payable; the effective liability is the sum of the two account balances at a given date. Contrast with *contra account*.

adjusted acquisition (historical) cost. Sometimes said of the *book value* of a *plant asset*. Also, cost adjusted to a *constant dollar* amount to reflect *general price level changes*.

adjusted bank balance of cash. The *balance* shown on the statement from the bank plus or minus amounts, such as for unrecorded deposits or outstanding checks, to reconcile the bank's balance with the correct cash balance. See *adjusted book balance of cash*.

adjusted basis. The *basis* used to compute gain or loss on disposition of an *asset* for tax purposes. Also, see *book value*.

adjusted book balance of cash. The *balance* shown in the firm's account for cash in bank plus or minus amounts, such as for *notes* collected by the bank or bank service charges, to reconcile the account balance with the correct cash balance. See *adjusted bank balance of cash*.

adjusted trial balance. *Trial balance* taken after *adjusting entries* but before *closing entries*. Contrast with *pre-* and *post-closing trial balances*. See *unadjusted trial balance* and *post-closing trial balance*. See also *work sheet*.

adjusting entry. An entry made at the end of an *accounting period* to record a *transaction* or other *accounting event*, which for some reason has not been recorded or has been improperly recorded during the accounting period. An entry to update the accounts. See *work sheet*.

adjustment. A change in an *account* produced by an *adjusting entry*. Sometimes the term is used to refer to the process of restating *financial statement* amounts to *constant dollars*.

administrative expense. An *expense* related to the enterprise as a whole as contrasted to expenses related to more specific functions such as manufacturing or selling.

admission of partner. Legally, when a new partner joins a *partnership*, the old partnership is dissolved and a new one comes into being. In practice, however, the old accounting records may be kept in use and the accounting entries reflect the manner in which the new partner joined the firm. If the new partner merely purchases the interest of another partner, the only accounting is to change the name for one capital account. If the new partner contributes *assets* and *liabilities* to the partnership, then the new assets must be recognized with debits and the liabilities and other source of capital, with credits. See *bonus method*.

ADR. See *asset depreciation range*.

advances from (by) customers. A preferred title for the *liability* account representing *receipts* of *cash* in advance of delivering the *goods* or rendering the *service* (that will cause *revenue* to be recognized). Sometimes called "deferred revenue" or "deferred income."

advances to affiliates. *Loans* by a parent company to a *subsidiary*. Frequently combined with "investment in subsidiary" as "investments and advances to subsidiary" and shown as a *noncurrent asset* on the parent's *balance sheet*. These advances are eliminated in *consolidated financial statements*.

advances to suppliers. A preferred term for the *asset account* representing *disbursements* of cash in advance of receiving *assets* or *services*.

adverse opinion. An *auditor's report* stating that the financial statements are not fair or are not in accord with *GAAP*.

affiliated company. Said of a company controlling or controlled by another company.

after closing. *Post-closing*; said of a *trial balance* at the end of the period.

after cost. Said of *expenditures* to be made subsequent to *revenue* recognition. For example, *expenditures* for *repairs* under warranty are after costs. Proper recognition of after costs involves a debit to expense at the time of the sale and a credit to an *estimated liability*. When the liability is discharged, the debit is to the estimated liability and the credit is to the assets consumed.

AG; Aktiengesellschaft. Germany. The form of a German company whose shares can trade on the stock exchange.

agency fund. An account for *assets* received by governmental units in the capacity of trustee or agent.

agency theory. A branch of economics relating the behavior of *principals* (such as owner non-managers or bosses) and their *agents* (such as nonowner managers or subordinates). The principal assigns responsibility and authority to the agent but the agent has his or her own risks and preferences different from those of the principal. The principal is unable to observe all activities of the agent. Both the principal and the agent must consider the differing risks and preferences in designing incentive contracts.

agent. One authorized to transact business, including executing contracts, for another.

aging accounts receivable. The process of classifying *accounts receivable* by the time elapsed since the claim came into existence for the purpose of estimating the amount of uncollectible accounts receivable as of a given date. See *sales contra, estimated uncollectibles* and *allowance for uncollectibles*.

aging schedule. A listing of *accounts receivable*, classified by age, used in *aging accounts receivable*.

AICPA. American Institute of Certified Public Accountants. The national organization that represents *CPAs*. See *AcSEC*. It oversees the writing and grading of the Uniform CPA Examination. Each state, however, sets its own requirements for becoming a CPA in that state. See *certified public accountant*.

all-capital earnings rate. *Rate of return on assets*.

all-inclusive (income) concept. Under this concept, no distinction is drawn between *operating* and *nonoperating revenues* and *expenses*; thus the only entries to retained earnings are for *net income* and *dividends*. Under this concept all *income, gains*, and *losses* are reported in the *income statement*; thus, events usually reported as *prior-period adjustments* and as *corrections of errors* are included in net income. This concept in its pure form is not the basis of *GAAP*, but *APB Opinions Nos. 9 and 30* move far in this direction. They do permit retained earnings entries for prior-period adjustments and correction of errors.

allocate. To spread a *cost* from one *account* to several accounts, to several products, or activities, or to several periods.

allocation base. *Joint costs* are assigned to *cost objectives* in some systematic fashion. The allocation base specifies the fashion. For example, the cost of a truck might be assigned to periods based on miles driven during the period; the allocation base is miles. Or, the cost of a factory supervisor might be assigned to product based on *direct labor* hours; the allocation base is direct labor hours.

allocation of income taxes. See *deferred income tax.*

allowance. A balance sheet *contra account* generally used for *receivables* and depreciable assets. See *sales* (or *purchase*) *allowance* for another use of this term.

allowance for funds used during construction. One principle of public utility regulation and rate setting is that customers should pay the full costs of producing the services (e.g., electricity) that they use, and nothing less. Thus an electric utility is even more careful than other businesses to capitalize into an *asset account* the full costs, but no more, of producing a new electric power generating plant. One of the costs of building a new plant is the *interest* cost on money tied up during construction. If *funds* are explicitly borrowed by an ordinary business, the journal entry for interest of $1,000 is typically:

Interest Expense...................	1,000	
Interest Payable		1,000
Interest expense for the period.		

If the firm is constructing a new plant, then another entry would be made capitalizing interest into the plant-under-construction account:

Construction Work in Progress	750	
Interest Expense		750
Capitalize relevant portion of interest relating to construction work in progress into the asset account.		

The cost of the *plant asset* is increased; when the plant is used, *depreciation* is charged; the interest will become an expense through the depreciation process in the later periods of use, not currently as the interest is paid. Thus the full cost of the electricity generated during a given period is reported as expense in that period. But suppose, as is common, that the electric utility does not explicitly borrow the funds, but uses some of its own funds, including funds raised from equity issues as well as from debt. Even though there is no explicit interest expense, there is the *opportunity cost* of the funds. Put another way, the cost of the plant under construction is not less in an economic sense just because the firm used its own cash, rather than borrowing. The public utility using its own funds, on which $750 of interest would be payable if the funds had been explicitly borrowed, will make the following entry:

Construction Work in Progress	750	
Allowance for Funds Used		
During Construction		750
Recognition of interest, an opportunity cost, on own funds used.		

The allowance account is a form of *revenue*, to appear on the income statement, and will be closed to Retained Earnings, increasing it. On the *funds statement*, it is an income or revenue item not producing funds and so must be subtracted from net income in deriving *funds provided by operations. SFAS No. 34* specifically prohibits nonutility companies from capitalizing the opportunity cost (interest) on own funds used into plant under construction.

allowance for uncollectibles (accounts receivable). A *contra* to Accounts Receivable that shows the estimated amount of *accounts receivable* that will not be collected. When such an allowance is used, the actual *write-off* of specific accounts receivable (*debit* allowance, *credit* specific account) does not affect *revenue* or *expense* at the time of the write off. The revenue reduction is recognized when *bad debt expense* is *debited* and the allowance is credited; the amount of the credit to the allowance may be based on a percentage of sales on account for a period of time or computed from *aging accounts receivable.* This contra account enables an estimate to be shown of the amount of receivables that will be collected without identifying specific uncollectible accounts. See *allowance method.*

allowance method. A method of attempting to *match* all *expenses* of a transaction with its associated *revenues.* Usually involves a debit to expense and a credit to an *estimated liability*, such as for estimated warranty expenditures, or a debit to a revenue (*contra*) account and a credit to an asset (*contra*) account, such as in some firms' accounting for uncollectible accounts. See *allowance for uncollectibles* for further explanation. When the allowance method is used for *sales discounts*, sales are recorded at *gross invoice* prices (not reduced by the amounts of discounts made available). An estimate of the amount of discounts to be taken is debited to a *revenue contra account* and *credited* to an allowance account, shown contra to *accounts receivable.*

American Accounting Association. AAA. An organization primarily for academic accountants, but open to all interested in accounting. It publishes *The Accounting Review.*

American Institute of Certified Public Accountants. See *AICPA.*

American Stock Exchange. AMEX. ASE. A public market where various corporate *securities* are traded.

AMEX. *American Stock Exchange.*

amortization. Strictly speaking, the process of liquidating or extinguishing ("bringing to death") a *debt* with a series of payments to the *creditor* (or to a *sinking fund*). From that usage has evolved a related use involving the accounting for the payments themselves: "amortization schedule" for a mortgage which is a table showing the allocation between *interest* and *principle.* The term has come to mean writing off ("liquidating") the cost of an asset. In this context it means the general process of *allocating acquisition cost* of an asset to either the periods of benefit as *expenses* or to *inventory* accounts as *product costs*. Called *depreciation* for *plant assets*, *depletion* for *wasting assets* (natural resources), and "amortization" for *intangibles*. *SFAC No. 6* refers to amortization as "the accounting process of reducing an amount by periodic payments or write-downs." The expressions "unamortized debt discount or premium" and "to amortize debt discount or premium" relate to *accruals*, not to *deferrals*. The expressions "amortization of long-term assets" and "to amortize long-term assets" refer to deferrals, not accruals. Contrast with *accretion*.

analysis of variances. See *variance analysis*.

annual report. A report for shareholders and other interested parties prepared once a year, includes a *balance sheet*, an *income statement*, a *statement of cash flows*, a reconciliation of changes in *owners' equity* accounts, a *summary of significant accounting principles*, other explanatory *notes*, the *auditor's report*, and, comments from management about the year's events. See *10-K* and *financial statements*.

annuitant. One who receives an *annuity*.

annuity. A series of payments, usually made at equally spaced time intervals.

annuity certain. An *annuity* payable for a definite number of periods. Contrast with *contingent annuity*.

annuity due. An *annuity* whose first payment is made at the start of period 1 (or at the end of period 0). Contrast with *annuity in arrears*.

annuity in advance. An *annuity due*.

annuity in arrears. An *ordinary annuity* whose first payment occurs at the end of the first period.

annuity method of depreciation. See *compound interest depreciation*.

antidilutive. Said of a *potentially dilutive security* that will increase *earnings per share* if it is *exercised* or *converted* into common stock. In computing *primary* and *fully diluted earnings per share*, antidilutive securities may not be assumed to be exercised or converted and hence do not increase reported earnings per share in a given period.

APB. Accounting Principles Board of the *AICPA*. It set *accounting principles* from 1959 through 1973, issuing 31 *APB Opinions* and 4 *APB statements*. It was superseded by the *FASB*.

APB Opinion. The name given to pronouncements of the *APB* that make up much of *generally accepted accounting principles*; there are 31 *APB Opinions*, issued from 1962 through 1973.

APB Statement. The *APB* issued four *Statements* between 1962 and 1970. The *Statements* were approved by at least two thirds of the Board, but they are recommendations, not requirements. For example, *Statement No. 3* (1969) suggested the publication of *constant dollar financial statements* but did not require them.

APBs. An abbreviation used for *APB Opinions*.

applied cost. A *cost* that has been *allocated* to a department, product, or activity; need not be based on actual costs incurred.

applied overhead. *Overhead costs* charged to departments, products or activities. Also called *absorbed overhead*.

appraisal. The process of obtaining a valuation for an *asset* or *liability* that involves expert opinion rather than evaluation of explicit market transactions.

appraisal method of depreciation. The periodic *depreciation* charge is the difference between the beginning and end-of-period appraised value of the *asset* if that difference is positive. If negative, there is no charge. Not based on *historical cost* nor, hence, generally accepted.

appreciation. An increase in economic worth caused by rising market prices for an *asset*. Contrast with *accretion*.

appropriated retained earnings. See *retained earnings, appropriated*.

appropriation. In governmental accounting, an *expenditure* authorized for a specified amount, purpose, and time.

appropriation account. In governmental accounting, an account set up to record specific authorizations to spend; it is credited with appropriation amounts. *Expenditures* during the period and *encumbrances* outstanding at the end of the period are closed (debited) to this account at the end of the period.

approximate net realizable value method. A method of assigning joint costs to *joint products* based on revenues minus *additional processing costs* of the end products.

ARB. *Accounting Research Bulletin*.

arbitrage. Strictly speaking, the simultaneous purchase in one market and sale in another of a *security* or commodity in hope of making a *profit* on price differences in the different markets. Often this term is loosely used when the item sold is somewhat different from the item purchased; for example, the sale of shares of *common stock* and the simultaneous purchase of a *convertible bond* that is convertible into identical common shares.

arm's length. Said of a transaction negotiated by unrelated parties, each acting in his or her own self-interest; the basis for a *fair market value* determination.

arrears. Said of *cumulative preferred stock dividends* that have not been declared up to the current date. See *annuity in arrears* for another context.

ARS. *Accounting Research Study.*

articles of incorporation. Document filed with state authorities by persons forming a corporation. When the document is returned with a certificate of incorporation, it becomes the corporation's *charter*.

articulate. Said of the relationship between any operating statement (for example, *income statement* or *statement of cash flows*) and *comparative balance sheets*, where the operating statement explains (or reconciles) the change in some major balance sheet category (for example, *retained earnings* or *working capital*).

ASE. *American Stock Exchange.*

ASR. *Accounting Series Release.*

assess. To value property for the purpose of property taxation; the assessment is computed by the taxing authority. To levy a charge on the owner of property for improvements thereto, such as for sewers or sidewalks.

assessed valuation. A dollar amount for real estate or other property used by a government as a basis for levying taxes. The amount may or may not bear some relation to *market value*.

asset. *SFAC No. 6* defines assets as "probable future economic benefits obtained or controlled by a particular entity as a result of past transactions. . . . An asset has three essential characteristics: (a) it embodies a probable future benefit that involves a capacity, singly or in combination with other assets, to contribute directly or indirectly to future net cash inflows, (b) a particular entity can obtain the benefit and control others' access to it, and (c) the transaction or other event giving rise to the entity's right to or control of the benefit has already occurred." A footnote points out that "probable" means that which can be reasonably expected or believed but is neither certain nor proved. May be *tangible* or *intangible*, *short-term* (current) or *long-term* (noncurrent).

asset depreciation range. ADR. The range of *depreciable lives* allowed by the *Internal Revenue Service* for a specific depreciable *asset*.

asset turnover. Net sales divided by average assets. See *ratio*.

assignment of accounts receivable. Transfer of the legal ownership of an *account receivable* through its sale. Contrast with *pledging* accounts receivable where the receivables serve as *collateral* for a *loan*.

ATB. *Accounting Terminology Bulletin.*

at par. Said of a *bond* or *preferred stock* issued or selling at its *face amount*.

attachment. The laying claim to the *assets* of a borrower or debtor by a lender or creditor when the borrower has failed to pay debts on time.

attest. Rendering of an *opinion* by an auditor that the *financial statements* are fair. This procedure is called the "attest function" of the CPA. See *fair presentation*.

attribute measured. When making physical measurements, such as of a person, one needs to decide the units with which to measure, such as inches or centimeters or pounds or grams. One chooses the attribute height or weight independently of the measuring unit English or metric. In conventional accounting the attribute measured is *historical cost* and the measuring unit is *nominal dollars*. Some theorists argue that accounting is more useful when the attribute measured is *current cost*. Others argue that accounting is more useful when the measuring unit is *constant dollars*. We think, as do others, that both changes from conventional accounting should be made. The attribute historical cost can be measured in nominal dollars or in constant dollars. The attribute current cost can also be measured in nominal dollars or constant dollars. Choosing between two attributes and two measuring units implies four different accounting systems. Each of these four has its uses.

attribute(s) sampling. The use of sampling technique in which each item selected is assessed on the basis of whether it has a particular qualitative characteristic in order to determine the rate of occurrence of this characteristic in the population. See also *estimation sampling*. Compare *variables sampling*.

audit. Systematic inspection of accounting records involving analyses, tests, and *confirmations*. See *internal audit*.

audit committee. A committee of the board of directors of a *corporation* usually consisting of outside directors who nominate the independent auditors and discuss the auditors' work with them. If the auditors believe certain matters should be brought to the attention of shareholders, the auditors first bring these matters to the attention of the audit committee.

Audit Guides.   See *Industry Audit Guides.*

audit program.   The procedures followed by the *auditor* in carrying out the *audit.*

audit trail.   A reference accompanying an *entry,* or *posting,* to an underlying source record or document. A good audit trail is essential for efficiently checking the accuracy of accounting entries. See *cross-reference.*

Auditing Research Monograph.   Publication series of the *AICPA.*

auditing standards.   A set of ten standards promulgated by the *AICPA,* including three general standards, three standards of field work, and four standards of reporting. According to the AICPA, these standards "deal with the measures of the quality of the performance and the objectives to be attained," rather than with specific auditing procedures.

Auditing Standards Advisory Council.   An *AICPA* committee.

Auditing Standards Board.   Operating committee of the *AICPA* promulgating auditing rules.

auditor.   One who checks the accuracy, fairness, and general acceptability of accounting records and statements and then *attests* to them.

auditor's opinion.   *Auditor's report.*

auditor's report.   The auditor's statement of the work done and an opinion of the *financial statements.* Opinions are usually unqualified ("clean"), but may be *qualified,* or the auditor may disclaim an opinion in the report. Often called the "accountant's report." See *adverse opinion.*

AudSEC.   The former Auditing Standards Executive Committee of the *AICPA,* now functioning as the *Auditing Standards Board.*

authorized capital stock.   The number of *shares* of stock that can be issued by a corporation; specified by the *articles of incorporation.*

average.   The arithmetic mean of a set of numbers; obtained by summing the items and dividing by the number of items.

average collection period of receivables.   See *ratio.*

average-cost flow assumption.   An *inventory flow assumption* where the cost of units is the *weighted average* cost of the *beginning inventory* and purchases. See *inventory equation.*

average tax rate.   The rate found by dividing *income tax expense* by *net income* before taxes. Contrast with *marginal tax rate, statutory tax rate.*

avoidable cost.   A *cost* that will cease if an activity is discontinued. An *incremental* or *variable cost.* See *programmed cost.*

B

backlog.   Orders for which insufficient *inventory* is on hand for current delivery and which will be filled in a later period.

backlog depreciation.   In *current cost accounting,* a problem arising for the *accumulated depreciation* on *plant assets.* Consider an *asset* costing $10,000 with a 10-year life depreciated with the *straight-line method.* Assume that a similar asset has a current cost of $10,000 at the end of the first year but $12,000 at the end of the second year. Assume that the depreciation charge is based on the average current cost during the year, $10,000 for the first year and $11,000 for the second. The depreciation charge for the first year is $1,000 and for the second is $1,100 (= .10 x $11,000), so the *accumulated depreciation account* is $2,100 after 2 years. Note that at the end of the second year, 20 percent of the asset's future benefits have been used, so the accounting records based on current costs must show a *net book value* of $9,600 (= .80 x $12,000), which would result if accumulated depreciation of $2,400 were subtracted from a current cost of $12,000. But the sum of the depreciation charges has been only $2,100. The *journal entry* to increase the accumulated depreciation account requires a *credit* to that account of $300. The question arises, what account is to be debited? That is the problem of backlog depreciation. Some theorists would *debit* an *income* account and others would *debit* a *balance sheet owners' equity* account without reducing current-period earnings. The answer to the question of what to do with the debit is closely tied to the problem of how *holding gains* are recorded. When the asset account is debited for $2,000 to increase the recorded amount from $10,000 to $12,000, a holding gain of $2,000, in this example, must be recorded with a credit. Many theorists believe that whatever account is credited for the holding gains is the same account that should be debited for backlog depreciation. Sometimes called "catch-up depreciation."

bad debt.   An *uncollectible account receivable;* see *bad debt expense* and *sales contra, estimated uncollectibles.*

bad debt expense.   The name for the *account debited* in both the *allowance method* for *uncollectibles* and the *direct write-off method.*

bad debt recovery. Collection, perhaps partial, of a specific account receivable previously written off as uncollectible. If the *allowance method* is used, the *credit* is usually to the *allowance* account. If the *direct write-off method* is used, the credit is to a *revenue account*.

bailout period. In a *capital budgeting* context, the total time that must elapse before net accumulated cash inflows from a project including potential *salvage value* of assets at various times equal or exceed the accumulated cash outflows. Contrast with *payback period*, which assumes completion of the project and uses terminal salvage value. Bailout is superior to payback because bailout takes into account, at least to some degree, the *present value* of the cash flows after termination date being considered. The potential salvage value at any time includes some estimate of the flows that can occur after that time.

balance. As a noun, the sum of *debit* entries minus the sum of *credit* entries in an *account*. If positive, the difference is called a debit balance; if negative, a credit balance. As a verb, to find the difference described above.

balance sheet. Statement of financial position that shows Total *Assets* = Total *Liabilities + Owners' Equity*. The *balance sheet accounts* compromising Total Assets are usually classified under the headings (1) *current assets*, (2) *investments*, (3) *property, plant, and equipment*, or (4) *intangible assets*. The balance sheet accounts compromising Total Liabilities are usually classified under the heading current liabilities or long-term liabilities.

balance sheet account. An account that can appear on a balance sheet. A *permanent account*; contrast with *temporary account*.

balloon. Most *mortgage* and *installment loans* require relative equal periodic payments. Sometimes, the loan requires relatively equal periodic payments with a large final payment. The large final payment is called a "balloon" payment. Such loans are called "balloon" loans. Although a *coupon bond* meets this definition, the term is seldom, if ever, applied to bond loans.

bank balance. The amount of the balance in a checking account shown on the *bank statement*. Compare with *adjusted bank balance* and see *bank reconciliation schedule*.

bank prime rate. See *prime rate*.

bank reconciliation schedule. A schedule that shows how the difference between the book balance of the cash in a bank account and the bank's statement can be explained. Takes into account the amount of such items as checks issued that have not cleared or deposits that have not been recorded by the bank as well as errors made by the bank or the firm.

bank statement. A statement sent by the bank to a checking account customer showing deposits, checks cleared, and service charges for a period, usually one month.

bankrupt. Said of a company whose *liabilities* exceed its *assets* where a legal petition has been filed and accepted under the bankruptcy law. A bankrupt firm is usually, but need not be, *insolvent*.

base stock method. A method of inventory valuation that assumes that there is a minimum normal or base stock of goods that must be kept on hand at all times for effective continuity of operations. This base quantity is valued at *acquisition cost* of the inventory on hand in the earliest period when inventory was on hand. The method is not allowable for income tax purposes and is no longer used, but is generally considered to be the forerunner of the *LIFO* method.

basic accounting equation. *Accounting equation.*

basis. *Acquisition cost*, or some substitute therefore, of an *asset* or *liability* used in computing gain or loss on disposition or retirement. *Attribute measured*. This term is used in both *financial* and *tax reporting*, but the basis of a given item need not be the same for both purposes.

basket purchase. Purchase of a group of *assets* (and *liabilities*) for a single price; *costs* must be assigned to each of the items so that the individual items can be recorded in the *accounts*.

bear. One who believes that security prices will fall. A "bear market" refers to a time when stock prices are generally declining. Contrast with *bull*.

bearer bond. See *registered bond* for contrast and definition.

beginning inventory. Valuation of *inventory* on hand at the beginning of the *accounting period*.

behavioral congruence. *Goal congruence.*

betterment. An *improvement*, usually *capitalized*.

bid. An offer to purchase, or the amount of the offer.

big bath. A *write-off* of a substantial amount of costs previously treated as *assets*. Usually caused when a corporation drops a line of business that required a large investment but that proved to be unprofitable. Sometimes used to describe a situation where a corporation takes a large write-off in one period in order to free later periods of gradual write-offs of those amounts. In this sense it frequently occurs when there is a change in top management.

Big Six. The six largest U.S. *public accounting (CPA)* partnerships; in alphabetical order: Arthur Andersen & Co.; Coopers & Lybrand; Deloitte & Touche; Ernst & Young; KPMG Peat Marwick; and Price Waterhouse.

bill. An *invoice* of charges and *terms of sale* for *goods* and *services*. Also, a piece of currency.

bill of materials. A specification of the quantities of *direct materials* expected to be used to produce a given job or quantity of output.

blocked currency. Currency whose holder by law cannot withdraw from the issuing country or exchange for the currency of another country.

board of directors. The governing body of a corporation elected by the shareholders.

bond. A certificate to show evidence of debt. The *par value* is the *principal* or face amount of the bond payable at maturity. The *coupon rate* is the amount of interest payable in one year divided by the principal amount. Coupon bonds have attached to them coupons that can be redeemed at stated dates for interest payments. Normally, bonds carry semiannual coupons.

bond conversion. The act of exchanging *convertible bonds* for *preferred* or *common stock*.

bond discount. From the standpoint of the issuer of a *bond* at the issue date, the excess of the *par value* of a bond over its initial sales price; at later dates, the excess of par over the sum of (initial issue price plus the portion of discount already *amortized*). From the standpoint of a bondholder, the difference between par value and selling price when the bond sells below par.

bond indenture. The contract between an issuer of *bonds* and the bondholders.

bond premium. Exactly parallel to *bond discount* except that the issue price (or current selling price) is higher than *par value*.

bond ratings. Ratings of corporate and *municipal bond* issues by Moody's Investors Service and by Standard & Poor's Corporation, based on the issuer's existing *debt* level, its previous record of payment, the *coupon rate* on the bonds, and the safety of the *assets* or *revenues* that are committed to paying off *principal* and *interest*. Moody's top rating is Aaa; Standard & Poor's is AAA.

bond redemption. Retirement of *bonds*.

bond refunding. To incur *debt*, usually through the issue of new *bonds*, intending to use the proceeds to retire an *outstanding* bond issue.

bond sinking fund. See *sinking fund*.

bond table. A table showing the current price of a *bond* as a function of the *coupon rate*, years to *maturity*, and effective *yield to maturity* (or *effective rate*).

bonus. Premium over normal *wage* or *salary*, paid usually for meritorious performance.

bonus method. When a new partner is admitted to a *partnership* and the new partner is to be credited with *capital* in excess proportion to the amount of *tangible* assets he or she contributes, two methods may be used to recognize this excess, say $10,000. First, $10,000 may be transferred from the old partners to the new one. This is the bonus method. Second, goodwill in the amount of $10,000 may be recognized as an asset with the credit to the new partner's capital account. This is the *goodwill method*. (Notice that the new partner's percentage of total ownership is not the same under the two methods.) If the new partner is to be credited with capital in smaller proportion than the amount of contribution, then there will be bonus or goodwill for the old partners.

book. As a verb, to record a transaction. As a noun, usually plural, the *journals* and *ledgers*. As an adjective, see *book value*.

book cost. *Book value.*

book inventory. An *inventory* amount that results, not from physical count, but from the amount of beginning inventory plus *invoice* amounts of net purchases less invoice amounts of *requisitions* or withdrawals; implies a *perpetual* method.

book of original entry. A *journal*.

book value. The amount shown in the books or in the *accounts* for an *asset*, *liability*, or *owners' equity* item. Generally used to refer to the *net* amount of an *asset* or group of assets shown in the account that records the asset and reductions, such as for *amortization*, in its cost. Of a firm, the excess of total assets over total liabilities. *Net assets.*

book value per share of common stock. Common *shareholders' equity* divided by the number of shares of *common stock outstanding*. See *ratio*.

bookkeeping. The process of analyzing and recording transactions in the accounting records.

boot. The additional money paid (or received) along with a used item in a trade-in or exchange transaction for another item. See *trade-in transaction*.

borrower. See *loan*.

branch. A sales office or other unit of an enterprise physically separated from the home office of the enterprise but not organized as a legally separate *subsidiary*. The term is rarely used to refer to manufacturing units.

branch accounting. An accounting procedure that enables the financial position and operations of each *branch* to be reported separately but later combined for published statements.

breakeven analysis. See *breakeven chart*.

breakeven chart. Two kinds of breakeven charts appear here. The charts are based on the information for a month shown below. Revenue is $30 per unit.

Cost Classification	Variable Cost, Per Unit	Fixed Cost, Per Month
Manufacturing costs:		
Direct material	$4	—
Direct labor	9	—
Overhead	4	$3,060
Total manufacturing costs	$17	$3,060
Selling, general and administrative costs .	5	1,740
Total costs	$22	$4,800

The cost-volume-profit graph presents the relationship of changes in volume to the amount of *profit*, or *income* . On such a graph, total *revenue* and total *costs* for each volume level are indicated and profit or loss at any volume can be read directly from the chart. The profit-volume graph does not show revenues and costs but more readily indicates profit (or loss) at various output levels. Two caveats should be kept in mind about these graphs. Although the curve depicting *variable cost* and total cost is shown as being a straight line for its entire length, it is likely that at low or high levels of output, variable cost would probably differ from $22 per unit. The variable cost figure was probably established by studies of operations at some broad central area of production, called the *relevant range*. For low (or high) levels of activity, the chart may not be applicable. For this reason, the total cost and profit-loss curves are sometimes shown as dotted lines at lower (or higher) volume levels. Second, this chart is simplified because it assumes a single product firm. For a multiproduct firm, the horizontal axis would have to be stated in dollars rather than in physical units of output. Breakeven charts for multiproduct firms necessarily assume that constant proportions of the several products are sold and changes in this mixture as well as in costs or selling prices would invalidate such a chart.

breakeven point. The volume of sales required so that total *revenues* and total *costs* are equal. May be expressed in units (*fixed costs/contribution per unit*) or in sales dollars [selling price per unit x (fixed costs/contribution per unit)].

budget. A financial plan that is used to estimate the results of future operations. Frequently used to help control future operations. In governmental operations, budgets often become the law.

budgetary accounts. In governmental accounting, the accounts that reflect estimated operations and financial condition, as affected by estimated *revenues, appropriations*, and *encumbrances*. In contrast to *proprietary accounts* that record the transactions.

A. Cost-Volume-Profit Graph

B. Profit-Volume Graph

budgetary control. Management of governmental (nongovernmental) unit in accordance with an official (approved) *budget* in order to keep total expenditures within authorized (planned) limits.

budgeted cost. See *standard cost* for definition and contrast.

budgeted statements. *Pro forma statements* prepared before the event or period occurs.

bull. One who believes that security prices will rise. A "bull market" refers to a time when stock prices are generally rising. Contrast with *bear*.

burden. See *overhead costs*.

burn rate. A new business usually begins life with cash-absorbing operating losses, but with a limited amount of cash. The "burn rate" measures how long the new business can survive before operating losses must stop or a new infusion of cash will be necessary. The measurement is ordinarily stated in terms of months.

business combination. As defined in *APB Opinion No. 16*, the bringing together into a single accounting *entity* of two or more incorporated or unincorporated businesses. The *merger* will be accounted for either with the *purchase method* or the *pooling-of-interests method*. See *conglomerate*.

business entity. *Entity. Accounting entity.*

bylaws. The rules adopted by the shareholders of a corporation that specify the general methods for carrying out the functions of the corporation.

by-product. A *joint product* whose sales value is so small relative to the sales value of the other joint product(s) that it does not receive normal accounting treatment. The costs assigned to by-products reduce the costs of the main product(s). By-products are allocated a share of joint costs such that the expected gain or loss upon their sale is zero. Thus, by-products are shown in the *accounts* at *net realizable value*.

C

CA. *Chartered accountant.*

call. An option to buy *shares* of a publicly-traded corporation at a fixed price during a fixed time span. Contrast with *put*.

call premium. See *callable bond*.

call price. See *callable bond*.

callable bond. A *bond* for which the issuer reserves the right to pay a specific amount, the call price, to retire the obligation before *maturity* date. If the issuer agrees to pay more than the *face amount* of the bond when called, the excess of the payment over the face amount is the "call premium."

Canadian Institute of Chartered Accountants. The national organization that represents *chartered accountants* in Canada.

cancelable lease. See *lease*.

capacity. Stated in units of product, the amount that can be produced per unit of time. Stated in units of input, such as *direct labor* hours, the amount of input that can be used in production per unit of time. This measure of output or input is used in allocating *fixed costs* if the amounts producible are normal, rather than maximum, amounts.

capacity cost. A *fixed cost* incurred to provide a firm with the capacity to produce or to sell. Consists of *standby costs* and *enabling costs*. Contrast with *programmed costs*.

capacity variance. *Production volume variance.*

capital. *Owners' equity* in a business. Often used, equally correctly, to mean the total assets of a business. Sometimes used to mean *capital assets*.

capital asset. Properly used, a designation for income tax purposes that describes property held by a taxpayer, except *cash*, inventoriable *assets*, goods held primarily for sale, most depreciable property, *real estate, receivables,* certain *intangibles,* and a few other items. Sometimes this term is imprecisely used to describe *plant* and *equipment*, which are clearly not capital assets under the income tax definition. Often the term is used to refer to an *investment* in *securities*.

capital budget. Plan of proposed outlays for acquiring long-term *assets* and the means of *financing* the acquisition.

capital budgeting. The process of choosing *investment* projects for an enterprise by considering the *present value* of cash flows and deciding how to raise the funds required by the investment.

capital consumption allowance. The term used for *depreciation expense* in national income accounting and the reporting of funds in the economy.

capital contributed in excess of par (or stated) value. A preferred title for the account that shows the amount received by the issuer for *capital stock* in excess of *par (or stated) value*.

capital expenditure (outlay). An *expenditure* to acquire long-term *assets*.

capital gain. The excess of proceeds over *cost*, or other *basis*, from the sale of a *capital asset* as defined by the Internal Revenue Code. If the capital asset has been held for a sufficiently long time before sale, then the tax on the gain is computed at a rate lower than is used for other gains and ordinary income.

capital lease. A *lease* treated by the *lessee* as both the borrowing of funds and the acquisition of an *asset* to be *amortized*. Both the *liability* and the asset are recognized on the balance sheet. Expenses consist of *interest* on the *debt* and *amortization* of the asset. The *lessor* treats the lease as the sale of the asset in return for a series of future cash receipts. Contrast with *operating lease*.

capital loss. A negative capital gain; see *capital gain*.

capital rationing. In a *capital budgeting* context, the imposing of constraints on the amounts of total capital expenditures in each period.

capital stock. The ownership shares of a corporation. Consists of all classes of *common* and *preferred stock*.

capital structure. The composition of a corporation's equities; the relative proportions of *short-term debt*, *long-term debt*, and *owners' equity*.

capital surplus. An inferior term for *capital contributed in excess of par (or stated) value*.

capitalization of a corporation. A term used by investment analysts to indicate *shareholders' equity* plus *bonds outstanding*.

capitalization of earnings. The process of estimating the economic worth of a firm by computing the *net present value* of the predicted *net income* (not *cash flows*) of the firm for the future.

capitalization rate. An *interest rate* used to convert a series of payments or receipts or earnings into a single *present value*.

capitalize. To record an *expenditure* that may benefit a future period as an *asset* rather than to treat the expenditure as an *expense* of the period of its occurrence. Whether or not expenditures for advertising or for research and development should be capitalized is controversial, but *SFAS No. 2* requires expensing of *R&D* costs. We believe expenditures should be capitalized if they lead to future benefits and thus meet the criterion to be an asset.

carryback, carryforward, carryover. The use of losses or tax credits in one period to reduce income taxes payable in other periods. There are two common kinds of carrybacks: for net operating losses and for *capital losses*. They are applied against taxable income. In general, carrybacks are for three years with the earliest year first. Operating losses can be carried forward for fifteen years. Corporate capital loss carryforwards are for five years. The capital loss for individuals can be carried forward indefinitely.

carrying cost. Costs (such as property taxes and insurance) of holding, or storing, *inventory* from the time of purchase until the time of sale or use.

carrying value (amount). *Book value*.

CASB. Cost Accounting Standards Board. A board of five members authorized by the U.S. Congress to "promulgate cost-accounting standards designed to achieve uniformity and consistency in the cost-accounting principles followed by defense contractors and subcontractors under federal contracts." The *principles* promulgated since 1970 by the CASB are likely to have considerable weight in practice where the *FASB* has not established a standard. Although the Congress allowed the CASB to go out of existence in 1980, its standards have the same force as before.

cash. Currency and coins, negotiable checks, and balances in bank accounts. For the *statement of cash flows*, "cash" also includes *marketable securities* held as *current assets*.

cash basis of accounting. In contrast to the *accrual basis of accounting*, a system of accounting in which *revenues* are recognized when *cash* is received and *expenses* are recognized as *disbursements* are made. No attempt is made to *match revenues* and *expenses* in determining *income*. See *modified cash basis*.

cash budget. A schedule of expected cash *receipts* and *disbursements*.

cash collection basis. The *installment method* for recognizing *revenue*. Not to be confused with the *cash basis of accounting*.

cash conversion cycle. *Cash cycle*.

cash cycle. The period of time that elapses during which *cash* is converted into *inventories*, inventories are converted into *accounts receivable*, and receivables are converted back into cash. Sometimes called *earnings cycle*.

cash disbursements journal. A specialized *journal* used to record *expenditures* by *cash* and by *check*. If a *check register* is also used, a cash disbursements journal records only expenditures of currency and coins.

cash discount. A reduction in sales or purchase price allowed for prompt payment.

cash dividend. See *dividend.*

cash equivalent value. A term used to describe the amount for which an *asset* could be sold. Also called *market value; fair market price (value).*

cash flow. Cash *receipts* minus *disbursements* from a given *asset,* or group of assets, for a given period. Financial analysts sometimes use this term to mean *net income + depreciation + depletion + amortization.* See also *operating cash flow* and *free cash flow.*

cash flow statement. *Statement of cash flows.*

cash provided by operations. An important subtotal in the *statement of cash flows.* This amount is the total of revenues producing *cash* less *expenses* requiring cash. Often, the amount is shown as *net income* plus expenses not requiring cash (such as depreciation charges) minus revenues not producing cash (such as revenues recognized under the *equity method* of accounting for a long-term investment). The statement of cash flows maintains the same distinctions between *continuing operations, discontinued operations,* and *income* or *loss* from *extraordinary items* as does the *income statement.*

cash receipts journal. A specialized *journal* used to record all *receipts* of *cash.*

cash (surrender) value of life insurance. An amount equal, not to the face value of the policy to be paid in event of death, but to the amount that could be realized if the policy were immediately canceled and traded with the insurance company for cash. If a firm owns a life insurance policy, the policy is reported as an asset at an amount equal to this value.

cash yield. See *yield.*

cashier's check. A bank's own *check* drawn on itself and signed by the cashier or other authorized official. It is a direct obligation of the bank. Compare with *certified check.*

catch-up depreciation. *Backlog depreciation.*

CCA. *Current cost accounting; current value accounting.*

central corporate expenses. General *overhead expenses* incurred in running the corporate headquarters and related supporting activities of a corporation. These expenses are treated as *period expenses.* Contrast with *manufacturing overhead.* A major problem in *line of business reporting* is the treatment of these expenses.

central processing unit (CPU). The component of a computer system that carries out the arithmetic, logic, and data transfer.

certificate. The document that is the physical embodiment of a *bond* or a *share of stock.* A term sometimes used for the *auditor's report.*

certified management accountant. *CMA.*

certificate of deposit. Federal law constrains the *rate of interest* that banks can pay. Under current law banks are allowed to pay a rate higher than the one allowed on a *time deposit* if the depositor promises to leave funds on deposit for several months or more. When the bank receives such funds, it issues a certificate of deposit. The depositor can withdraw the funds before maturity if a penalty is paid.

certified check. The *check* of a depositor drawn on a bank on the face of which the bank has inserted the words "accepted" or "certified" with the date and signature of a bank official. The check then becomes an obligation of the bank. Compare with *cashier's check.*

certified financial statement. A financial statement attested to by an independent *auditor* who is a *CPA.*

certified internal auditor. See *CIA.*

certified public accountant. CPA. An accountant who has satisfied the statutory and administrative requirements of his or her jurisdiction to be registered or licensed as a public accountant. In addition to passing the Uniform CPA Examination administered by the *AICPA,* the CPA must meet certain educational, experience, and moral requirements that differ from jurisdiction to jurisdiction. The jurisdictions are each of the 50 states, the District of Columbia, Guam, Puerto Rico, and the Virgin Islands.

CGA. Canada. Certified General Accountant. An accountant who has satisfied the experience, education, and examination requirements of the Certified General Accountants' Association.

chain discount. A series of *discount* percentages; for example, if a chain discount of 10 and 5 percent is quoted, then the actual, or *invoice,* price is the nominal, or list, price times .90 times .95, or 85.5 percent of invoice price.

change fund. Coins and currency issued to cashiers, delivery drivers, and so on.

changes, accounting. See *accounting changes.*

changes in financial position. See *statement of cash flows.*

charge. As a noun, a *debit* to an account; as a verb, to debit.

charge off. To treat as a *loss* or *expense* an amount originally recorded as an *asset*; use of this term implies that the charge is not in accord with original expectations.

chart of accounts. A list of names and numbers, systematically organized, of *accounts*.

charter. Document issued by a state government authorizing the creation of a corporation.

chartered accountant. CA. The title used in Australia, Canada, and the United Kingdom for an accountant who has satisfied the requirements of the institute of his or her jurisdiction to be qualified to serve as a *public accountant*. In Canada, each provincial institute or order has the right to administer the examination and to set the standards of performance and ethics for Chartered Accountants in its province. For a number of years, however, the provincial organizations have pooled their rights to qualify new members through the Inter-provincial Education Committee and the result is that there are nationally set and graded examinations given in English and French. Deviation from the pass/fail grade awarded by the Board of Examiners (a subcommittee of the Inter-provincial Education Committee) is rare.

check. The Federal Reserve Board defines a check as "a *draft* or order upon a bank or banking house purporting to be drawn upon a deposit of funds for the payment at all events of a certain sum of money to a certain person therein named or to him or his order or to bearer and payable instantly on demand." It must contain the phrase "pay to the order of." The amount shown on the check's face must be clearly readable, and it must have the signature of the drawer. Checks need not be dated, although they usually are. The *balance* in the *cash account* is usually reduced when a check is issued, not later when it clears the bank and reduces cash in bank. See *remittance advice*.

check register. A *journal* to record *checks* issued.

CIA. Certified Internal Auditor. One who has satisfied certain requirements of the *Institute of Internal Auditors* including experience, ethics, education, and passing examinations.

CICA. *Canadian Institute of Chartered Accountants*.

CIF. Cost, insurance, and freight; a term used in contracts along with the name of a given port to indicate that the quoted price includes insurance, handling, and freight charges up to delivery by the seller at the given port.

circulating capital. *Working capital*.

clean opinion. See *auditor's report*.

clean surplus concept. The notion that the only entries to the *retained earnings* account are to record *net income* and *dividends*. See *comprehensive income*. Contrast with *current operating performance concept*. This concept, with minor exceptions, is now controlling in *GAAP*. (See *APB Opinions Nos.* 9 and 30.)

clearing account. An account containing amounts to be transferred to another account(s) before the end of the *accounting period*. Examples are the *income summary* account (whose balance is transferred to *retained earnings*) and the purchases account (whose balance is transferred to *inventory* or to *cost of goods sold*).

close. As a verb, to transfer the *balance* of a *temporary* or *contra* or *adjunct* account to the main account to which it relates; for example, to transfer *revenue* and *expense* accounts directly, or through the *income summary* account, to an *owners' equity* account, or to transfer *purchase discounts* to purchases.

closed account. An *account* with equal *debits* and *credits*, usually as a result of a *closing entry*. See *ruling an account*.

closing entries. The *entries* that accomplish the transfer of balances in *temporary accounts* to the related *balance sheet accounts*. See *work sheet*.

closing inventory. *Ending inventory*.

CMA. Certified Management Accounting certificate. Awarded by the *Institute of Certified Management Accountants* of the *National Association of Accountants* to those who pass a set of examinations and meet certain experience and continuing education requirements.

CoCoA. *Continuously contemporary accounting*.

coding of accounts. The numbering of *accounts*, as for a *chart of accounts*, which is necessary for computerized accounting.

coinsurance. Insurance policies that protect against hazards such as fire or water damage often specify that the owner of the property may not collect the full amount of insurance for a loss unless the insurance policy covers at least some specified "coinsurance" percentage, usually about 80 percent, of the *replacement cost* of the property. Coinsurance clauses induce the owner to carry full, or nearly full, coverage.

COLA. Cost-of-living adjustment. See *indexation*.

collateral. *Assets* pledged by a *borrower* that will be given up if the *loan* is not paid.

collectible. Capable of being converted into *cash*; now, if due; later, otherwise.

combination. See *business combination*.

comfort letter. A letter in which an auditor conveys negative assurances as to unaudited financial statements in a prospectus or draft financial statements included in a preliminary prospectus.

commercial paper. *Short-term notes* issued by corporate borrowers.

commission. Remuneration, usually expressed as a percentage, to employees based upon an activity rate, such as sales.

committed costs. *Capacity costs*.

Committee on Accounting Procedure. CAP. Predecessor of the *APB*. The *AICPA's* principles-promulgating body from 1939 through 1959. Its 51 pronouncements are called *Accounting Research Bulletins*.

common cost. *Cost* resulting from use of *raw materials*, a facility (for example, plant or machines), or a service (for example, fire insurance) that benefits several products or departments and must be allocated to those products or departments. Common costs result when multiple products are produced together although they could be produced separately; joint costs occur when multiple products are of necessity produced together. Many writers use common costs and *joint costs* synonymously. See *joint costs*, *indirect costs*, *overhead* and *sterilized allocation*.

common dollar accounting. *Constant dollar accounting*.

common monetary measuring unit. For U.S. corporations, the dollar. See also *stable monetary unit assumption* and *constant dollar accounting*.

common shares. *Shares* representing the class of owners who have residual claims on the *assets* and *earnings* of a *corporation* after all *debt* and *preferred shareholders'* claims have been met.

common stock equivalent. A *security* whose primary value arises from its ability to be exchanged for *common shares*; includes *stock options*, *warrants*, and also *convertible bonds* or *convertible preferred stock* whose *effective interest rate* at the time of issue is less than two-thirds the average Aa corporate bond yield. See *bond ratings*.

common size statement. A *percentage statement* usually based on total *assets* or *net sales* or *revenues*.

company wide control. See *control system*.

comparative (financial) statements. *Financial statements* showing information for the same company for different times, usually two successive years. Nearly all published financial statements are in this form. Contrast with *historical summary*.

compensating balance. When a bank lends funds to a customer, it often requires that the customer keep on deposit in his or her checking account an amount equal to some percentage—say, 20 percent—of the loan. The amount required to be left on deposit is the compensating balance. Such amounts effectively increase the *interest rate*. The amounts of such balances must be disclosed in *notes* to the *financial statements*.

completed contract method. Recognizing *revenues* and *expenses* for a job or order only when it is finished, except that when a loss on the contract is expected, revenues and expenses are recognized in the period when the loss is first forecast. This term is generally used only for long-term contracts. It is otherwise equivalent to the *sales basis* of *revenue recognition*.

completed sales basis. See *sales basis of revenue recognition*.

compliance audit. Objectively obtaining and evaluating evidence regarding assertions, actions, and events to ascertain the degree of correspondence between them and established performance criteria.

compliance procedure. An *audit* procedure used to gain evidence as to whether the prescribed internal controls are operating effectively.

composite cost of capital. See *cost of capital*.

composite depreciation. *Group depreciation* of dissimilar items.

composite life method. *Group depreciation*, which see, for items of unlike kind. The term may be used when a single item, such as a crane, which consists of separate units with differing service lives, such as the chassis, the motor, the lifting mechanism, and so on, is depreciated as a whole rather than treating each of the components separately.

compound entry. A *journal entry* with more than one *debit* or more than one *credit*, or both. See *trade-in transaction* for an example.

compound interest. *Interest* calculated on *principal* plus previously undistributed interest.

compound interest depreciation. A method designed to hold the *rate of return* on an asset constant. First find the *internal rate of return* on the cash inflows and outflows of the asset. The periodic depreciation charge is the cash flow for the period less the internal rate of return multiplied by the asset's *book value* at the beginning of the period. When the cash flows from the asset are constant over time, the method is sometimes called the "annuity method" of depreciation.

compounding period. The time period for which *interest* is calculated. At the end of the period, the interest may be paid to the lender or added (that is, converted) to principal for the next interest-earning period, which is usually a year or some portion of a year.

comprehensive budget. *Master budget.*

comprehensive income. Defined in *SFAS No. 3* as "the change in equity (net assets) of an entity during a period from transactions and other events and circumstances from nonowner sources. It includes all changes in equity during a period except those resulting from investments by owners and distributions to owners." In this definition, "equity" means *owners' equity.*

comptroller. Same meaning and pronunciation as *controller.*

conceptual framework. A coherent system of interrelated objectives and fundamentals, promulgated by the *FASB* primarily through its *SFAC* publications, expected to lead to consistent standards for *financial accounting* and reporting.

confidence level. The measure of probability that the actual characteristics of the population lie within the stated precision of the estimate derived from a sampling process. A sample estimate may be expressed in the following terms: "Based on the sample, we are 95% sure [confidence level] that the true population value is within the range of X to Y [precision]". *See precision.*

confirmation. A formal memorandum delivered by the customers or suppliers of a company to its independent *auditor* verifying the amounts shown as receivable or payable. The confirmation document is originally sent by the auditor to the customer. If the auditor asks that the document be returned whether the *balance* is correct or incorrect, then it is called a "positive confirmation." If the auditor asks that the document be returned only if there is an error, it is called a "negative confirmation."

conglomerate. *Holding company.* This term is used when the owned companies are in dissimilar lines of business.

conservatism. A *reporting objective* that calls for anticipation of all *losses* and *expenses* but defers recognition of *gains* or *profits* until they are *realized* in *arm's-length* transactions. In the absence of certainty, events are to be reported in a way that tends to minimize cumulative income.

consignee. See *on consignment.*

consignment. See *on consignment.*

consignor. See *on consignment.*

consistency. Treatment of like *transactions* in the same way in consecutive periods so that financial statements will be more comparable than otherwise. The reporting policy implying that procedures, once adopted, should be followed from period to period by a reporting *entity.* See *accounting changes* for the treatment of inconsistencies.

consol. A *bond* that never matures; a *perpetuity* in the form of a bond. Originally issued by Great Britain after the Napoleonic wars to consolidate debt issues of that period. The term arose as an abbreviation for "consolidated annuities."

consolidated financial statements. Statements issued by legally separate companies that show financial position and income as they would appear if the companies were one economic *entity.*

constant dollar. A hypothetical unit of *general purchasing power*, denoted "C$" by the *FASB.*

constant dollar accounting. Accounting where items are measured in *constant dollars.* See *historical cost/constant dollar accounting* and *current cost/constant dollar accounting.*

constant dollar date. The time at which the *general purchasing power* of one *constant dollar* is exactly equal to the *general purchasing power* of one *nominal dollar*; that is, the date when C$1 = $1. When the constant dollar date is mid-period, then the nominal amounts of *revenues* and *expenses* spread evenly throughout the period are equal to their constant dollar amounts, but end-of-period *balance sheet* amounts measured in constant mid-period dollars differ from their nominal dollar amounts. When the constant dollar date is at the end of the period, then the constant dollar and nominal dollar amounts on a balance sheet for that date are identical.

constrained share company. Canada. A public company whose *charter* specifies that at least a certain prescribed percentage of the shares must be beneficially owned by Canadian citizens or by corporations resident in Canada.

constructive receipt. An item is included in taxable income when the taxpayer can control funds whether or not cash has been received. For example, *interest* added to *principal* in a savings account is deemed by the *IRS* to be constructively received.

Consumer Price Index. CPI. A *price index* computed and issued monthly by the Bureau of Labor Statistics of the U.S. Department of Labor. The index attempts to track the price level of a group of goods and services purchased by the average consumer. The CPI is used in *constant dollar accounting*. Contrast with *GNP Implicit Price Deflator*.

contingency. A potential *liability*; if a specified event were to occur, such as losing a lawsuit, a liability would be recognized. The contingency is merely disclosed in notes, rather than shown in the balance sheet. *SFAS No. 5* requires treatment as a contingency until the outcome is "probable" and the amount of payment can be reasonably estimated, perhaps within a range. When the outcome becomes probable (the future event is "likely" to occur) and the amount can be reasonably estimated (using the lower end of a range if only a range can be estimated), then the liability is recognized in the accounts, rather than being disclosed in the notes. *Gain* contingencies are not recorded in the accounts, but are merely disclosed in notes.

contingent annuity. An *annuity* whose number of payments depends upon the outcome of an event whose timing is uncertain at the time the annuity is set up; for example, an annuity payable until death of the *annuitant*. Contrast with *annuity certain*.

contingent issue (securities). Securities issuable to specific individuals upon the occurrence of some event, such as the firm's attaining a specified level of earnings.

contingent liability. *Contingency*. This term is to be avoided because it refers to something that is not a *liability* on the *balance sheet*.

continuing appropriation. A governmental *appropriation* automatically renewed without further legislative action until it is altered or revoked or expended.

continuing operations. See *income from continuing operations*.

continuity of operations. The assumption in accounting that the business *entity* will continue to operate long enough for current plans to be carried out. The *going-concern assumption*.

continuous budget. A *budget* that perpetually adds a period in the future as the period just ended is dropped.

continuous compounding. *Compound interest* where the *compounding period* is every instant of time. See *e* for the computation of the equivalent annual or periodic rate.

continuous inventory method. The *perpetual inventory* method.

Continuously Contemporary Accounting. CoCoA. A name coined by the Australian theorist, Raymond J. Chambers, to indicate a combination of *current value ac-*

counting where amounts are measured in *constant dollars* and based on *exit values*.

contra account. An *account*, such as *accumulated depreciation*, that accumulates subtractions from another account, such as machinery. Contrast with *adjunct account*.

contributed capital. The sum of the balances in *capital stock* accounts plus *capital contributed in excess of par (or stated) value* accounts. Contrast with *donated capital*.

contributed surplus. An inferior term for *capital contributed in excess of par value*.

contribution approach. Method of preparing *income statements* that separates *variable costs* from *fixed costs* in order to emphasize the importance of cost behavior patterns for purposes of planning and control.

contribution margin. *Revenue* from *sales* less all variable *expenses*. Contrast with *gross margin*.

contribution margin ratio. *Contribution margin* divided by *net sales*; usually measured from the price and cost of a single unit.

contribution per unit. Selling price less *variable costs* per unit.

contributory. Said of a *pension plan* where employees, as well as employers, make payments to a pension *fund*. Note that the provisions for *vesting* are applicable only to the employer's payments. Whatever the degree of vesting of the employer's payments, the employee typically gets back all of his or her payments, with interest, in case of death, or other cessation of employment, before retirement.

control (controlling) account. A summary *account* with totals equal to those of entries and balances that appear in individual accounts in a *subsidiary ledger*. Accounts Receivable is a control account backed up with an account for each customer. The balance in a control account should not be changed unless a corresponding change is made in one of the subsidiary accounts.

control system. A device for ensuring that actions are carried out according to plan or for safeguarding *assets*. A system for ensuring that actions are carried out according to plan can be designed for a single function within the firm, called "operational control;" for autonomous segments within the firm that generally have responsibility for both revenues and costs, called "divisional control;" or for activities of the firm as a whole, called "company-wide control." Systems designed for safeguarding *assets* are called "internal control" systems.

controllable cost. A *cost* whose amount can be influenced by the way in which operations are carried out, such as advertising costs, which are controlled by marketing executives. These costs can be *fixed* or *variable*. See *programmed costs* and *managed costs*.

controlled company. A company, a majority of whose voting shares is held by an individual or corporation. Effective control can sometimes be exercised when less than 50 percent of the shares is owned.

controller. The title often used for the chief accountant of an organization. Often spelled *comptroller*.

conversion. The act of exchanging a convertible security for another security.

conversion audit. An examination of change-over procedures, and new accounting procedures and files, that takes place when a significant change in the accounting system (e.g., a change from a manual to a computerized system or a change of computers) has occurred.

conversion cost. *Direct labor* costs plus factory *overhead* costs incurred in producing a product. That is, the cost to convert raw materials to finished products. *Manufacturing cost*.

conversion period. *Compounding period*. Also, period during which a *convertible bond* or *convertible preferred stock* can be converted into *common stock*.

convertible bond. A *bond* that may be converted into a specified number of shares of *capital stock* during the *conversion period*.

convertible preferred stock. *Preferred shares* that may be converted into a specified number of shares of *common stock*.

co-operative. An incorporated organization formed for the benefit of its members (owners) who are either producers or consumers in order to acquire for them profits or savings that otherwise accrue to middlemen. Members exercise control on the basis of one vote per member.

co-product. A product sharing production facilities with another product. For example, if an apparel manufacturer produces shirts and jeans on the same line, these are co-products. Co-products are distinguished from *joint products* and *by-products* which, by their very nature must be produced together, such as the various grades of wood produced in a lumber factory.

copyright. Exclusive right granted by the government to an individual author, composer, playwright, and the like for the life of the individual plus 50 years. If the copyright is granted to a firm, then the right extends 75 years after the original publication. The *economic life* of a copyright

may be considerably less than the legal life as, for example, the copyright of this book.

corner. The control of a quantity of shares or a commodity that is sufficient in a free market to enable the holder effectively to control the market price.

corporation. A legal entity authorized by a state to operate under the rules of the entity's *charter*.

correcting entry. An *adjusting entry* where an improperly recorded *transaction* is properly recorded. Not to be confused with entries that correct *accounting errors*.

correction of errors. See *accounting errors*.

cost. The sacrifice, measured by the *price* paid or required to be paid, to acquire *goods* or *services*. See *acquisition cost* and *replacement cost*. The term "cost" is often used when referring to the valuation of a good or service acquired. When "cost" is used in this sense, a cost is an *asset*. When the benefits of the acquisition (the goods or services acquired) expire, the cost becomes an *expense* or *loss*. Some writers, however, use cost and expense as synonyms. Contrast with *expense*.

cost accounting. Classifying, summarizing, recording, reporting, and allocating current or predicted *costs*. A subset of *managerial accounting*.

Cost Accounting Standards Board. See *CASB*.

cost accumulation. Bringing together, usually in a single *account*, all *costs* of a specified activity. Contrast with *cost allocation*.

cost allocation. Assigning *costs* to individual products or time periods. Contrast with *cost accumulation*.

cost-based transfer price. A *transfer price* based on *historical costs*.

cost behavior. The functional relation between changes in activity and changes in *cost*. For example, *fixed* versus *variable costs*; *linear* versus *curvilinear cost*.

cost/benefit criterion. Some measure of *costs* compared to some measure of *benefits* for a proposed undertaking. If the costs exceed the benefits, then the undertaking is judged not worthwhile. This criterion will not give good decisions unless all costs and benefits flowing from the undertaking are estimated.

cost center. A unit of activity for which *expenditures* and *expenses* are accumulated.

cost effective. Among alternatives, the one whose benefit, or payoff, per unit of cost is highest. Sometimes said of an action whose expected benefits exceed expected costs whether or not there are other alternatives with larger benefit/cost ratios.

cost estimation. The process of measuring the functional relation between changes in activity levels and changes in cost.

cost flow assumption. See *flow assumption.*

cost flows. Costs passing through various classifications within an entity. See *flow of costs* for a diagram.

cost method (for investments). Accounting for an investment in the *capital stock* or *bonds* of another company where the investment is shown at *acquisition cost,* and only *dividends* declared or *interest receivable* is treated as *revenue.*

cost method (for treasury stock). The method of showing *treasury stock* in a *contra account* to all other items of *shareholders' equity* in an amount equal to that paid to reacquire the stock.

cost objective. Any activity for which a separate measurement of *costs* is desired. Examples include departments, products, and territories.

cost of capital. *Opportunity cost* of funds invested in a business. The rate of return required to be earned on an asset before the rational owner will devote that asset to a particular purpose. Sometimes measured as the average rate per year a company must pay for its *equities.* In efficient capital markets, the *discount rate* that equates the expected *present value* of all future cash flows to common shareholders with the market value of common stock at a given time.
The cost of capital is often measured by taking a *weighted average* of the firm's *debt* and various *equity securities.* The measurement so derived is sometimes called the "composite cost of capital," and some analysts confuse this measurement of the cost of capital with the cost of capital itself. For example, if the equities of a firm include substantial amounts for the *deferred income tax liability,* the composite cost of capital will underestimate the true cost of capital—the required rate of return on a firm's assets—because the deferred income tax liability has no explicit cost.

cost of goods manufactured. The sum of all costs allocated to products completed during a period; includes materials, labor, and *overhead.*

cost of goods purchased. Net purchase price of goods acquired plus costs of storage and delivery to the place where the items can be productively used.

cost of goods sold. Inventoriable *costs* that are *expensed* because the units are sold; equals *beginning inventory* plus *cost of goods purchased* or *manufactured* minus *ending inventory.*

cost of sales. Generally refers to *cost of goods sold;* occasionally, to *selling expenses.*

cost or market, whichever is lower. See *lower of cost or market.*

cost percentage. One less *markup percentage. Cost* of *goods available for sale* divided by selling prices of goods available for sale (when FIFO is used). With *LIFO, cost* of *purchases* divided by selling price of purchases. See *markup* for further detail on inclusions in calculation of cost percentage.

cost pool. *Indirect cost pool.*

cost principle. The *principle* that requires reporting *assets* at *historical* or *acquisition cost,* less accumulated *amortization.* This principle is based on the assumption that cost is equal to *fair market value* at the date of acquisition and subsequent changes are not likely to be significant.

cost-recovery-first method. A method of *revenue* recognition that credits *inventory* as collections are received until all costs are recovered. Only after costs are completely recovered is *income* recognized. To be used in financial reporting only when the total amount of collections is highly uncertain. Can never be used in income tax reporting. Contrast with the *installment method* where *constant* proportions of each collection are credited both to cost and to income.

cost sheet. Statement that shows all the elements comprising the total cost of an item.

cost terminology. The word "cost" appears in many accounting terms. The accompanying exhibit classifies some of these by the distinctions the terms are used to make. Joel Dean was, to our knowledge, the first to attempt such distinctions; we have used some of his ideas here. Some terms have more detailed discussion under their own listings.

cost-to-cost. The *percentage-of-completion method* where the estimate of completion is the ratio of costs incurred to date divided by total costs expected to be incurred for the entire project.

cost-volume-profit analysis. A study of the sensitivity of *profits* to changes in units sold (or produced), assuming some *semivariable costs* in the cost structure.

cost-volume-profit graph (chart). A graph that shows the relation between *fixed costs, contribution per unit, breakeven point,* and *sales.* See *breakeven chart.*

Cost Terminology: Distinctions among Terms Containing the Word "Cost"

Terms (Synonyms Given in Parentheses)			Distinctions and Comments
			1. The following pairs of terms distinguish the basis measured in accounting.
Historical Cost (Acquisition Cost)	vs.	Current Cost	A distinction used in financial accounting. Current cost can be used more specifically to mean replacement cost, net realizable value, or present value of cash flows. "Current cost" is often used narrowly to mean replacement cost.
Historical Cost (Actual Cost)	vs.	Standard Cost	The distinction between historical and standard costs arises in product costing for inventory valuation. Some systems record actual costs while others record the standard costs.
			2. The following pairs of terms denote various distinctions among historical costs. For each pair of terms, the sum of the two kinds of costs equals total historical cost used in financial reporting.
Variable Cost (Constant Cost)	vs.	Fixed Cost	Distinction used in breakeven analysis and in designing cost accounting systems, particularly for product costing. See (4), below, for a further subdivision of fixed costs and (5), below, for an economic distinction closely paralleling this one.
Traceable Cost (Joint Cost)	vs.	Common Cost	Distinction arises in allocating manufacturing costs to product. Common costs are allocated to product, but the allocations are more-or-less arbitrary. The distinction also arises in segment reporting and in separating manufacturing from nonmanufacturing costs.
Direct Cost	vs.	Indirect Cost	Distinction arises in designing cost accounting systems and in product costing. Direct costs can be traced directly to a cost object, (e.g., a product, a responsibility center) whereas indirect costs cannot.
Out-of-Pocket Cost (Outlay Cost; Cash Cost)	vs.	Book Cost	Virtually all costs recorded in financial statements require a cash outlay at one time or another. The distinction here separates expenditures to occur in the future from those already made and is used in making decisions. Book costs, such as for depreciation, reduce income without requiring a future outlay of cash. The cash has already been spent. See future v. past costs in (5), below.
Incremental Cost (Marginal Cost; Differential Cost)	vs.	Unavoidable Cost (Inescapable Cost; Sunk Cost)	Distinction used in making decisions. Incremental costs will be incurred (or saved) if a decision is made to go ahead (or to stop) some activity, but some activity, but not otherwise. Unavoidable costs will be reported in financial statements whether the decision is made to go ahead or not, because cash has already been spent or committed. Not all unavoidable costs are book costs, as, for example, a salary promised but not yet earned, that will be paid even if a no-go decision is made.
			The economist restricts the term marginal cost to the cost of producing one more unit. Thus the next unit has a marginal cost; the next week's output has an incremental cost. If a firm produces and sells a new product, the related new costs would properly be called incremental, not marginal. If a factory is closed, the costs saved are incremental, not marginal.
Escapable Cost (Unavoidable Cost)	vs.	Inescapable Cost	Same distinction as incremental v. sunk costs, but this pair is used only when the decision maker is considering stopping something ceasing to produce a product, closing a factory, or the like. See next pair.
Avoidable Cost	vs.	Unavoidable Cost	A distinction sometimes used in discussing the merits of variable and absorption costing. Avoidable costs are treated as product cost and unavoidable costs are treated as period expenses under variable costing.

Terms (Synonyms Given in Parentheses)		Distinctions and Comments
Controllable Cost	vs. Uncontrollable	The distinction here is used in assigning responsibility and in setting bonus Costincentive plans. All costs can be affected by someone in the entity; those who design incentive schemes attempt to hold a person responsible for a cost only if that person can influence the amount of the cost.

3. In each of the following pairs, used in historical cost accounting, the word "cost" appears in one of the terms where "expense" is meant. The distinction is between *expense* and *asset*.

Expired Cost	vs. Unexpired Cost	
Product Cost	vs. Period Cost	The terms distinguish product cost from period expense. When a given asset is used, is its cost converted into work in process and then into finished goods on the balance sheet until the goods are sold, or is it an expense shown on this period's income statement? Product costs appear on the income statement as part of cost of goods sold in the period when the goods are sold. Period expenses appear on the income statement with an appropriate caption for the item in the period when the cost is incurred or recognized.

4. The following subdivisions of fixed (historical) costs are used in analyzing operations. The relation between the components of fixed costs is:

$$\text{Fixed Costs} = \text{Capacity Costs} + \text{Programmed Costs}$$

Semifixed + Fixed Costs + "Pure" Fixed Costs   Fixed Portions of Semivariable Costs   Standby + Enabling Costs   Enabling Costs

Capacity Cost	vs. Programmed Cost	Capacity costs give a firm the capability to produce or to sell. Programmed costs, such as for advertising or research and development, may not be essential, but once a decision to incur them is made, they become fixed costs.
Standby Cost	vs. Enabling Cost	Standby costs will be incurred whether capacity, once acquired, is used or not, such as property taxes and depreciation on a factory. Enabling costs, such as for security force, can be avoided if the capacity is unused.
Semifixed Cost	vs. Semivariable Cost	A cost fixed over a wide range but that can change at various levels is a semifixed cost or "step cost." An example is the cost of rail lines from the factory to the main rail line where fixed cost depends on whether there are one or two parallel lines, but are independent of the number of trains run per day. Semivariable costs combine a strictly fixed component cost plus a variable component. Telephone charges usually have a fixed monthly component plus a charge related to usage.

5. The following pairs of terms distinguish among economic uses or decision making uses or regulatory uses of cost terms.

Fully Absorbed Cost vs.	Variable Cost (Direct Cost)	Fully absorbed costs refer to costs where fixed costs have been allocated to units or departments as required by generally accepted accounting principles. Variable costs, in contrast, may be more relevant for making decisions, such as in setting prices.
Fully Absorbed Cost vs.	Full Cost	In full costing, all costs, manufacturing costs as well as central corporate express (including financing expenses) are allocated to product or divisions. In full absorption costing, only manufacturing costs are allocated to product. Only in full costing will revenues, expenses, and income summed over all products or divisions equal corporate revenues, expenses, and income.

Cost Terminology: Distinctions among Terms Containing the Word "Cost"

Terms (Synonyms Given in Parentheses)			Distinctions and Comments
Opportunity Cost	vs.	Outlay Cost (Out-of-pocket Cost)	Opportunity cost refers to the economic benefit foregone by using a resource for one purpose instead of for another. The outlay cost of the resource will be recorded in financial records. The distinction arises because a resource is already in the possession of the entity with a recorded historical cost. Its economic value to the firm, opportunity cost, generally differs from the historical cost; it can be either larger or smaller.
Future Cost	vs.	Past Cost	Effective decision making analyzes only present and future outlay costs, or out-of-pocket costs. Opportunity costs are relevant for profit maximizing; past costs are used in financial reporting.
Short-Run Cost	vs.	Long-Run Cost	Short-run costs vary as output is varied for a given configuration of plant and equipment. Long-run costs can be incurred to change that configuration. This pair of terms is the economic analog of the accounting pair, see (2) above, variable and fixed costs. The analogy is not perfect because some short-run costs are fixed, such as property taxes on the factory, from the point of view of break-even analysis.
Imputed Cost	vs.	Book Cost	In a regulatory setting some costs, for example the cost of owners' equity capital, are calculated and used for various purposes; these are imputed costs. Imputed costs are not recorded in the historical costs accounting records for financial reporting. Book costs are recorded.
Average Cost	vs.	Marginal Cost	The economic distinction equivalent to fully absorbed cost of product and direct cost of product. Average cost is total cost divided by number of units. Marginal cost is the cost to produce the next unit (or the last unit).
Incremental Cost	vs.	Variable Cost	Whether a cost changes or remains fixed depends on the activity basis being considered. Typically, but not invariably, costs are said to be variable or fixed with respect to an activity basis such as changes in production levels. Typically, but not invariably, costs are said to be incremental or not with respect to an activity basis such as the undertaking of some new venture. For example, consider the decision to undertake the production of food processors, rather than food blenders, which the manufacturer has been making. To produce processors requires the acquisition of a new machine tool. The cost of the new machine tool is incremental with respect to a decision to produce food processors instead of food blenders, but, once acquired, becomes a fixed cost of producing food processors. If costs of direct labor hours are going to be incurred for the production of food processors or food blenders, whichever is produced (in a scenario when not both are to be produced), such costs are variable with respect to production measured in units, but not incremental with respect to the decision to produce processors rather than blenders. This distinction is often blurred in practice, so a careful understanding of the activity basis being considered is necessary for understanding of the concepts being used in a particular application.

costing. The process of calculating the cost of activities, products, or services. The British word for *cost accounting*.

coupon. That portion of a *bond* document redeemable at a specified date for *interest* payments. Its physical form is much like a ticket; each coupon is dated and is deposited at a bank, just like a check, for collection or is mailed to the issuer's agent for collection.

coupon rate. Of a *bond*, the amount of annual coupons divided by par value. Contrast with *effective rate*.

covenant. A promise with legal validity.

CPA. See *certified public accountant*. The *AICPA* suggests that no periods be shown in the abbreviation.

CPI. *Consumer price index*.

CPP. Current purchasing power; usually used as an adjective modifying the word "accounting" to mean the accounting that produces *constant dollar financial statements*.

Cr. Abbreviation for *credit*.

credit. As a noun, an entry on the right-hand side of an *account*. As a verb, to make an entry on the right-hand side of an account. Records increases in *liabilities, owner's equity, revenues* and *gains*; records decreases in *assets* and *expenses*. See *debit and credit conventions*. Also the ability or right to buy or borrow in return for a promise to pay later.

credit bureau. An organization paid by its clients to gather and evaluate data on the ability of a person to meet financial obligations.

credit loss. The amount of *accounts receivable* that is, or is expected to become, *uncollectible*.

credit memorandum. A document used by a seller to inform a buyer that the buyer's *account receivable* is being credited (reduced) because of *errors, returns,* or *allowances*. Also, the document provided by a bank to a depositor to indicate that the depositor's balance is being increased because of some event other than a deposit, such as the collection by the bank of the depositor's *note receivable*.

creditor. One who lends.

Critical Path Method. A method of *network analysis* in which normal duration time is estimated for each activity within a project. The critical path identifies the shortest completion period based on the most time-consuming sequence of activities from the beginning to the end of the network. Compare *PERT*.

cross-reference (index). A number placed by each *account* in a *journal entry* indicating the *ledger* account to which

the entry is posted and placing in the ledger the page number of the journal where the entry was made. Used to link the *debit* and *credit* parts of an entry in the ledger accounts back to the original entry in the journal. See *audit trail*.

cross-section analysis. Analysis of *financial statements* of various firms for a single period of time; contrast with time-series analysis where statements of a given firm are analyzed over several periods of time.

Crown corporation. Canada and the United Kingdom. A corporation that is ultimately accountable through a Minister of the Crown to Parliament or a legislature for the conduct of its affairs.

cum div. (dividend). The condition of shares whose quoted market price includes a declared but unpaid dividend. This condition pertains between the declaration date of the dividend and the record date. Compare *ex div. (dividend)*.

cum rights. The condition of securities whose quoted market price includes the right to purchase new securities. (Compare *ex rights*.)

cumulative dividend. Preferred stock *dividends* that, if not paid, accrue as a commitment that must be paid before dividends to common shareholders can be declared.

cumulative preferred shares. *Preferred* shares with *cumulative dividend* rights.

current asset. *Cash* and other *assets* that are expected to be turned into cash, sold, or exchanged within the normal operating cycle of the firm or one year, whichever is longer. One year is the usual period for classifying asset balances on the balance sheet. Current assets include *cash, marketable securities, receivables, inventory,* and *current prepayments*.

current cost. *Cost* stated in terms of current values (of *productive capacity*) rather than in terms of *acquisition cost*. See *net realizable value, current selling price*.

current cost accounting. The *FASB's* term for *financial statements* where the *attribute measured* is *current cost*.

current cost/nominal dollar accounting. Accounting based on *current cost* valuations measured in *nominal dollars*. Components of *income* include an *operating margin* and *holding gains and losses*.

current exit value. *Exit value*.

current fund. In governmental accounting, a synonym for *general fund*.

current funds. *Cash* and other assets readily convertible into cash. In governmental accounting, funds spent for operating purposes during the current period. Includes *general*, *special revenue*, *debt service*, and *enterprise funds*.

current (gross) margin. See *operating margin (based on current costs)*.

current liability. A debt or other obligation that must be discharged within a short time, usually the *earnings cycle* or one year, normally by expending *current assets*.

current operating performance concept. The notion that reported *income* for a period ought to reflect only ordinary, normal, and recurring operations of that period. A consequence is that *extraordinary* and nonrecurring items are entered directly in the Retained Earnings account. Contrast with *clean surplus concept*. This concept is no longer acceptable. (See *APB Opinions Nos. 9* and *30*.)

current ratio. Sum of *current assets* divided by sum of *current liabilities*. See *ratio*.

current realizable value. *Realizable value*.

current replacement cost. Of an *asset*, the amount currently required to acquire an identical asset (in the same condition and with the same service potential) or an asset capable of rendering the same service at a current *fair market price*. If these two amounts differ, the lower is usually used. Contrast with *reproduction cost*.

current selling price. The amount for which an *asset* could be sold as of a given time in an *arm's-length* transaction, rather than in a forced sale.

current service costs. *Service costs* of a *pension plan*.

current value accounting. The form of accounting where all assets are shown at *current replacement cost (entry value)* or *current selling price* or *net realizable value (exit value)* and all *liabilities* are shown at *present value*. Entry and exit values may be quite different from each other so there is no general agreement on the precise meaning of current value accounting.

current yield. Of a *bond*, the annual amount of *interest coupons* divided by current market price of the bond. Contrast with *yield to maturity*.

currently attainable standard cost. *Normal standard cost*.

curvilinear (variable) cost. A continuous, but not necessarily linear (straight-line), functional relation between activity levels and *costs*.

customers' ledger. The *ledger* that shows accounts receivable of individual customers. It is the *subsidiary ledger* for the *controlling account*, Accounts Receivable.

cutoff rate. *Hurdle rate*.

D

data bank. An organized file of information, such as customer name and address file, used in and kept up to date by a processing system.

data base. A comprehensive collection of interrelated information stored together in computerized form to serve several applications.

data base management system. Generalized software programs used to handle physical storage and manipulation of data bases.

days of average inventory on hand. See *ratio*.

days of grace. The days allowed by law or contract for payment of a debt after its due date.

DCF. *Discounted cash flow*.

DDB. *Double-declining-balance depreciation*.

debenture bond. A *bond* not secured with *collateral*.

debit. As a noun, an entry on the left-hand side of an *account*. As a verb, to make an entry on the left-hand side of an account. Records increases in *assets* and *expenses*; records decreases in *liabilities, owners' equity*, and *revenues*. See *debit and credit conventions*.

debit and credit conventions. The equality of the two sides of the *accounting equation* is maintained by recording equal amounts of *debits* and *credits* for each *transaction*. The conventional use of the *T-account* form and the rules for debit and credit in *balance sheet accounts* are summarized as follows.

Any Asset Account

Opening Balance Increase + Dr.	Decrease − Cr.
Ending Balance	

Any Liability Account

Decrease	Opening Balance
–	Increase
Dr.	+
	Cr.
	Ending Balance

Any Owners' Equity Account

Decrease	Opening Balance
–	Increase
Dr.	+
	Cr.
	Ending Balance

Revenue and expense accounts belong to the owners' equity group. The relationship and the rules for debit and credit in these accounts can be expressed as follows.

Any Owners' Equity Account

Decrease		Increase	
–		+	
Dr.		Cr.	
Expenses		Revenues	
Dr.	Cr.	Dr.	Cr.
+	–	–	+
*			*

* Normal balance prior to closing

debit memorandum. A document used by a seller to inform a buyer that the seller is debiting (increasing) the amount of the buyer's *account receivable*. Also, the document provided by a bank to a depositor to indicate that the depositor's *balance* is being decreased because of some event other than payment for a *check*, such as monthly service charges or the printing of checks.

debt. An amount owed. The general name for *notes, bonds, mortgages,* and the like that are evidence of amounts owed and have definite payment dates.

debt-equity ratio. Total *liabilities* divided by total equities. See *ratio*. Sometimes the denominator is merely total shareholders' equity. Sometimes the numerator is restricted to *long-term debt*.

debt capital. *Noncurrent liabilities.* See *debt financing* and contrast with *equity financing*.

debt financing. Raising *funds* by issuing *bonds, mortgages,* or *notes*. Contrast with *equity financing*. *Leverage.*

debt guarantee. See *guarantee*.

debt ratio. *Debt-equity ratio.*

debt service fund. In governmental accounting, a *fund* established to account for payment of *interest* and *principal* on all general-obligation *debt* other than that payable from special *assessments*.

debt service requirement. The amount of cash required for payments of *interest*, current maturities of *principal* on outstanding *debt*, and payments to *sinking funds* (corporations) or to the *debt service fund* (governmental).

debtor. One who borrows.

decentralized decision making. A manager of a business unit is given responsibility for that unit's *revenues* and *costs*, and is free to make decisions about prices, sources of supply, and the like, as though the unit were a separate business owned by the manager. See *responsibility accounting* and *transfer price*.

declaration date. Time when a *dividend* is declared by the *board of directors*.

declining balance depreciation. The method of calculating the periodic *depreciation* charge by multiplying the *book value* at the start of the period by a constant percentage. In pure declining-balance depreciation the constant percentage is $1 - \sqrt[n]{s/c}$, where n is the *depreciable life*, s is *salvage value*, and c is *acquisition cost*. See *double-declining balance depreciation*.

deep discount bonds. Said of *bonds* selling much below (exactly how much is not clear) *par value*.

defalcation. *Embezzlement.*

default. Failure to pay *interest* or *principal* on a *debt* when due.

defeasance. *Interest rates* have increased over the past several decades. Consequently, the *market value* of *debt* outstanding is substantially less than its *book value* for many firms. In *historical cost accounting* for debt retirements, retiring debt with a *cash* payment less than the book value of the debt results in a gain (generally, an *extraordinary item*). Many firms would like to retire the outstanding debt issues and report the gain. Two factors impede doing so: (1) the gain can be a taxable event generating adverse *income tax* consequences; and (2) the transactions costs in retiring all of the debt can be large, in part because not all debt holders can easily be located or persuaded to sell back their bonds to the issuer. The process of "defeasance" is the economic equivalent to retiring a debt issue that saves the issuer from adverse tax consequences and actually having to locate and retire the bonds. The process works as follows. The debt issuing firm turns over to an independent trustee, such as a bank, amounts of cash or low-risk government bonds sufficient to make all debt service payments on the outstanding debt, including bond retirements, in return for the trustee's commitment to make all debt service payments. The debt issuer effectively retires the outstanding debt. It debits the liability account, credits Cash or Marketable Securities, as appropriate, and credits Extraordinary Gain on Debt Retirement. The trustee is free to retire debt or make debt service payments, whichever it chooses. For income tax purposes, however, the firm's debt is still outstanding. The firm will have taxable interest *deductions* for its still outstanding debt and taxable interest *revenue* on the investments held by the trustee for debt service. In law, the term "defeasance" means "a rendering null and void." This process described here renders the outstanding debt economically null and void, without causing a taxable event.

defensive interval. A financial *ratio* equal to the number of days of normal cash *expenditures* covered by *quick assets*. It is defined as

$$\frac{\text{Quick Assets}}{\frac{\text{All Expenses Except Amoritzation and}}{\text{Others Not Using Funds}}}{365}$$

The denominator of the ratio is the cash expenditure per day. This ratio has been found useful in predicting *bankruptcy*.

deferral. The accounting process concerned with past *cash receipts* and *payments*; in contrast to *accrual*. Recognizing a liability resulting from a current cash receipt (as for magazines to be delivered) or recognizing an asset from a current cash payment (or for prepaid insurance or a long-term depreciable asset).

deferral method. See *flow-through method* (of accounting for the *investment credit*) for definition and contrast.

deferred annuity. An *annuity* whose first payment is made sometime after the end of the first period.

deferred asset. *Deferred charge.*

deferred charge. *Expenditure* not recognized as an *expense* of the period when made but carried forward as an *asset* to be *written off* in future periods, such as for advance rent payments or insurance premiums. See *deferral*.

deferred cost. *Deferred charge.*

deferred credit. Sometimes used to indicate *advances from customers*.

deferred debit. *Deferred charge.*

deferred expense. *Deferred charge.*

deferred gross margin. *Unrealized gross margin.*

deferred income. *Advances from customers.*

deferred income tax (liability). An *indeterminate term liability* that arises when the pretax income shown on the tax return is less than what it would have been had the same *accounting principles* and *cost basis* for *assets* and *liabilities* been used in tax returns as used for financial reporting. *SFAS* No. 96 requires that the firm debit income tax *expense* and credit deferred income tax with the amount of the taxes delayed by using different accounting principles in tax returns from those used in financial reports. See *temporary difference, timing difference,* and *permanent difference.* See *installment sales.* If, as a result of temporary differences, cumulative taxable income exceeds cumulative reported income before taxes, the deferred income tax account will have a *debit* balance and will be reported as a *deferred charge.*

deferred revenue. Sometimes used to indicate *advances from customers*.

deferred tax. See *deferred income tax*.

deficit. A *debit balance* in the Retained Earnings account; presented on the balance sheet in a *contra account* to shareholders' equity. Sometimes used to mean negative *net income* for a period.

defined-benefit plan. A *pension plan* where the employer promises specific dollar amounts to each eligible employee; the amounts usually depend on a formula that takes into account such things as the employee's earnings, years of employment, and age. The employer's cash contributions and pension expense are adjusted in relation to *actuarial* experience in the eligible employee group and investment performance of the pension *fund*. Sometimes called a "fixed-benefit" pension plan. Contrast with *money purchase plan*.

defined contribution plan. A *money purchase (pension) plan* or other arrangement, based on formula or discretion, where the employer makes cash contributions to eligible individual employee *accounts* under the terms of a written plan document. Profit-sharing pension plans are of this type.

deflation. A period of declining *general price changes*.

demand deposit. *Funds* in a *checking account* at a bank.

demand loan. See *term loan* for definition and contrast.

denial of opinion. Canada. The statement that an *auditor*, for reasons arising in the *audit*, is unable to express an opinion as to whether the *financial statements* provide *fair presentation.*

denominator volume. Capacity measured in expected number of units to be produced this period; divided into *budgeted fixed costs* to obtain fixed costs applied per unit of product.

dependent variable. See *regression analysis.*

depletion. Exhaustion or *amortization* of a *wasting asset,* or *natural resource.* Also see *percentage depletion.*

depletion allowance. See *percentage depletion.*

deposit method (of revenue recognition). This method of *revenue* recognition does not differ from the *completed sale* or *completed contract method.* In some contexts such as retail land sales, the customer must make substantial payments while still having the right to back out of the deal and receive a refund. When there is uncertainty about whether the deal will be completed but a cash collection is made by the seller, the seller must *credit* deposits, a *liability account,* rather than *revenue.* (In this regard, the accounting differs from the completed contract method where the account credited is offset against the *work-in-process inventory* account.) When the *sale* becomes complete, a revenue account is credited and the deposit account is *debited.*

deposit, sinking fund. Payments made to a *sinking fund.*

deposits (by customers). A *liability* arising upon receipt of *cash* (as in a bank, or in a grocery store when the customer pays cash for soft-drink bottles to be repaid when the bottles are returned).

deposits in transit. Deposits made by a firm but not yet reflected on the *bank statement.*

depreciable cost. That part of the *cost* of an asset, usually *acquisition cost* less *salvage value,* that is to be charged off over the life of the asset through the process of *depreciation.*

depreciable life. For an *asset,* the time period or units of activity (such as miles driven for a truck) over which *depreciable cost* is to be allocated. For tax returns, depreciable life may be shorter than estimated *service life.*

depreciation. *Amortization of plant assets;* the process of allocating the cost of an asset to the periods of benefit—the *depreciable life.* Classified as a *production cost* or a *period expense,* depending upon the asset and whether *absorption* or *variable costing* is used. Depreciation methods described in this glossary include the *annuity method, appraisal method, composite method,*

compound interest method, production method, replacement method, retirement method, straight line method, sinking fund method, and *sum-of-the-years'-digits method.*

depreciation reserve. An inferior term for *accumulated depreciation.* See *reserve.* Do not confuse with a replacement *fund.*

Descartes' rule of signs. In a *capital budgeting* context, the rule says that a series of cash flows will have a nonnegative number of *internal rates of return.* The number is equal to the number of variations in the sign of the cash flow series or is less than that number by an even integer. Consider the following series of cash flows, the first occurring now and the others at subsequent yearly intervals: -100, -100, +50, +175, -50, +100. The internal rates of return are the numbers for r that satisfy the equation

$$-100 - \frac{100}{(1+r)} + \frac{50}{(1+r)^2} + \frac{175}{(1+r)^3} - \frac{50}{(1+r)^4} + \frac{100}{(1+r)^5} = 0$$

The series of cash flows has three variations in sign: a change from minus to plus, a change from plus to minus, and a change from minus to plus. The rule says that this series must have either one or three internal rates of return; in fact, it has only one, about 12 percent. See *reinvestment rate* for guidance in solving this problem.

detective controls. *Internal controls* designed to detect, or maximize the chance of detection of, errors and other irregularities. Compare *preventive controls.*

determination. See *determine.*

determine. The verb "determine" and the noun "determination" are often used (in our opinion, overused) by accountants and those who describe the accounting process. A leading dictionary associates the following meanings with the verb "determine": settle, decide, conclude, ascertain, cause, affect, control, impel, terminate, and decide upon. In addition, accounting writers can mean any one of the following: measure, allocate, report, calculate, compute, observe, choose, and legislate. In accounting, there are two distinct sets of meanings—those encompassed by the synonym "cause or legislate" and those encompassed by the synonym "measure." The first set of uses conveys the active notion of causing something to happen and the second set of uses conveys the more passive notion of observing something that someone else has caused to happen. An accountant who speaks of cost or income "determination" generally means measurement or observation, not causation; management and economic conditions cause costs and income to be what they are. One who speaks of accounting principles "determination" can mean choosing or applying (as in "determining depreciation charges" from an allowable set) or causing to be acceptable (as in the *FASB* "determining" the accounting for *leases*). In the long run, income is cash in less cash out, so management and economic conditions "determine" (cause) income to be what it is. In the short run, reported income is a function of accounting principles chosen and applied, so the accountant "determines" (measures) income. A question such as "Who determines income?" has, therefore, no unambiguous answer. The meaning of "an accountant determining acceptable accounting principles" is also vague. Does the clause mean merely choosing one from the set of generally acceptable principles, or does it mean using professional judgment to decide that some of the generally accepted principles are not correct under the current circumstances? We try never to use "determine" unless we mean "cause." Otherwise we use "measure," "report," "calculate," "compute," or whatever specific verb seems appropriate. We suggest that careful writers will always "determine" to use the most specific verb to convey meaning. "Determine" is seldom the best choice of words to describe a process where those who make decisions often differ from those who apply technique.

development stage enterprise. As defined in *SFAS* No. 7, a firm whose planned principal *operations* have not commenced or, having commenced, have not generated significant *revenue*. Such enterprises should be so identified, but no special *accounting principles* apply to them.

differential analysis. Analysis of *incremental costs*.

differential cost. *Incremental cost*. If a total cost curve is smooth (in mathematical terms, differentiable), then the curve graphing the derivative of the total cost curve is often said to show differential costs, the cost increments associated with infinitesimal changes in volume.

dilution. A potential reduction in *earnings per share* or *book value* per share by the potential *conversion* of securities or by the potential exercise of *warrants* or *options*.

dilutive. Said of a *security* that would reduce *earnings per share* if it were exchanged for *common stock*.

dipping into LIFO layers. See *LIFO inventory layer*.

direct access. Access to computer storage where information can be located directly, regardless of its position in the storage file. Compare *sequential access*.

direct cost. Cost of *direct material* and *direct labor* incurred in producing a product. See *prime cost*. In some accounting literature, this term is used to mean the same thing as *variable cost*.

direct costing. Another, less-preferred, term for *variable costing*.

direct labor (material) cost. Cost of labor (material) applied and assigned directly to a product; contrast with *indirect labor (material)*.

direct labor variance. *Price* and *quantity variances* for direct labor in *standard costs systems*.

direct method. See *statement of cash flows*.

direct posting. A method of bookkeeping where *entries* are made directly in *ledger accounts*, without the use of a *journal*.

direct write-off method. See *write-off method*.

disbursement. Payment by *cash* or by *check*. See *expenditure*.

DISC. Domestic International Sales Corporation. A U.S. *corporation*, usually a *subsidiary*, whose *income* is primarily attributable to exports. *Income tax* on 50 percent of a DISC's income is usually deferred for a long period. Generally, this results in a lower overall corporate tax for the *parent* than would otherwise be incurred.

disclaimer of opinion. An *auditor's report* stating that an opinion cannot be given on the *financial statements*. Usually results from *material* restrictions on the scope of the audit or from material uncertainties about the accounts that the auditor cannot resolve at the time of the audit.

disclosure. The showing of facts in *financial statements, notes* thereto, or the *auditor's report*.

discontinued operations. See *income from discontinued operations*.

discount. In the context of *compound interest, bonds* and *notes*, the difference between *face* or *future value* and *present value* of a payment. In the context of *sales* and *purchases*, a reduction in price granted for prompt payment. See also *chain discount, quantity discount*, and *trade discount*.

discount factor. The reciprocal of one plus the *discount rate*. If the discount rate is 10 percent per period, the discount factor for three periods is $1/(1.10)^3 = (1.10)^{-3} = 0.75131$.

discount rate. *Interest rate* used to convert future payments to *present values*.

discounted bailout period. In a *capital budgeting* context, the total time that must elapse before discounted value of net accumulated cash flows from a project, including potential *salvage value* at various times of assets, equals or exceeds the *present value* of net accumulated cash outflows. Contrast with *discounted payback period*.

discounted cash flow. DCF. Using either the *net present value* or the *internal rate of return* in an analysis to measure the value of future expected cash *expenditures* and *receipts* at a common date. In discounted cash flow analysis, choosing the alternative with the largest *internal rate of return* may give wrong answers when there are *mutually exclusive projects* and the amounts of initial investment are quite different for two of the projects. Consider, to take an unrealistic example to illustrate the point, a project involving an initial investment of $1, with an *IRR* of 60 percent and another project involving an initial investment of $1 million with an IRR of 40 percent. Under most conditions, most firms will prefer the second project to the first, but choosing the project with the larger IRR will lead to undertaking the first, not the second. This shortcoming of choosing between alternatives based on the magnitude of the internal rate or return, rather than based on the magnitude of the *net present value* of the cash flows, is called the "scale effect."

discounted payback period. The shortest amount of time which must elapse before the discounted present value of cash inflows from a project, excluding potential *salvage value* equals the discounted *present value* of the cash outflows.

discounting a note. See *note receivable discounted* and *factoring.*

discounts lapsed (lost). The sum of *discounts* offered for prompt payment that were not taken (or allowed) because of expiration of the discount period. See *terms of sale.*

discovery sampling. Acceptance sampling whereby an entire population is accepted if and only if the sample contains no disparities.

discovery value accounting. See *reserve recognition accounting.*

discretionary costs. *Programmed costs.*

Discussion Memorandum. A neutral discussion of all the issues concerning an accounting problem of current concern to the *FASB*. The publication of such a document usually implies that the FASB is considering issuing an *SFAS* or *SFAC* on this particular problem. The discussion memorandum brings together material about the particular problem to facilitate interaction and comment by those interested in the matter. It may lead to an *Exposure Draft.*

dishonored note. A *promissory note* whose maker does not repay the loan at *maturity* for a *term loan*, or on demand, for a *demand loan.*

disintermediation. Federal law regulates the maximum *interest rate* that both banks and savings and loan associations can pay for *time deposits*. When free-market interest rates exceed the regulated interest ceiling for such time deposits, some depositors withdraw their funds and invest them elsewhere at a higher interest rate. This process is known as "disintermediation."

distributable income. The portion of conventional accounting net income that can be distributed to owners (usually in the form of *dividends*) without impairing the physical capacity of the firm to continue operations at current levels. Pretax distributable income is conventional pretax income less the excess of *current cost* of goods sold and *depreciation* charges based on the replacement cost of *productive capacity* over cost of goods sold and depreciation on an *acquisition cost basis*. Contrast with *sustainable income.* See *inventory profit.*

distributable surplus. Canada and the United Kingdom. The statutory designation to describe the portion of the proceeds of the issue of shares without *par value* not allocated to share capital.

distributed processing. Processing in a complex computer information network, in which data relevant only to individual locations is processed locally, while information required elsewhere is transmitted either to the central computer or to local a computer for further processing.

distribution expense. *Expense* of selling, advertising, and delivery activities.

dividend. A distribution of assets generated from *earnings* to owners of a corporation; it may be paid in cash (cash dividend), with stock (stock dividend), with property, or with other securities (dividend in kind). Dividends, except stock dividends, become a legal liability of the corporation when they are declared. Hence, the owner of stock ordinarily recognizes *revenue* when a dividend, other than a stock dividend, is declared. See also *liquidating dividend* and *stock dividend.*

dividend yield. *Dividends* declared for the year divided by market price of the stock as of a given time of the year.

dividends in arrears. Dividends on *cumulative preferred stock* that have not been declared in accordance with the preferred stock contract. Such arrearages must usually be cleared before dividends on *common stock* can be declared.

dividends in kind. See *dividend.*

division. A more or less self-contained business unit which is part of a larger family of business units under common control.

divisional control. See *control system.*

divisional reporting. *Line-of-business reporting.*

dollar sign rules. In presenting accounting statements or schedules, place a dollar sign beside the first figure in each column and beside any figure below a horizontal line drawn under the preceding figure.

dollar-value LIFO method. A form of *LIFO* inventory accounting with inventory quantities (*layers*) measured in dollar, rather than physical, terms. Adjustments to account for changing prices are made by use of specific price indexes appropriate for the kinds of items in the inventory.

Domestic International Sales Corporation. See *DISC*.

donated capital. A *shareholders' equity* account credited when contributions, such as land or buildings, are freely given to the company. Do not confuse with *contributed capital*.

double entry. The system of recording transactions that maintains the equality of the accounting equation; each entry results in recording equal amounts of *debits* and *credits*.

double-declining-balance depreciation. DDB. *Declining-balance depreciation*, which see, where the constant percentage used to multiply by book value in computing the depreciation charge for the year is $2/n$ and n is the *depreciable life* in periods. *Salvage value* is omitted from the depreciable amount. Thus if the asset cost $100 and has a depreciable life of 5 years, the depreciation in the first year would be $40 = 2/5 x $100, in the second would be $24 = 2/5 x ($100 - $40), and in the third year would be $14.40 = 2/5 x ($100 - $40 - $24). By the fourth year, the remaining undepreciated cost could be depreciated under the straight line method at $10.80 = 1/2 x ($100 - $40 - $24 - $14.40) per year for tax purposes.

double T-account. *T-account* with an extra horizontal line showing a change in the account balance to be explained by the subsequent entries into the account, such as:

Plant

42,000	

This account shows an increase in the asset account, plant, of $42,000 to be explained. Such accounts are useful in preparing the *statement of cash flows*; they are not a part of the formal record-keeping process.

double taxation. Corporate income is subject to the corporate income tax and the aftertax income, when distributed to owners as dividends, is subject to the personal income tax.

doubtful accounts. *Accounts receivable* estimated to be *uncollectible*.

Dr. The abbreviation for *debit*.

draft. A written order by the first party, called the drawer, instructing a second party, called the drawee (such as a bank) to pay a third party, called the payee. See also *check, cashier's check, certified check, NOW account, sight draft,* and *trade acceptance*.

drawee. See *draft*.

drawer. See *draft*.

drawing account. A *temporary account* used in *sole proprietorships* and *partnerships* to record payments to owners or partners during a period. At the end of the period, the drawing account is closed by crediting it and debiting the owner's or partner's share of income or, perhaps, his or her capital account.

drawings. Payments made to a *sole proprietor* or to a *partner* during a period. See *drawing account*.

driver. A determinant of costs incurred. Examples include order processing, issuing an engineering change order, changing the production schedule, and stopping production to change machine settings. The notion arises primarily in product costing, particularly *activity-based costing*.

drop ship. Ordinarily a manufacturer sends goods to a distributor who sends the goods to its customer. If the distributor asks the manufacturer to send an order directly to the customer, the shipment is called a "drop shipment" and the goods are said to be "drop shipped."

dry-hole accounting. See *reserve recognition accounting* for definition and contrast.

dual transactions assumption (fiction). In presenting the *statement of cash flows*, some transactions not involving *cash* accounts are reported as though cash was generated and then used. For example, the issue of *capital stock* in return for the *asset*, land, is reported in the statement of cash flows as though stock were issued for *cash* and cash were used to acquire land. Other examples of transactions that require the dual transaction fiction are the issue of the *mortgage* in return for a noncurrent asset and the issue of stock to bondholders on *conversion* of their *convertible bonds*.

dual transfer prices. The *transfer price charged* to the buying *division* differs from that *credited* to the selling division. Such prices make sense when the selling division has excess capacity and, as usual, the *incremental cost* to produce the goods or services being transferred is less than their *fair market value*.

duality. The axiom of *double entry* record keeping that every *transaction* is broken down into equal *debit* and *credit* amounts.

E

e. The base of natural logarithms; 2.718281828459045 . . . . If *interest* is compounded continuously during a period at stated rate of *r* per period, then the effective *interest rate* is equivalent to interest compounded once per period at rate *i* where $i = e^r - 1$. Tables of e^r are widely available. If 12 percent annual interest is compounded continuously, the effective annual rate is $e^{.12} - 1 = 12.75$ percent.

earned surplus. A term once used, but no longer considered proper, for *retained earnings*.

earnings. *Income*, or sometimes *profit*.

earnings cycle. The period of time that elapses for a given firm, or the series of transactions, during which *cash* is converted into *goods* and *services*, goods and services are sold to customers, and customers pay for their purchases with cash. Also known as *cash cycle*.

earnings per share (of common stock). *Net income* to common shareholders (net income minus *preferred dividends*) divided by the average number of *common shares* outstanding; see also *primary earnings per share* and *fully diluted earnings per share*. See *ratio*.

earnings per share (of preferred stock). *Net income* divided by the average number of *preferred shares* outstanding during the period. This ratio indicates how well the preferred dividends are covered or protected; it does not indicate a legal share of *earnings*. See *ratio*.

earnings, retained. See *retained earnings*.

earnings statement. *Income statement*.

earn-out. An agreement between two merging firms under which the amount of payment by the acquiring firm to the acquired firm's shareholders depends on the future earnings of the acquired firm or, perhaps of the *consolidated entity*.

easement. The acquired right or privilege of one person to use, or have access to, certain property of another. For example, a public utility's right to lay pipes or lines under property of another and to service those facilities.

economic depreciation. Decline in *current cost* of an *asset* during a period.

economic entity. See *entity*.

economic life. The time span over which the benefits of an *asset* are expected to be received. The economic life of a *patent*, *copyright*, or *franchise* may be less than the legal life. *Service life*.

economic order quantity. In mathematical *inventory* analysis, the optimal amount of stock to order when inventory is reduced to a level called the "reorder point." If *A* represents the *incremental cost* of placing a single order, *D* represents the total demand for a period of time in units, and *H* represents the incremental holding cost during the period per unit of inventory, then the economic order quantity $Q = \sqrt{2AD/H}$. Q is sometimes called the "optimal lot size."

ED. *Exposure Draft*.

EDP. Abbreviation for *electronic data processing*.

effective interest method. A systematic method for computing *interest expense* (or *revenue*) that makes the interest expense for each period divided by the amount of the net *liability* (*asset*) at the beginning of the period equal to the *yield rate* on the bond at the time of issue (acquisition). Interest for a period is yield rate (at time of issue) multiplied by the net liability (asset) at the start of the period. The *amortization* of discount or premium is the *plug* to give equal *debits* and *credits*. (Interest expense is a debit and the amount of coupon payments is a credit.)

effective (interest) rate. Of a bond, the *internal rate of return* or *yield to maturity* at the time of issue. Contrast with *coupon rate*. If the bond is issued for a price below *par*, the effective rate is higher than the coupon rate; if it is issued for a price greater than par, then the effective rate is lower than the coupon rate. In the context of *compound interest*, the concept arises when the *compounding period* on a *loan* differs from one year, such as a nominal interest rate of 12 percent compounded monthly. The effective interest is the single rate that could use at the end of the year to multiply the *principal* at the beginning of the year and give the same amount as results from compounding interest each period during the year. For example, if 12 percent per year is compounded monthly, the effective annual interest rate is 12.683 percent. That is, if you compound $100 each month at 1 percent per month, the $100 will grow to $112.63 at the end of the year. In general, if the nominal rate is *r* percent per year and is compounded *m* times per year, then the effective rate is $(1 + r/m)^m - 1$.

efficiency variance. A term used for the *quantity variance* for labor or *variable overhead* in a *standard cost system*.

efficient market hypothesis. The supposition in finance that securities' prices reflect all available information and react nearly instantaneously and in an unbiased fashion to new information.

EITF. *Emerging Issues Task Force.*

eligible. Under income tax legislation, a term that restricts or otherwise alters the meaning of another tax or accounting term, generally to signify that the related assets or operations are entitled to specified tax treatment.

eliminations. *Work sheet* entries to prepare *consolidated statements* that are made to avoid duplicating the amounts of *assets, liabilities, owners' equity, revenues,* and *expenses* of the consolidated *entity* when the accounts of the *parent* and *subsidiaries* are summed.

Emerging Issues Task Force. EITF. A group convened by the *FASB* to deal more rapidly with accounting issues than the FASB's due process procedures can allow. The task force comprises about 20 members from public accounting, industry, and several trade associations. It meets every six weeks. Meetings are chaired by the FASB's director of research. Several FASB board members usually attend and participate. The chief accountant of the *SEC* has indicated that the SEC will require that published financial statements follow guidelines set by a consensus of the EITF. The EITF requires that nearly all of its members agree on a position before that position is given the label of "consensus." Since 1984, the EITF has become one of the promulgators of *GAAP*.

employee stock option. See *stock option.*

Employee Stock Ownership Trust (or Plan). See *ESOT.*

employer, employee payroll taxes. See *payroll.*

enabling costs. A type of *capacity cost* that will stop being incurred if operations are shut down completely but must be incurred in full if operations are carried out at any level. Costs of a security force or of a quality control inspector for an assembly line might be examples. Contrast with *standby costs.*

encumbrance. In governmental accounting, an anticipated *expenditure*, or *funds* restricted for anticipated expenditure, such as for outstanding purchase orders. *Appropriations* less expenditures less outstanding encumbrances yields unencumbered balance.

ending inventory. The *cost* of *inventory* on hand at the end of the *accounting period*, often called "closing inventory." The dollar amount of inventory to be carried to the subsequent period.

endorsee. See *endorser.*

endorsement. See *draft.* The *payee* signs the draft and transfers it to a fourth party, such as the payee's bank.

endorser. The *payee* of a *note* or *draft* signs it, after writing "Pay to the order of X," transfers the note to person X, and presumably receives some benefit, such as cash, in return. The payee who signs over the note is called the endorser and person X is called the endorsee. The endorsee then has the rights of the payee and may in turn become an endorser by endorsing the note to another endorsee.

engineering method (of cost estimation). Estimates of unit costs of product built up from study of the materials, labor and *overhead* components of the production process.

enterprise. Any business organization, usually defining the accounting *entity*.

enterprise fund. A *fund* established by a governmental unit to account for acquisition, operation, and maintenance of governmental services that are supposed to be self-supporting from user charges, such as for water or airports.

entity. A person, *partnership, corporation,* or other organization. The *accounting entity* for which accounting statements are prepared may not be the same as the entity defined by law. For example, a *sole proprietorship* is an accounting entity but the individual's combined business and personal assets are the legal entity in most jurisdictions. Several affiliated corporations may be separate legal entities while *consolidated financial statements* are prepared for the group of companies operating as a single economic entity.

entity theory. The view of the corporation that emphasizes the form of the *accounting equation* that says *assets = equities.* Contrast with *proprietorship theory.* The entity theory is less concerned with a distinct line between *liabilities* and *shareholders' equity* than is the proprietorship theory. Rather, all equities are provided to the corporation by outsiders who merely have claims of differing legal standings. The entity theory implies using a *multiple-step* income statement.

entry value. The *current cost* of acquiring an asset or service at a *fair market price. Replacement cost.*

EOQ. *Economic order quantity.*

EPS. *Earnings per share.*

EPVI. *Excess present value index.*

equalization reserve. An inferior title for the allowance or *estimated liability* account when the *allowance method* is used for such things as maintenance expenses. Periodically, maintenance *expense* is debited and the allowance is credited. As maintenance *expenditures* are actually incurred, the allowance is debited and cash or the other asset expended is credited.

equities. *Liabilities* plus *owners' equity*. See *equity*.

equity. A claim to *assets*; a source of assets. *SFAS No. 3* defines equity as "the residual interest in the assets of an entity that remains after deducting its liabilities." Usage may be changing so that "equity" will exclude liabilities. We prefer to keep the broader definition, including liabilities, because there is no other single word that serves this useful purpose.

equity financing. Raising *funds* by issuance of *capital stock*. Contrast with *debt financing*.

equity method. A method of accounting for an *investment* in the stock of another company in which the proportionate share of the earnings of the other company is debited to the investment account and credited to a *revenue* account as earned. When *dividends* are received, *cash* is debited and the investment account is credited. Used in reporting when the investor owns sufficient shares of stock of an unconsolidated company to exercise significant control over the actions of that company. One of the few instances where revenue is recognized without a change in *working capital*.

equity ratio. *Shareholders' equity* divided by total *assets*. See *ratio*.

equivalent production. *Equivalent units*.

equivalent units (of work). The number of units of completed output that would require the same costs as were actually incurred for production of completed and partially completed units during a period. Used primarily in *process costing* calculations to measure in uniform terms the output of a continuous process.

ERISA. Employee Retirement Income Security Act of 1974. The federal law that sets most *pension plan* requirements.

error accounting. See *accounting errors*.

escalator clause. A clause inserted in a purchase or rental contract which permits, under specified conditions, upward adjustments of price or allowances.

escapable cost. *Avoidable costs*.

ESOP. Employee Stock Ownership Plan. See *ESOT*.

ESOT. Employee Stock Ownership Trust. A trust *fund* created by a corporate employer that can provide certain tax benefits to the corporation while providing for

employee stock ownership. The corporate employer can contribute up to 25 percent of its payroll per year to the trust. The contributions are *deductions* from otherwise taxable income for federal *income tax* purposes. The assets of the trust must be used for the benefit of employees—for example, to fund death or retirement benefits. The assets of the trust are usually the *common stock*, sometimes nonvoting, of the corporate employer. As an example of the potential *tax shelter*, consider the case of a corporation with $1 million of *debt* outstanding, which it wishes to retire, and an annual payroll of $2 million. The corporation sells $1 million of common stock to the ESOT. The ESOT borrows $1 million with the loan guaranteed by, and therefore a *contingency* of, the corporation. The corporation uses the $1 million proceeds of the stock issue to retire its outstanding debt. (The debt of the corporation has been replaced with the debt of the ESOT.) The corporation can contribute $500,000 (= .25 x $2 million payroll) to the ESOT each year and treat the contribution as a deduction for tax purposes. After a little more than two years, the ESOT has received sufficient funds to retire its loan. The corporation has effectively repaid its original $1 million debt with pretax dollars. Assuming an income tax rate of 40 percent, it has saved $400,000 (= .40 x $1 million) of aftertax dollars *if* the $500,000 expense for the contribution to the ESOT for the pension benefits of employees would have been made, in one form or another, anyway. Observe that the corporation could use the proceeds ($1 million in the example) of the stock issued to the ESOT for any of several different purposes: financing expansion, replacing plant assets, or acquiring another company. Basically this same form of pretax dollar financing through pensions is "almost" available with any corporate pension plan, but with one important exception. The trustees of an ordinary pension trust must invest the assets "prudently" and if they do not, they are personally liable to employees. Current judgment about "prudent" investment requires diversification—pension trust assets should be invested in a wide variety of investment opportunities. (Not more than 10 percent of a pension trust's assets can ordinarily be invested in the parent's common stock.) Thus the ordinary pension trust cannot, in practice, invest all, or even most, of its assets in the parent corporation's stock. This constraint does not apply to the investments of an ESOT. All ESOT assets may be invested in the parent company's stock. The ESOT also provides a means for closely held corporations to achieve wider ownership of shares without *going public*. The laws enabling ESOTs provide for independent professional appraisal of shares not traded in public markets and for transactions between the corporation and the ESOT or between the ESOT and the employees to be based on the appraised values of the shares.

estate planning. The arrangement of an individual's affairs to facilitate the passage of assets to beneficiaries and to minimize taxes upon death.

estimated expenses. See *after cost*.

estimated liability. The preferred terminology for estimated costs to be incurred for such uncertain things as repairs under *warranty*. An estimated liability appears on the *balance sheet*. Contrast with *contingency*.

estimated revenue. A term used in governmental accounting to designate revenue expected to accrue during a period whether or not it will be collected during the period. A *budgetary account* is usually established at the beginning of the budget period.

estimated salvage value. Synonymous with *salvage value* of an *asset* before its retirement.

estimates, changes in. See *accounting changes*.

estimation sampling. The use of sampling technique whereby a qualitative or quantitative characteristic of the population is inferred from the occurrence of that characteristic in the sample drawn. See *attribute(s) sampling*; *variables sampling*.

EURL; Entreprise unipersonnelle à responsabilité limitée. France. Similar to *SARL*, but has only one shareholder.

ex rights. The condition of securities whose quoted market price no longer includes the right to purchase new securities, such rights having expired or been retained by the vendor. Compare *cum rights*.

except for. Qualification in *auditor's report*, usually caused by a change, approved by the auditor, from one acceptable accounting principle or procedure to another.

excess present value. In a *capital budgeting* context, *present value* of (anticipated net cash inflows minus cash outflows including initial cash outflow) for a project.

excess present value index. *Present value* of future *cash* inflows divided by initial cash outlay.

exchange. The generic term for a transaction (or more technically, a reciprocal transfer) between one entity and another. In another context, the name for a market, such as the New York Stock Exchange.

exchange gain or loss. The phrase used by the *FASB* for *foreign exchange gain or loss*.

exchange rate. The *price* of one country's currency in terms of another country's currency. For example, the British pound sterling might be worth \$1.60 at a given time. The exchange rate would be stated as "one pound is worth one dollar and sixty cents" or "one dollar is worth £.625 (= £1/\$1.60)."

excise tax. Tax on the manufacture, sale, or consumption of a commodity.

ex-dividend. Said of a stock at the time when the declared *dividend* becomes the property of the person who owned the stock on the *record date*. The payment date follows the ex-dividend date.

executory contract. A mere exchange of promises. An agreement providing for payment by a payor to a payee upon the performance of an act or service by the payee, such as a labor contract. Obligations under such contracts generally are not recognized as *liabilities*.

exemption. A term used for various amounts subtracted from gross income in computing taxable income. Not all such subtractions are called "exemptions." See *tax deduction*.

exercise. When owners of an *option* or *warrant* purchase the security that the option entitles them to purchase, they have exercised the option or warrant.

exercise price. See *option*.

exit value. The proceeds that would be received if assets were disposed of in an *arm's-length transaction*. *Current selling price*. *Net realizable value*.

expected value. The mean or arithmetic *average* of a statistical distribution or series of numbers.

expected value of (perfect) information. Expected *net benefits* from an undertaking with (perfect) information minus expected net benefits of the undertaking without (perfect) information.

expendable fund. In governmental accounting, a *fund* whose resources, *principal*, and earnings may be distributed.

expenditure. Payment of *cash* for goods or services received. Payment may be made either at the time the goods or services are received or at a later time. Virtually synonymous with *disbursement* except that disbursement is a broader term and includes all payments for goods or services. Contrast with *expense*.

expense. As a noun, a decrease in *owners' equity* caused by the using up of *assets* in producing *revenue* or carrying out other activities that are part of the entity's *operations*. A "gone" asset or *net asset*; an expired cost. The amount is the *cost* of the assets used up. Do not confuse with *expenditure* or *disbursement*, which may occur before, when, or after the related expense is recognized. Use the word "cost" to refer to an item that still has service potential and is an asset. Use the word "expense" after the asset's service potential has been used.

As a verb, to designate a past or current expenditure as a current expense.

expense account.   An *account* to accumulate *expenses*; such accounts are closed at the end of the accounting period. A *temporary owners' equity* account. Also used to describe a listing of expenses by an employee submitted to the employer for reimbursement.

experience rating.   A term used in insurance, particularly unemployment insurance, to denote changes from ordinary rates to reflect extraordinarily large or small amounts of claims over time by the insured.

expired cost.   An *expense* or a *loss*.

Exposure Draft. ED.   A preliminary statement of the *FASB* (or *APB* between 1962 and 1973) that shows the contents of a pronouncement the Board is considering making effective.

external reporting.   Reporting to shareholders and the public, as opposed to internal reporting for management's benefit. See *financial accounting* and contrast with *managerial accounting*.

extraordinary item.   A *material expense* or *revenue* item characterized both by its unusual nature and infrequency of occurrence that is shown along with its income tax effects separately from ordinary income and *income from discontinued operations* on the *income statement*. A *loss* from an earthquake would probably be classified as an extraordinary item. Gain (or loss) on retirement of *bonds* is treated as an extraordinary item under the terms of *SFAS No. 4*.

F

face amount (value).   The nominal amount due at *maturity* from a *bond* or *note* not including contractual interest that may also be due on the same date. The corresponding amount of a stock certificate is best called the *par* or *stated value*, whichever is applicable.

factoring.   The process of buying *notes* or *accounts receivable* at a *discount* from the holder to whom the debt is owed; from the holder's point of view, the selling of such notes or accounts. When a single note is involved, the process is called "discounting a note."

factory.   Used synonymously with *manufacturing* as an adjective.

factory burden.   Manufacturing *overhead*.

factory cost.   *Manufacturing cost*.

factory expense.   Manufacturing *overhead*. *Expense* is a poor term in this context because the item is a *product cost*.

factory overhead.   Usually an item of *manufacturing cost* other than *direct labor* or *direct materials*.

fair market price (value).   Price (value) negotiated at *arm's-length* between a willing buyer and a willing seller, each acting rationally in his or her own self interest. May be estimated in the absence of a monetary transaction.

fair presentation (fairness).   When the *auditor's report* says that the *financial statements* "present fairly . . . ," the auditor means that the accounting alternatives used by the entity are all in accordance with *GAAP*. In recent years, however, courts are finding that conformity with *generally accepted accounting principles* may be insufficient grounds for an opinion that the statements are fair. *SAS No. 5* requires that the auditor judge the accounting principles used "appropriate in the circumstances" before attesting to fair presentation.

FASB. Financial Accounting Standards Board.   An independent board responsible, since 1973, for establishing *generally accepted accounting principles*. Its official pronouncements are called *"Statements of Financial Accounting Concepts" ("SFAC")*, *"Statements of Financial Accounting Standards" ("SFAS")*, and *"Interpretations."* See also *Discussion Memorandum* and *Technical Bulletin*.

FASB Interpretation.   An official statement of the *FASB* interpreting the meaning of *Accounting Research Bulletins*, *APB Opinions*, and *Statements of Financial Accounting Standards*.

FASB Technical Bulletin.   See *Technical Bulletin*.

favorable variance.   An excess of actual *revenues* over expected revenues. An excess of *standard cost* over actual cost.

federal income tax.   *Income tax* levied by the U.S. government on individuals and corporations.

Federal Insurance Contributions Act.   See *FICA*.

Federal Unemployment Tax Act.   See *FUTA*.

feedback.   The process of informing employees about how their actual performance compares with the expected or desired level of performance in the hope that the information will reinforce desired behavior and reduce unproductive behavior.

FEI.   *Financial Executives Institute*.

FICA. Federal Insurance Contributions Act.   The law that sets *"Social Security" taxes* and benefits.

fiduciary. Someone responsible for the custody or administration of property belonging to another, such as an executor (of an estate), agent, receiver (in *bankruptcy*), or trustee (of a trust).

FIFO. *First-in, first-out;* the *inventory flow assumption* by which *ending inventory* cost is computed from most recent purchases and *cost of goods sold* is computed from oldest purchases including beginning inventory. See *LISH*. Contrast with *LIFO*.

finance. As a verb, to supply with *funds* through the *issue* of stocks, bonds, notes, or mortgages, or through the retention of earnings.

financial accounting. The accounting for *assets, equities, revenues,* and *expenses* of a business. Primarily concerned with the historical reporting of the *financial position* and operations of an *entity* to external users on a regular, periodic basis. Contrast with *managerial accounting*.

Financial Accounting Foundation. The independent foundation (committee) that raises funds to support the *FASB* and *GASB*.

Financial Accounting Standards Advisory Council. A committee giving advice to the *FASB* on matters of strategy and emerging issues.

Financial Accounting Standards Board. *FASB*.

Financial Executives Institute. An organization of financial executives, such as chief accountants, *controllers,* and treasurers, of large businesses.

financial expense. An *expense* incurred in raising or managing *funds*.

financial flexibility. As defined by *SFAC No. 5,* "the ability of an entity to take effective actions to alter amounts and timing of cash flows so it can respond to unexpected needs and opportunities."

financial forecast. See *financial projection* for definition and contrast.

financial leverage. See *leverage*.

financial position (condition). Statement of the *assets* and *equities* of a firm displayed as a *balance sheet*.

financial projection. An estimate of *financial position,* results of *operations,* and changes in cash flows for one or more future periods based on a set of assumptions. If the assumptions are not necessarily the most likely outcomes, then the estimate is called a "projection." If the assumptions represent the most probable outcomes, then the estimate is called a "forecast." "Most probable" means

that the assumptions have been evaluated by management and that they are management's judgment of the most likely set of conditions and most likely outcomes.

financial ratio. See *ratio*.

financial reporting objectives. FASB *Statement of Financial Accounting Concepts No. 1* sets out the broad objectives of financial reporting that are intended to guide the development of specific *accounting standards*.

Financial Reporting Release. Series of releases, issued by the SEC since 1982. Replaces the *Accounting Series Releases.* See *SEC*.

financial statements. The *balance sheet, income statement, statement of retained earnings, statement of cash flows,* statement of changes in *owners' equity accounts,* and *notes* thereto.

financial structure. *Capital structure.*

financial year. The term for *fiscal year* in Australia and the United Kingdom.

financing activities. Obtaining resources from (a) owners and providing them with a return on and a return of their *investment* and (b) *creditors* and repaying amounts borrowed (or otherwise settling the obligation). See *statement of cash flows*.

financing lease. *Capital lease.*

finished goods (inventory account). Manufactured product ready for sale; a *current asset (inventory) account.*

firm. Informally, any business entity. (Strictly speaking, a firm is a *partnership*.)

first in, first out. See *FIFO*.

fiscal year. A period of 12 consecutive months chosen by a business as the *accounting period* for annual reports. May or may not be a *natural business year* or a calendar year.

FISH. An acronym, conceived by George H. Sorter, for *first in, still here.* FISH is the same cost flow assumption as *LIFO*. Many readers of accounting statements find it easier to think about inventory questions in terms of items still on hand. Think of LIFO in connection with *cost of goods sold* but of FISH in connection with *ending inventory.* See *LISH*.

fixed assets. *Plant assets.*

fixed assets turnover. *Sales* divided by average total *fixed assets.*

fixed benefit plan. A *defined-benefit (pension) plan.*

fixed budget. A plan that provides for specified amounts of *expenditures* and *receipts* that do not vary with activity levels. Sometimes called a "static budget." Contrast with *flexible budget.*

fixed charges earned (coverage) ratio. *Income* before *interest expense* and *income tax expense* divided by interest expense.

fixed cost (expense). An *expenditure* or *expense* that does not vary with volume of activity, at least in the short run. See *capacity costs,* which include *enabling costs* and *standby costs,* and *programmed costs* for various subdivisions of fixed costs. See *cost terminology.*

fixed interval sampling. A method of choosing a sample in which the first item is selected from the population randomly, with the remaining sample items drawn at equally spaced intervals. Compare *variable sampling.*

fixed liability. *Long-term* liability.

fixed manufacturing overhead applied. The portion of *fixed manufacturing overhead cost* allocated to units produced during a period.

fixed overhead variance. Difference between *actual fixed manufacturing costs* and fixed manufacturing costs applied to production in a *standard costing system.*

flexible budget. *Budget* that projects receipts and expenditures as a function of activity levels. Contrast with *fixed budget.*

flexible budget allowance. With respect to manufacturing overhead, the total cost that should have been incurred at the level of activity actually experienced during the period.

float. *Checks* whose amounts have been *added* to the depositor's bank account, but not yet subtracted from the *drawer's* bank account.

flow. The change in the amount of an item over time. Contrast with *stock.*

Flow of Costs (and Sales Revenue)

*The credit in the entry to record these items is usually to a payable; for all others, the credit is usually to an asset, or to an asset contra account.
**When sales to customers are recorded, the Sales account is credited. The debit is usually to Cash or Accounts Receivable.

flow assumption. When a *withdrawal* is made from *inventory*, the cost of the withdrawal must be computed by a flow assumption if *specific identification* of units is not used. The usual flow assumptions are *FIFO, LIFO,* and *weighted average*.

flow of costs. *Costs* passing through various classifications within an *entity*. See the accompanying diagram for a summary of *product* and *period cost* flows.

flow-through method. Accounting for the *investment credit* to show all income statement benefits of the credit in the year of acquisition, rather than spreading them over the life of the asset acquired, called the "deferral method." The *APB* preferred the deferral method in *Opinion No. 2* (1962) but accepted the flow-through method in *Opinion No. 4* (1964). The term is also used in connection with *depreciation* accounting where *straight-line method* is used for financial reporting and an *accelerated* method for tax reporting. Followers of the flow-through method would not recognize a *deferred tax liability. APB Opinion No. 11* prohibits the use of the flow-through approach in financial reporting although it has been used by some regulatory commissions.

FOB. Free on board some location (for example, FOB shipping point; FOB destination); the *invoice* price includes delivery at seller's expense to that location. Title to goods usually passes from seller to buyer at the FOB location.

folio. A page number or other identifying reference used in posting to indicate the source of entry.

footing. Adding a column of figures.

footnotes. More detailed information than that provided in the *income statement, balance sheet, statement of retained earnings,* and *statement of cash flows;* these are considered an integral part of the statements and are covered by the *auditor's report.* Sometimes called "notes."

forecast. See *financial projection* for definition and contrast.

foreclosure. The borrower fails to make a required payment on a *mortgage;* the lender takes possession of the property for his or her own use or sale. Assume that the lender sells the property but the proceeds of sale are insufficient to cover the outstanding balance on the loan at the time of foreclosure. Under the terms of most mortgages, the lender becomes an unsecured creditor of the borrower for the still-unrecovered balance of the loan.

foreign currency. For *financial statements* prepared in a given currency, any other currency.

foreign exchange gain or loss. Gain or loss from holding *net* foreign *monetary items* during a period when the *exchange rate* changes.

Foreign Sales Corporation. See *FSC*.

forfeited share. A share to which a subscriber has lost title because of nonpayment of a *call*.

Form 10-K. See *10-K*.

forward exchange contract. An agreement to exchange at a specified future date currencies of different countries at a specified rate call the "forward rate".

forward price. The price of a commodity for delivery at a specified future date. Compare *spot price*.

franchise. A privilege granted or sold, such as to use a name or to sell products or services.

free cash flow. Financial statement analysts use this term to mean *cash flow + interest expense + income tax expense*.

free on board. *FOB*.

freight-in. The *cost* of freight or shipping incurred in acquiring *inventory*, preferably treated as a part of the cost of *inventory*. Often shown temporarily in an *adjunct account* that is closed at the end of the period with other purchase accounts to the inventory account by the acquirer.

freight-out. The *cost* of freight or shipping incurred in selling *inventory*, treated by the seller as a selling *expense* in the period of sale.

FSC. Foreign Sales Corporation. A foreign *corporation* engaging in certain export activities some of whose *income* is exempt from U.S. federal *income tax*. A U.S. corporation need pay no income taxes on *dividends* distributed by an FSC out of *earnings* attributable to certain foreign income.

full absorption costing. The method of *costing* which assigns all types of manufacturing costs (*direct material, direct labor, fixed* and *variable overhead*) to units produced; required by *GAAP*. Also called "absorption costing." Contrast with *variable costing*.

full costing. full costs. The total cost of producing and selling a unit. Full cost per unit equals *full absorption cost* per unit plus *marketing, administrative, interest,* and other *central corporate expenses,* per unit. The sum of full costs for all units equals total costs of the firm. Often used in *long-term* profitability and pricing decisions.

full disclosure. The reporting policy requiring that all significant or *material* information is to be presented in the financial statements. See *fair presentation*.

fully diluted earnings per share. Smallest *earnings per share* figure on *common stock* that can be obtained by computing an earnings per share for all possible combinations of assumed *exercise* or *conversion* of *potentially dilutive securities*. Must be reported on the *income statement* if it is less than 97 percent of earnings available to common shareholders divided by the average number of common shares outstanding during the period.

fully vested. Said of a *pension plan* when an employee (or his or her estate) has rights to all the benefits purchased with the employer's contributions to the plan even if the employee is not employed by this employer at the time of death or retirement.

function. In governmental accounting, said of a group of related activities for accomplishing a service or regulatory program for which the governmental unit is responsible. In mathematics, a rule for associating a number, called the dependent variable, with another number (or numbers), called independent variable(s).

functional classification. *Income statement* reporting form in which *expenses* are reported by functions, that is, cost of goods sold, administrative expenses, financing expenses, selling expenses; contrast with *natural classification*.

fund. An *asset* or group of assets set aside for a specific purpose. See also *fund accounting*.

fund accounting. The accounting for resources, obligations, and *capital* balances, usually of a not-for-profit or governmental *entity*, which have been segregated into *accounts* representing logical groupings based on legal, donor, or administrative restrictions or requirements. The groupings are described as "funds." The accounts of each fund are *self-balancing* and from them a *balance sheet* and an operating statement for each fund can be prepared. See *fund* and *fund balance*.

fund balance. In governmental accounting, the excess of assets of a *fund* over its liabilities and reserves; the not-for-profit equivalent of *owners' equity*.

funded. Said of a *pension plan* or other obligation when *funds* have been set aside for meeting the obligation when it becomes due. The federal law for pension plans requires that all *normal costs* be funded as recognized. In addition, *prior service cost* of pension plans must be funded over 30 or over 40 years, depending on the circumstances.

funding. Replacing *short-term* liabilities with *long-term* debt.

funds. Generally *working capital*; current assets less current liabilities. Sometimes used to refer to *cash* or to cash and *marketable securities*.

funds provided by operations. See *cash provided by operations*.

funds statement. An informal name often used for the *statement of cash flows*.

funny money. Said of securities such as *convertible preferred stock, convertible bonds, options*, and *warrants* that have aspects of *common stock* equity but that did not reduce reported *earnings per share* prior to the issuance of *APB Opinions No. 9* in 1967 and *No. 15* in 1969.

FUTA. Federal Unemployment Tax Act which provides for taxes to be collected at the federal level, to help subsidize the individual states' administration of their unemployment compensation programs.

future value. Value at a specified future date of a sum increased at a specified *interest rate*.

G

GAAP. *Generally accepted accounting principles.* A plural noun.

GAAS. *Generally accepted auditing standards.* A plural noun. Not to be confused with *GAS*.

gain. Increase in *owners' equity* caused by a transaction not part of a firm's typical, day-to-day operations and not part of owners' *investment* or *withdrawals*. The term "gain" (or "*loss*") is distinguished in two separate ways from related terms. First, gains (and losses) are generally used for nonoperating, incidental, peripheral, or nonroutine transactions: gain on sale of land in contrast to *gross margin* on *sale* of *inventory*. Second, gains and losses are *net* concepts, not gross concepts: gain or loss results from subtracting some measure of *cost* from the measure of inflow. *Revenues* and *expenses*, on the other hand, are gross concepts; their difference is a net concept. Gain is nonroutine and net, *profit* or *margin* is routine and net; revenue is routine and gross. Loss is net but can be either routine ("loss on sale of inventory") or not ("loss on disposal of segment of business").

gain contingency. See *contingency*.

GAS. *Goods available for sale.* Not to be confused with *GAAS*.

GASB. Governmental Accounting Standards Board. An independent body responsible, since 1982, for establishing accounting standards for state and local government units. It is part of the *Financial Accounting Foundation*, parallel to the *FASB*, and currently consists of five members.

GbR; Gesellschaft des bürgerlichen Rechtes. Germany. A *partnership* whose members agree to share in specific aspects of their own separate business pursuits, such as an office. This partnership has no legal form and is not a separate accounting *entity*.

gearing. British term for *financial leverage*.

gearing adjustment. Consider a firm, part of whose assets are *noncurrent liabilities* and who has experience *holding gains* on its *assets* during a period. All of the increase in wealth caused by the holding gains belongs to the owners; none typically belongs to the lenders. Some British accounting authorities believe that published *income statements* should show the part of the holding gain financed with debt in *income* for the period. That part is called the "gearing adjustment."

general debt. Debt of a governmental unit legally payable from general revenues and backed by the full faith and credit of the governmental unit.

general expenses. *Operating expenses* other than those specifically assigned to cost of goods sold, selling, and administration.

general fixed asset (group of accounts). Accounts showing those long-term assets of a governmental unit not accounted for in *enterprise, trust,* or intragovernmental service funds.

general fund. Assets and liabilities of a nonprofit entity not specifically earmarked for other purposes; the primary operating fund of a governmental unit.

general journal. The formal record where transactions, or summaries of similar transactions, are recorded in *journal entry* form as they occur. Use of the adjective "general" usually implies only two columns for cash amounts or that there are also various *special journals*, such as a *check register* or *sales journal*, in use.

general ledger. The name for the formal *ledger* containing all of the financial statement accounts. It has equal debits and credits as evidenced by the *trial balance*. Some of the accounts in the general ledger may be *controlling accounts*, supported by details contained in *subsidiary ledgers*.

general partner. Member of *partnership* personally liable for all debts of the partnership; contrast with *limited partner*.

general price index. A measure of the aggregate prices of a wide range of goods and services in the economy at one time relative to the prices during a base period. See *consumer price index* and *GNP Implicit Price Deflator*. Contrast with *specific price index*.

general price level-adjusted statements. See *constant dollar accounting*.

general price level changes. Changes in the aggregate prices of a wide range of goods and services in the economy. These price changes are measured using a *general price index*. Contrast with *specific price changes*.

general purchasing power. The command of the dollar over a wide range of goods and services in the economy. The general purchasing power of the dollar is inversely related to changes in a general price index. See *general price index*.

general purchasing power accounting. See *constant dollar accounting*.

generally accepted accounting principles. GAAP. As previously defined by the *APB* and now by the *FASB*, the conventions, rules, and procedures necessary to define accepted accounting practice at a particular time; includes both broad guidelines and relatively detailed practices and procedures.

generally accepted auditing standards. GAAS. The standards, as opposed to particular procedures, promulgated by the *AICPA* (in *Statements on Auditing Standards*) that concern "the auditor's professional quantities" and "the judgment exercised by him in the performance of his examination and in his report." Currently, there are ten such standards: three general ones (concerned with proficiency, independence, and degree of care to be exercised), three standards of field work, and four standards of reporting. The first standard of reporting requires that the *auditor's report* state whether or not the *financial statements* are prepared in accordance with *generally accepted accounting principles*. Thus the typical auditor's report says that the examination was conducted in accordance with generally accepted auditing standards and that the statements are prepared in accordance with generally accepted accounting principles. See *auditor's report*.

geographic segment. A single operation or a group of operations located in a particular geographic area, that generate revenue, incur costs and have assets employed in or associated with generating such revenue.

GIE; Groupement d'intérêt économique. France. A joint venture, normally used for exports and research and development pooling.

GmbH; Gesellschaft mit beschränkter Haftung. Germany. A private company with unlimited number of shareholders. Transfer of ownership can take place only with the consent of other shareholders. Contrast with *AG*.

GNP Implicit Price Deflator (Index). A *price index* issued quarterly by the Office of Business Economics of the U.S. Department of Commerce. This index attempts to trace the price level of all *goods and services* comprising the *gross national product*. Contrast with *consumer price index*.

goal congruence. All members of an organization have incentives to perform for a common interest, such as *shareholder* wealth maximization for a *corporation*.

going-concern assumption. For accounting purposes a business is assumed to remain in operation long enough for all its current plans to be carried out. This assumption is part of the justification for the *acquisition cost* basis, rather than a *liquidation* or *exit value* basis of accounting.

going public. Said of a business when its *shares* become widely traded, rather than being closely held by relatively few shareholders. Issuing shares to the general investing public.

goods. Items of merchandise, supplies, raw materials, or finished goods. Sometimes the meaning of "goods" is extended to include all *tangible* items, as in the phrase "goods and services."

goods available for sale. The sum of *beginning inventory* plus all acquisitions of *merchandise* or *finished goods* during an *accounting period*.

goods in process. *Work in process.*

goodwill. The excess of cost of an acquired firm (or operating unit) over the current *fair market value* of the separately identifiable *net assets* of the acquired unit. Before goodwill is recognized, all identifiable assets, whether or not on the books of the acquired unit, must be given a *fair market value*. For example, a firm has developed a *patent* which is not recognized on its books because of *SFAS* No. 2. If another company acquires the firm, the acquirer will recognize the patent at an amount equal to its estimated fair market value before computing goodwill. Informally, the term is used to indicate the value of good customer relations, high employee morale, a well-respected business name, and so on, that are expected to result in greater than normal earning power.

goodwill method. A method of accounting for the *admission* of a new partner to a *partnership* when the new partner is to be credited with a portion of capital different from the value of the *tangible* assets contributed as a fraction of tangible assets on the partnership. See *bonus method* for a description and contrast.

Governmental Accounting Standards Advisory Council. A group that consults with the *GASB* on agenda, technical issues and the assignment of priorities to projects. It consists of more than a dozen members representing various areas of expertise.

Governmental Accounting Standards Board. *GASB.*

GPL. General price level; usually used as an adjective modifying the word "accounting" to mean *constant dollar accounting*.

GPLA. General price level-adjusted accounting; *constant dollar accounting*.

GPP. General purchasing power; usually used as an adjective modifying the word "accounting" to mean *constant dollar accounting*.

graded vesting. Said of a *pension plan* where not all employee benefits are currently *vested*. By law, the benefits must become vested according to one of several formulas as time passes.

grandfather clause. An exemption in new accounting *pronouncements* exempting transactions that occurred before a given date from the new accounting treatment. For example, *APB Opinion No. 17*, adopted in 1970, exempted *goodwill* acquired before 1970 from required *amortization*. The term "grandfather" appears in the title to *SFAS No. 10*.

gross. Not adjusted or reduced by deductions or subtractions. Contrast with *net*.

gross margin. *Net sales* minus *cost of goods sold*.

gross margin percent. $100 \times (1 - cost\ of\ goods\ sold/net\ sales) = 100 \times (gross\ margin/net\ sales)$.

gross national product. GNP. The market value within a nation for a year of all goods and services produced as measured by final sales of goods and services to individuals, corporations, and governments plus the excess of exports over imports.

gross price method (of recording purchase or sales discounts). The *purchase* (or *sale*) is recorded at its *invoice price*, not deducting the amounts of *discounts* available. Discounts taken are recorded in a *contra* account to purchases (or sales). Information on discounts lapsed is not made available, and for this reason, most firms prefer the *net price method* of recording purchase discounts.

gross profit. *Gross margin.*

gross profit method. A method of estimating *ending inventory* amounts. *Cost of goods sold* is measured as some fraction of sales; the *inventory equation* is then used to value *ending inventory*.

gross profit ratio. *Gross margin* divided by *net sales*.

gross sales. All *sales* at *invoice* prices, not reduced by *discounts*, *allowances*, *returns*, or other adjustments.

group depreciation. A method of calculating *depreciation* charges where similar assets are combined, rather than depreciated separately. No gain or loss is recognized on retirement of items from the group until the last item in the group is sold or retired. See *composite life method*.

guarantee. A promise to answer for payment of debt or performance of some obligation if the person liable for the debt or obligation fails to perform. A guarantee is a *contingency* of the *entity* making the promise. Often, the words "guarantee" and "warranty" are used to mean the same thing. In precise usage, however, "guarantee" means promise to fulfill the promise of some person to perform a contractual obligation such as to pay a sum of money, whereas "warranty" is most often used to refer to promises about pieces of machinery or other products. See *warranty*.

H

half-year convention. An assumption used in *tax accounting* under *ACRS*, and sometimes in *financial accounting*, that *depreciable assets* were acquired at mid-year of the year of acquisition. When this convention is used, the *depreciation charge* for the year is computed as one-half the charge that would be used if the assets had been acquired at the beginning of the year.

hardware. The physical equipment or devices forming a computer and peripheral equipment.

hash total. A control used to establish accuracy of data processing, whereby a total of data is made by adding values which would not normally be added together (e.g., the sum of a list of part numbers) and subsequently compared to a computer-generated total of the same values.

Hasselback. An annual directory of accounting faculty at colleges and universities, which gives information about the faculty's training and fields of specialization. The directory has been compiled since the late 1970's by James R. Hasselback of Florida State University and is distributed by Prentice-Hall of Englewood Cliffs, New Jersey.

hidden reserve. The term refers to an amount by which *owners' equity* has been understated, perhaps deliberately. The understatement arises from an undervaluation of *assets* or overvaluation of *liabilities*. By undervaluing assets on this period's *balance sheet*, *net income* in some future period can be made to look artificially high by disposing of the asset: actual *revenues* less artificially low cost of assets sold yields artificially high net income. There is no *account* that has this title.

hire-purchase agreement. A lease containing a purchase option.

historical cost. *Acquisition cost; original cost; a sunk cost.*

historical cost/constant dollar accounting. Accounting based on *historical cost* valuations measured in *constant dollars*. *Nonmonetary items* are restated to reflect changes in the *general purchasing power* of the dollar since the time the specific *assets* were acquired or *liabilities* were incurred. A *gain* or *loss* is recognized on *monetary items* as they are held over time periods when the general purchasing power of the dollar changes.

historical summary. A part of the *annual report* to shareholders that shows important items, such as *net income*, *revenues*, *expenses*, *asset* and *equity* totals, *earnings per share*, and the like, for five or ten periods including the current one. Usually not as much detail is shown in the historical summary as in *comparative statements*, which typically report as much detail for the two preceding years as for the current year. Annual reports may contain both comparative statements and a historical summary.

holdback. A portion of the progress payments called for under the terms of a contract which the customer need not pay until the contractor has fulfilled the contract or satisfied financial obligations to subcontractors.

holding company. A company that confines its activities to owning *stock* in, and supervising management of, other companies. A holding company usually owns a controlling interest in, that is more than 50 percent of the voting stock of, the companies whose stock it holds. Contrast with *mutual fund*. See *conglomerate*. In British usage, the term refers to any company with controlling interest in another company.

holding gain or loss. Difference between end-of-period price and beginning-of-period price of an asset held during the period. Realized holding gains and losses are not ordinarily separately reported in financial statements. Unrealized gains are not usually reflected in income at all. Some unrealized losses, such as on inventory or marketable securities, are reflected in income or *owners' equity* as the losses occur; see *lower of cost or market*. See *inventory profit* for further refinement, including *gains* on *assets* sold during the period.

holding gain or loss net of inflation. Increase or decrease in the *current cost* of an asset while it is held measured in units of *constant dollars*.

horizontal analysis. *Time-series analysis.*

horizontal integration. The extension of activity by an organization in the same general line of business or expansion into supplementary, complementary, or compatible products. Compare with *vertical integration*.

house account. An account with a customer who does not pay sales commissions.

human resource accounting. A term used to describe a variety of proposals that seek to report and emphasize the importance of human resources—knowledgeable, trained, and loyal employees— in a company's earning process and total assets.

hurdle rate. Required rate of return in a *discounted cash flow* analysis.

hybrid security. *Security*, such as a *convertible bond*, containing elements of both *debt* and *owners' equity.*

hypothecation. The *pledging* of property, without transfer of title or possession, to secure a loan.

I

I. *Identity matrix.*

IAA. *Interamerican Accounting Association.*

ICMA. *Institute of Certified Management Accountants.* See *CMA* and *National Association of Accountants.*

ideal standard costs. *Standard costs* set equal to those that would be incurred under the best possible conditions.

identity matrix. A square *matrix* with ones on the main diagonal and zeros elsewhere; a matrix I such that for any other matrix A, IA = AI = A. The matrix equivalent to the number one.

IIA. *Institute of Internal Auditors.*

implicit interest. *Interest* not paid or received. See *interest, imputed.* All transactions involving the deferred payment or receipt of cash involve interest, whether explicitly stated or not. The implicit interest on a single-payment *note* is the difference between the amount collected at maturity less the amount lent at the start of the loan. The implicit *interest rate* per year can be computed from

$$\left[\frac{\text{Cash Received at Maturity}}{\text{Cash Lent}} \right]^{(1/t)} - 1$$

where t is the term of the loan in years; t need not be an integer.

imprest fund. *Petty cash fund.*

improvement. An *expenditure* to extend the useful life of an *asset* or to improve its performance (rate of output, cost) over that of the original asset. Such expenditures are *capitalized* as part of the asset's cost. Sometimes called "betterment." Contrast with *maintenance* and *repair.*

imputed cost. A cost that does not appear in accounting records, such as the *interest* that could be earned on cash spent to acquire inventories rather than, say, government bonds. Or, consider a firm that owns the buildings it occupies. This firm has an imputed cost for rent in an amount equal to what it would have to pay to use similar buildings owned by another. *Opportunity cost.*

imputed interest. See *interest, imputed.*

incentive compatible compensation. Said of a compensation plan for managers that induces them to act for the interests of owners while acting in their own interests. For example, consider a time of rising prices and increasing inventories when using a *LIFO cost flow assumption* implies having to pay lower *income taxes* than would *FIFO.* A bonus scheme for managers based on accounting *net income* would not be incentive compatible because the owners will be better off under LIFO, while managers will be better off if they report using FIFO. See *LIFO conformity rule.* See *goal congruence.*

income. *Excess of revenues* and *gains* over *expenses* and *losses* for a period; *net income.* Sometimes used with an appropriate modifier to refer to the various intermediate amounts shown in a *multiple-step income statement.* Sometimes used to refer to revenues, as in "rental income." See *comprehensive income.*

income accounts. *Revenue* and *expense accounts.*

income before taxes. On the *income statement,* the difference between all *revenues* and *expenses* except *income tax* expense. Contrast with *net income* and *taxable income.*

income determination. See *determine.*

income distribution account. *Temporary account* sometimes debited when *dividends* are declared; closed to *retained earnings.*

income from continuing operations. As defined by APB *Opinion No. 30,* all *revenues* less all *expenses* except for the following: results of operations (including *income tax* effects) that have been or will be discontinued; *gains* or *losses,* including income tax effects, on disposal of segments of the business; gains or losses, including income tax effects, from *extraordinary items*; and the cumulative effect of *accounting changes.*

income from discontinued operations. *Income,* net of tax effects, from parts of the business that have been discontinued during the period or are to be discontinued in the near future. Such items are reported on separate line of the *income statement* after *income from continuing operations* but before *extraordinary items*.

income (revenue) bond. See *special revenue debt*.

income smoothing. A method of timing business *transactions* or choosing *accounting principles* so that variations in reported *income* from year to year are reduced from what they would otherwise be. Although income smoothing is an objective of some managements, it is not an official *accounting principle* or *reporting objective*.

income statement. The statement of *revenues, expenses, gains,* and *losses* for the period ending with *net income* for the period. The *earnings-per-share* amount is usually shown on the income statement; the *reconciliation* of beginning and ending balances of *retained earnings* may also be shown in a combined statement of income and retained earnings. See *income from continuing operations, income from discontinued operations, extraordinary items, multiple-step, single-step.*

income summary. An *account* used in problem solving that serves as a surrogate for the *income statement*. All *revenues* are closed to the Income Summary as *credits* and all *expenses,* as *debits*. The *balance* in the account, after all other *closing entries* are made, is then closed to the retained earnings or other *owners' equity* account and represents *net income* for the period.

income tax. An annual tax levied by the federal and other governments on the income of an entity.

income tax allocation. See *deferred tax liability* and *tax allocation: intrastatement.*

incremental. An adjective used to describe the change in *cost, expense, investment, cash flow, revenue, profit,* and the like if one or more units are produced or sold or if an activity is undertaken.

incremental cost. See *incremental.*

indenture. See *bond indenture.*

independence. The mental attitude required of the *CPA* in performing the *attest* function. It implies impartiality and that the members of the auditing CPA firm own no stock in the corporation being audited.

independent accountant. The *CPA* who performs the *attest* function for a firm.

independent variable. See *regression analysis.*

indeterminate-term liability. A *liability* lacking the criterion of being due at a definite time. This term is our own coinage to encompass the *minority interest.*

indexation. An attempt by lawmakers or parties to a contract to cope with the effects of *inflation*. Amounts fixed in law or contracts are "indexed" when these amounts change as a given measure of price changes. For example, a so-called escalator clause (COLA—cost of living allowance or adjustment) in a labor contract might provide that hourly wages will be increased as the *Consumer Price Index* increases. Many economists have suggested the indexation of numbers fixed in the income tax laws. If, for example, the personal exemption is $1,000 at the start of the period, prices rise by 10 percent during the period, and the personal exemption is indexed, then the personal exemption would automatically rise to $1,100 (= $1,000 + .10 x $1,000) at the end of the period.

indirect cost pool. Any grouping of individual costs that are not identified with a *cost objective.*

indirect costs. Costs of production not easily associated with the production of specific goods and services; *overhead costs*. May be *allocated* on some arbitrary basis to specific products or departments.

indirect labor (material) cost. An *indirect cost* for labor (material) such as for supervisors (supplies).

indirect method. See *statement of cash flows.*

individual proprietorship. *Sole proprietorship.*

Industry Audit Guide. A series of publications by the *AICPA* providing specific accounting and *auditing principles* for specialized situations. Audit guides have been issued covering government contractors, state and local government units, investment companies, finance companies, brokers and dealers in securities, and many others.

inescapable cost. A *cost* that is not *avoidable*. A *cost* that is not *avoidable* because of an action. For example, if two operating rooms in a hospital are closed, but security is still employed, the security costs are "inescapable" with respect to the decision to close the operating rooms.

inflation. A time of generally rising prices.

inflation accounting. Strictly speaking, *constant dollar accounting*. Some writers use the term, incorrectly, to mean *current cost accounting.*

information circular. Canada. A document, accompanying the notice of a shareholders' meeting, prepared in connection with the solicitation of proxies by or on behalf of the management of the corporation. It contains information concerning the persons making the solicitation, election of directors, appointment of auditors and other particulars of matters to be acted upon at the meeting.

information system. A system, sometimes formal and sometimes informal, for collecting, processing, and communicating data that are useful for the managerial functions of decision making, planning, and control, and for financial reporting under the *attest* requirement.

inherent interest rate. *Implicit interest* rate.

insolvent. Unable to pay debts when due. Said of a company even though *assets* exceed *liabilities*.

installment. Partial payment of a debt or collection of a receivable, usually according to a contract.

installment contracts receivable. The name used for *accounts receivable* when the *installment method* of recognizing revenue is used. Its *contra account, unrealized gross margin*, is shown on the balance sheet as a subtraction from the amount receivable.

installment (sales) method. Recognizing *revenue* and *expense* (or *gross margin*) from a sales transaction in proportion to the fraction of the selling price collected during a period. Allowed by the *IRS* for income tax reporting, but acceptable in *GAAP* (*APB Opinion No. 10*) only when cash collections are uncertain. See *realized* (and *unrealized*) *gross margin*.

installment sales. Sales on account where the buyer promises to pay in several separate payments, called *installments*. Sometimes are, but need not be, accounted for on the *installment method*. If installment sales are accounted for with the sales *basis of revenue recognition* for financial reporting but with the installment method for income tax returns, then a *deferred income tax liability* arises.

Institute of Certified Management Accountants. See *ICMA*.

Institute of Internal Auditors. IIA. The national association of accountants who are engaged in internal auditing and are employed by business firms. Administers a comprehensive professional examination; those who pass qualify to be designated CIA, certified internal auditor.

insurance. A contract for reimbursement of specific losses; purchased with insurance premiums. Self-insurance is not insurance but merely the willingness to assume risk of incurring losses while saving the premium.

intangible asset. A nonphysical, *noncurrent* right that gives a firm an exclusive or preferred position in the marketplace. Examples are a *copyright, patent, trademark, goodwill, organization costs, capitalized* advertising cost, computer programs, licenses for any of the preceding, government licenses

(e.g., broadcasting or the right to sell liquor), *leases*, franchises, mailing lists, exploration permits, import and export permits, construction permits, and marketing quotas.

Interamerican Accounting Association. IAA. An organization, headquartered in Mexico City, devoted to facilitating interaction between accounting practitioners in Central America, North America, and South America.

intercompany elimination. See *eliminations*.

intercompany profit. If one *affiliated company* sells to another, and the goods remain in the second company's *inventory* at the end of the period, then the first company's *profit* has not been realized by a sale to an outsider. That profit is called "intercompany profit" and is eliminated from net *income* in *consolidated income statements* or when the *equity method* is used.

intercompany transaction. *Transaction* between *parent company* and *subsidiary* or between subsidiaries in a *consolidated entity* whose effects are eliminated in preparing *consolidated financial statements*. See *intercompany profit*.

intercorporate investment. A given *corporation* owns *shares* or *debt* issued by another.

interdepartment monitoring. One of the advantages of allocating *service department* costs to *production departments* is that those charged with the costs will have an incentive to control the costs incurred in the service department.

interest. The charge or cost for using money; expressed as a rate per period, usually one year, the "interest rate." See *effective interest rate* and *nominal interest rate*.

interest, imputed. If a borrower merely promises to pay a single amount, sometime later than the present, then the present value (computed at a *fair market* interest rate, called the "imputed interest rate") of the promise is less than the *face amount* to be paid at *maturity*. The difference between the face amount and the present value of a promise is called imputed interest. See also *imputed cost*.

interest factor. One plus the *interest* rate.

interest method. See *effective interest method*.

interest rate. See *interest*.

interfund accounts. In governmental accounting, the accounts that show transactions between funds, especially interfund receivables and payables.

interim statements. Statements issued for periods less than the regular, annual *accounting period*. Most corporations are required to issue interim statements on a quarterly basis. The basic issue in preparing interim reports is whether their purpose is to report on the interim period (1) as a self-contained accounting period or (2) as an integral part of the year of which they are a part so that forecasts of annual performance can be made. For example, assume that at the end of the first quarter, a retailer has depleted its *inventory* so that *LIFO cost of goods sold* is artificially low and *net income* is artificially high, relative to their amounts if purchases for inventory had been "normal" and equal to or greater than sales. The retailer expects to purchase inventory sufficiently large so that when cost of goods sold is computed for the year, there will be no *dips into old LIFO layers* and income will not be artificially high. Under the first approach, the quarterly income will be computed from cost of goods sold using data for the dips that have actually occurred by the end of the quarter. Under the second, quarterly income will be computed from cost of goods sold assuming that purchases were equal to "normal" amounts and that there are no dips into old LIFO layers. *APB Opinion No. 28* and the *SEC* require that interim reports be constructed largely to satisfy the second purpose.

internal audit.   An *audit* conducted by employees to ascertain whether *internal control* procedures are working, as opposed to an external audit conducted by a *CPA*.

internal control.   See *control system.*

internal rate of return. IRR.   The discount rate that equates the net *present value* of a stream of cash outflows and inflows to zero.

internal reporting.   Reporting for management's use in planning and control; contrast with *external reporting* for financial statement users.

Internal Revenue Service. IRS.   Agency of the U.S. Treasury Department responsible for administering the Internal Revenue Code and for collecting income and certain other taxes.

International Accounting Standards Committee.   An organization that promotes the establishment of international accounting standards.

interperiod tax allocation.   See *deferred income tax liability.*

interpolation.   The estimation of an unknown number intermediate between two (or more) known numbers.

Interpretations.   See *FASB Interpretations.*

in the black (red).   Operating at a profit (loss).

intrastatement tax allocation.   See *tax allocation: intrastatement.*

inventoriable costs.   *Costs* incurred that are added to the cost of manufactured products. *Product costs* (*assets*) as opposed to *period expenses.*

inventory.   As a noun, the *balance* in an asset *account* such as raw materials, supplies, work in process, and finished goods. As a verb, to calculate the *cost* of goods on hand at a given time or to physically count items on hand.

inventory equation.   *Beginning inventory* + net additions - withdrawals = ending inventory. Ordinarily, additions are net purchases and withdrawals are *cost of goods sold.* Notice that ending inventory, to be shown on the balance sheet, and cost of goods sold, to be shown on the income statement, are not independent of each other. The larger is one, the smaller must be the other. In valuing inventories, beginning inventory and net purchases are usually known. In some inventory methods (for example, some applications of the *retail inventory method*), costs of goods sold is measured and the equation is used to find the cost of ending inventory. In most methods, cost of ending inventory is measured and the equation is used to find the cost of goods sold (withdrawals). In *current cost* (in contrast to *historical cost*) accounting *additions* (in the equation) include holding gains, whether realized or not. Thus the current cost inventory equation is: Beginning Inventory (at Current Cost) + Purchases (where Current Cost is Historical Cost) + Holding Gains (whether Realized or Not) - Ending Inventory (at Current Cost) = Cost of Goods Sold (Current Cost).

inventory holding gains.   See *inventory profit.*

inventory layer.   See *LIFO inventory layer.*

inventory profit.   This term has several possible meanings. Consider the data in the accompanying illustration. The *historical cost* data are derived in the conventional manner; the firm uses a *FIFO cost flow assumption.* The *current cost* data are assumed, but are of the kind that the FASB suggests in *SFAS No. 89.* The term *income from continuing operations* refers to revenues less expenses based on current, rather than historical, costs. To that subtotal add realized holding gains to arrive at realized (conventional) income. To that, add unrealized holding gains to arrive at *economic income.* The term "inventory profit" often refers (for example in some *SEC* releases) to the realized holding gain, $110 in the illustration. The amount of inventory profit will usually be material when FIFO is used and prices are rising. Sometimes, the term refers to the total *holding gain,* $300 (= $110 + $190, both realized and unrealized), but this meaning is less often used. In periods of rising prices and increasing inventories, the realized holding gains under a FIFO cost flow assumption will be substantially larger than under LIFO. In the illustration, for example, assume under LIFO that the historical cost of goods sold is $4,800, that historical LIFO cost of beginning inventory is $600, and that historical LIFO cost of ending inventory is $800. Then income from continuing operations, based on current costs, remains $350 (= $5,200 - $4,850), realized holding gains are $50 (= $4,850 - $4,800), realized income is $400 (= $350 + $50), the unrealized holding gain for the year is $250 [= ($1,550 - $800) - ($1,100 - $600)], and economic income is $650 (= $350 + $50 + $250). Because the only real effect of the cost flow assumption is to split the total holding gain into realized and unrealized portions, economic income is the same, independent of the cost flow assumption. The total of holding gains is $300 in the illustration. The choice of cost flow assumption merely determines the portion reported as realized.

Inventory Profit Illustration

	(Historical) Acquisition Cost Assuming FIFO	Current Cost
Assumed Data		
Inventory, 1/1	$ 900	$1,100
Inventory, 12/31	1,150	1,550
Cost of Goods Sold for Year .	4,740	4,850
Sales for Year	$5,200	$5,200
INCOME STATEMENT FOR YEAR		
Sales	$5,200	$5,200
Cost of Goods Sold	4,740	4,850
(1) Income from Continuing Operations		$ 350
Realized Holding Gains		110[a]
(2) Realized Income = Conventional Net Income (under FIFO)	$ 460	$ 460
Unrealized Holding Gain		190[b]
(3) Economic Income		$ 650

[a]Realized holding gain during a period is current cost of goods sold less historical cost of goods sold; the realized holding gain for the year under FIFO is $110 = $4,850 − $4,750. Some refer to this as inventory profit"

[b]The total unrealized holding gain at any time is current cost of inventory on hand at that time less historical cost of that inventory. The unrealized holding gain during a period is unrealized holding gain at the end of the period less the unrealized holding gain at the beginning of the period. Unrealized holding gain prior to this year is $200 = $1,100 − $900. Unrealized holding gain during this year = ($1,550 − 1,160) − ($1,100 − $900) = $390 − $200 = $190.

inventory turnover. Number of times the average *inventory* has been sold during a period; *cost of goods sold* for a period divided by average inventory for the period. See *ratio*.

invested capital. *Contributed capital*.

investee. A company whose *stock* is owned by another.

investing activities. Lending money and collecting *principal* (but not *interest*, which is an *operating activity*) on those loans; acquiring and selling *securities* or productive *assets* expected to produce *revenue* over several *periods*.

investment. An *expenditure* to acquire property or other *assets* in order to produce *revenue*; the asset so acquired; hence a *current* expenditure made in anticipation of future income. Said of *securities* of other companies held for the long term and appearing in a separate section of the *balance sheet*; in this context, contrast with *marketable securities*.

investments. A balance sheet heading for tangible assets held for periods longer than the operating cycle and not used in revenue production (assets not meeting the definitions of *current assets* or *property, plant, and equipment*).

investment center. A *responsibility center*, with control over *revenues, costs,* and *assets*.

investment credit. A reduction in income tax liability sometimes granted by the federal government to firms that buy new equipment. This item is a credit, in that it is deducted from the tax bill, not from pretax income. The tax credit has been a given percentage of the purchase price of certain assets purchased. The actual rules and rates have changed over the years. As of 1988, there is no investment credit. See *flow-through method* and *carryforward*.

investment tax credit. *Investment credit*.

investment turnover ratio. This term means the same thing as *total assets turnover ratio*, but is sometimes used for a *division*.

invoice. A document showing the details of a sale or purchase transaction.

I.O.U. An informal document acknowledging a debt, setting out the amount of the debt and signed by the debtor.

IRR. *Internal rate of return*.

IRS. *Internal Revenue Service*.

isoprofit line. On a graph delimiting feasible production possibilities of two products that require the use of the same limited resources, a line showing all feasible production possibility combinations with the same *profit* or, perhaps, *contribution margin*.

issue. When a corporation exchanges its stock (or bonds) for cash or other assets, the corporation is said to issue, not sell, that stock (or bonds). Also used in the context of withdrawing supplies or materials from inventory for use in operations and the drawing of a *check*.

issued shares. Those shares of *authorized capital stock* of a *corporation* that have been distributed to the shareholders. See *issue*. Shares of *treasury stock* are legally issued but are not considered to be *outstanding* for the purpose of voting, *dividend declarations*, and *earnings-per-share* calculations.

J

JIT. See *just-in-time inventory*.

job cost sheet. A schedule showing actual or budgeted inputs for a special order.

job development credit. The name used for the *investment credit* in the 1971 tax law, since repealed, on this subject.

job (-order) costing. Accumulation of *costs* for a particular identifiable batch of product, known as a job, as it moves through production.

joint cost. Cost of simultaneously producing or otherwise acquiring two or more products, called joint products, that must, by the nature of the process, be produced or acquired together, such as the cost of beef and hides of cattle. Generally, the joint costs of production are allocated to the individual products in proportion to their respective sales value at the *splitoff* point. Other examples include central *corporate expenses*, *overhead* of a department when several products are manufactured, and *basket purchases*. See *common cost*. See *sterilized allocation*.

joint cost allocation. See *joint cost*.

joint product. One of two or more outputs with significant value produced by a process that must be produced or acquired simultaneously. See *by-product* and *joint cost*.

journal. The place where transactions are recorded as they occur. The book of original entry.

journal entry. A dated recording in a *journal*, showing the accounts affected, of equal *debits* and *credits*, with an explanation of the *transaction*, if necessary.

Journal of Accountancy. A monthly publication of the *AICPA*.

Journal of Accounting and Economics. Scholarly journal published three times a year by the Graduate School of Management of the University of Rochester.

Journal of Accounting Research. Scholarly journal containing articles on theoretical and empirical aspects of accounting. Published three times a year by the Graduate School of Business of the University of Chicago.

journal voucher. A *voucher* documenting (and sometimes authorizing) a transaction, leading to an entry in the *journal*.

journalize. To make an entry in a journal.

judgment(al) sampling. A method of choosing a sample in which the selection of items to be examined is determined subjectively, as contrasted to selection by statistical methods. Compare *random sampling*.

junk bond. A low-rated *bond* that lacks the merit and characteristics of an investment-grade bond. It offers high yields—typically in excess of 15 percent per year—but also possesses high risk of default. Sometimes referred to, less pejoratively, as a "high-yield bond."

just-in-time inventory (production); JIT. System of managing *inventory* for manufacturing where each component is purchased or manufactured just before it is used. Contrast with systems where many parts are acquired or manufactured in advance of needs. JIT systems have much smaller, ideally no, carrying costs for inventory, but run higher risks of incurring *stockout* costs.

K

K. Two to the tenth power (2^{10} or 1,024), when referring to computer storage capacity. It is derived from the prefix "kilo" which represents 1,000 in decimal notation.

KG; Kommanditgesellschaft. Germany. Similar to a general partnership (*OHG*) except that some of its members may limit their liability. One of the partners must be a *general partner* with unlimited liability.

kiting. This term means slightly different things in banking and auditing contexts. In both, however, it refers to the wrongful practice of taking advantage of the *float*—the time that elapses between the deposit of a *check* in one bank and its collection at another. In the banking context, an individual deposits in Bank A a check written on Bank B. He (or she) then writes checks against the deposit created in Bank A. Several days later, he deposits in Bank B a check written on Bank A, to cover the original check written on Bank B. Still later, he deposits in Bank A a check written on Bank B. The process of covering the deposit in Bank A with a check written on Bank B and vice versa is continued until an actual deposit of cash can be arranged. In the auditing context, kiting refers to a form of *window dressing* where the amount of the account Cash in Bank is made to appear larger than it actually is by depositing in Bank A a check written on Bank B without recording the check written on Bank B in the *check register* until after the close of the *accounting period*.

know-how. Technical or business information of the type defined under *trade secret*, but that is not maintained as a secret. The rules of accounting for this asset are the same as for other *intangibles*.

L

labor variances. The *price* (or *rate*) and *quantity* (or *usage*) *variances* for *direct labor* inputs in a *standard cost system*.

laid-down cost. Canada and the United Kingdom. The sum of all direct costs incurred for procurement of goods up to the time of physical receipt, such as invoice cost plus customs and excise duties, freight and cartage.

land. An *asset shown at acquisition cost* plus the *cost* of any nondepreciable *improvements*. In accounting, implies use as a plant or office site, rather than as a *natural resource*, such as timberland or farm land.

lapping (accounts receivable). The theft, by an employee, of cash sent in by a customer to discharge the latter's *payable*. The theft from the first customer is concealed by using cash received from a second customer. The theft from the second customer is concealed by using the cash received from a third customer, and so on. The process is continued until the thief returns the funds or can make the theft permanent by creating a fictitious *expense* or receivable write-off, or until the fraud is discovered.

lapse. To expire; said of, for example, an insurance policy or discounts made available for prompt payment that are not taken.

last-in, first-out. See *LIFO*.

layer. See *LIFO inventory layer*.

lead time. The time that elapses between placing an order and receipt of the *goods or services* ordered.

learning curve. A mathematical expression of the phenomenon that incremental unit costs to produce decrease as managers and labor gain experience from practice.

lease. A contract calling for the lessee (user) to pay the lessor (owner) for the use of an asset. A cancelable lease is one the lessee can cancel at any time. A noncancelable lease requires payments from the lessee for the life of the lease and usually has many of the economic characteristics of *debt financing*. Most long-term noncancelable leases meet the usual criteria to be classified as a *liability* but some leases entered into before 1977 need not be shown as a liability. *SFAS No. 13* and the *SEC* require disclosure in notes to the financial statements of the commitments for long-term noncancelable leases. See *capital lease* and *operating lease*.

leasehold. The *asset* representing the right of the *lessee* to use leased property. See *lease* and *leasehold improvement*.

leasehold improvement. An *improvement* to leased property. Should be *amortized* over *service life* or the life of the lease, whichever is shorter.

least and latest rule. Pay the least amount of taxes as late as possible within the law to minimize the *present value* of tax payments for a given set of operations.

ledger. A book of accounts. See *general ledger* and *subsidiary ledger*; contrast with *journal*. Book of final entry.

legal capital. The amount of *contributed capital* that, according to state law, must remain permanently in the firm as protection for creditors.

legal entity. See *entity*.

lender. See *loan*.

lessee. See *lease*.

lessor. See *lease*.

letter stock. Privately placed *common shares*; so called because the *SEC* requires the purchaser to sign a letter of intent not to resell the shares.

leverage. "Operating leverage" refers to the tendency of *net income* to rise at a faster rate than sales when there are *fixed costs*. A doubling of sales, for example, usually implies a more than doubling of net income. "Financial leverage" (or "capital leverage") refers to the increased rate of return on *owners' equity* (see *ratio*) when an investment earns a return larger than the after-tax *interest rate* paid for *debt* financing. Because the interest charges on debt are usually fixed, all *incremental* income benefits owners but none of the income benefits debtors. When "leverage" is used without a qualifying adjective, it usually refers to financial leverage and means the use of *long-term* debt in securing *funds* for the *entity*.

leveraged lease. A special form of lease involving three parties: a *lender*, a *lessor*, and a *lessee*. The lender, such as a bank or insurance company, lends a portion, say 80 percent, of the cash required for acquiring the *asset*. The lessor puts up the remainder, 20 percent, of the cash required. The lessor acquires the asset with the cash, using the asset as security for the loan and leases it to the lessee on a *noncancelable* basis. The lessee makes periodic lease payments to the lessor, who in turn makes payments on the loan to the lender. Typically, the lessor has no obligation for the debt to the lender other than transferring a portion of the receipts from the lessee. If the lessee should default on required lease payments, then the lender can repossess the leased asset. The lessor is usually entitled to deductions for tax purposes for *depreciation* on the asset, for *interest expense* on the loan from the lender, and for any *investment credit*. The lease is leveraged in the sense that the lessor, who enjoys most of the risks and rewards of ownership, usually borrows most of the funds needed to acquire the asset. *See leverage.*

liability. An obligation to pay a definite (or reasonably definite) amount at a definite (or reasonably definite) time in return for a past or current benefit. That is, the obligation arises from other than an *executory contract*. A probable future sacrifice of economic benefits arising from present obligations of a particular *entity* to *transfer assets* or to provide services to other entities in the future as a result of past *transactions* or events. *SFAC No. 6* says that "probable" refers to that which can reasonably be expected or believed but is neither certain nor proved. A liability has three essential characteristics: (1) the entity has an obligation to transfer assets or services at a specified or determinable date, (2) it has little or no discretion to avoid the transfer, and (3) the event causing the obligation has already happened; that is, is not executory.

lien. The right of person A to satisfy a claim against person B by holding B's property as security or by seizing B's property.

life annuity. A *contingent annuity* in which payments cease at death of a specified person(s), usually the *annuitant(s)*.

LIFO. *Last-in, first-out.* An *inventory* flow assumption where the *cost of goods sold* is the cost of the most recently acquired units and the *ending inventory cost* is computed from costs of the oldest units; contrast with *FIFO*. In periods of rising prices and increasing inventories, LIFO leads to higher reported expenses and therefore lower reported income and lower balance sheet inventories than does FIFO. See also *FISH* and *inventory profit*.

LIFO conformity rule. The *IRS* requires that companies that use a *LIFO cost flow assumption for income taxes* also use LIFO in computing *income* reported in *fi-*nancial statements* and forbids disclosure of *pro forma* results from using any other cost flow assumption.

LIFO, dollar-value method. See *dollar-value LIFO method.*

LIFO inventory layer. The *ending inventory* for a period is likely to be larger than the *beginning inventory*. Under a *LIFO cost flow assumption*, this increase in physical quantities is assigned a cost computed from the prices of the earliest purchases during the year. The LIFO inventory then consists of layers, sometimes called "slices," which typically consist of relatively small amounts of physical quantities from each of the past several years. Each layer carries the prices from near the beginning of the period when it was acquired. The earliest layers will typically (in periods of rising prices) have prices much less than current prices. If inventory quantities should decline in a subsequent period, the latest layers enter cost of goods sold first.

LIFO reserve. *Unrealized holding gain* in *ending inventory*: current or *FIFO historical* cost of ending inventory less LIFO *historical cost*. See *reserve*; a better term for this concept is "excess of current cost over LIFO historical cost."

limited liability. Shareholders of corporations are not personally liable for debts of the company.

limited partner. Member of a *partnership* not personally liable for debts of the partnership; every partnership must have at least one *general partner* who is fully liable.

line of business reporting. See *segment reporting.*

line of credit. An agreement with the bank or set of banks for short-term borrowing on demand.

linear programming. A mathematical tool for finding profit maximizing (or cost minimizing) combinations of products to produce when there are several products that can be produced but there are linear constraints on the resources available in the production processes or on maximum and minimum production requirements.

liquid. Said of a business with a substantial amount (the amount is unspecified) of *working capital*, especially *quick assets*.

liquid assets. *Cash, current marketable securities*, and, sometimes, *current receivables*.

liquidating dividend. *Dividend* declared in the winding up of a business to distribute the assets of the company to the shareholders. Usually treated by recipient as a return of *investment*, not as *revenue*.

liquidation.   Payment of a debt. Sale of assets in closing down a business or a segment thereof.

liquidation value per share.   The amount each *share* of stock will receive if the corporation is dissolved. For *preferred stock* with a liquidation preference, a stated amount per share.

liquidity.   Refers to the availability of *cash*, or near cash resources, for meeting a firm's obligations.

LISH.   An acronym, conceived by George H. Sorter, for *last in, still here*. LISH is the same cost flow assumption as *FIFO*. Many readers of accounting statements find it easier to think about inventory questions in terms of items still on hand. Think of FIFO in connection with *cost of goods sold* but of LISH in connection with *ending inventory*. See *FISH*.

list price.   The published or nominally quoted price for goods.

list price method.   See *trade-in transaction*.

loan.   An arrangement where the owner of property, called the lender, allows someone else, called the borrower, the use of the property for a period of time that is usually specified in the agreement setting up the loan. The borrower promises to return the property to the lender and, often, to make a payment for use of the property. Generally used when the property is *cash* and the payment for its use is *interest*.

long-lived (term) asset.   An asset whose benefits are expected to be received over several years. A *noncurrent* asset, usually includes *investments, plant assets*, and *intangibles*.

long-run. long-term.   A term denoting a time or time periods in the future. How far in the future depends on context. For some securities traders, "long-term" can mean anything beyond the next hour or two. For most managers, it means anything beyond the next year or two. For government policy makers, it can mean anything beyond the next decade or two.

long-term (construction) contract accounting.   The *percentage of completion method* of *revenue* recognition. Sometimes used to mean the *completed contract method*.

long-term debt ratio.   *Noncurrent liabilities* divided by total *assets*.

long-term liability (debt).   *Noncurrent liability*.

long-term solvency risk.   The risk that a firm will not have sufficient *cash* to pay its *debts* sometime in the *long run*.

loophole.   Imprecise term meaning a technicality allowing a taxpayer (or *financial statements*) to circumvent a law's (or *GAAP*'s) intent without violating its letter.

loss.   Excess of *cost* over net proceeds for a single transaction; negative *income* for a period. A cost expiration that produced no *revenue*. See *gain* for a discussion of related and contrasting terms.

loss contingency.   See *contingency*.

lower of cost or market.   A basis for valuation of *inventory* or *marketable equity securities*. The inventory value is set at the lower of *acquisition cost* or *current replacement cost* (market), subject to the following constraints: First, the market value of an item used in the computation cannot exceed its *net realizable value*—an amount equal to selling price less reasonable costs to complete production and to sell the item. Second, the market value of an item used in the computation cannot be less than the net realizable value minus the normal *profit* ordinarily realized on disposition of completed items of this type. The lower-of-cost-or-market valuation is chosen as the lower of acquisition *cost* or replacement cost (*market*) subject to the upper and lower bounds on replacement cost established in the first two steps. Thus,

Market Value	=	Midvalue of (Replacement Cost, Net Realizable Value, Net Realizable Value less Normal Profit Margin)
Lower of Cost or Market Valuation	=	Minimum (Acquisition Cost, Market Value).

The accompanying exhibit illustrates the calculation of the lower-of-cost-or-market valuation for four inventory items. Notice that each of the four possible outcome occurs once in determining lower of cost or market. Item 1 uses acquisition cost; item 2 uses net realizable value; item 3 uses replacement cost; and item 4 uses net realizable value less normal profit.

Lower of cost or market cannot be used for inventory on tax returns in a combination with a *LIFO cost flow assumption*. In the context of inventory, once the asset is written down, a new "original cost" basis is established and subsequent increases in market value are ignored in the accounts.

In the context of *marketable equity securities*, the method is applied separately to short-term and long-term portfolios of securities. Losses in market value on the short-term portfolio (and any subsequent recoveries in value up to original cost) are reported as part of *income from continuing operations* for the period. For the long-term portfolio, the losses (and subsequent recoveries, if any) are *debited* (or *credited*) directly to an *owners' equity contra account*. Note that hyphens are not used when the term is used as a noun but hyphens are used when the term is used as an adjectival phrase.

	Item			
	1	**2**	**3**	**4**
Calculation of Market Value				
(a) Replacement Cost	$92	$96	$92	$96
(b) Net Realizable Value . . .	95	95	95	95
(c) Net Realizable Value Less Normal Profit Margin [=(b) - $9]	86	86	86	86
(d) Market = Midvalue [(a), (b), (c)]	92	95	92	95
Calculation of Lower of Cost or Market				
(e) Acquisition Cost	90	97	96	90
(f) Market [= (d)]	92	95	92	95
(g) Lower of Cost or Market = Minimum [(e), (f)]	90	95	92	90

Ltd.; Limited. United Kingdom. A private limited corporation. The name of a private limited company must include the word "Limited" or its abbreviation "Ltd."

lump-sum acquisition. *Basket purchase.*

M

MACRS. Modified *accelerated cost recovery system.* Some writers use "modified" to distinguish the 1986 amendments from the original 1981 law.

MD&A. *Management discussion and analysis* section of *financial statements.*

maintenance. *Expenditures* undertaken to preserve an *asset's* service potential for its originally intended life; these expenditures are treated as *period expenses* or *product costs*; contrast with *improvement.* See *repair.*

make-or-buy decision. A managerial decision about whether the firm should produce a product internally or purchase it from others. Proper make-or-buy decisions in the short run result when *incremental costs* are the only costs considered in decision making.

maker (of note) (of check). One who signs a *note* to borrow. One who signs a *check*; in this context synonymous with drawer; see *draft.*

management. Executive authority that operates a business.

management accounting. See *managerial accounting.*

Management Accounting. Monthly publication of the *NAA.*

management audit. An audit conducted to ascertain whether the objectives, policies, and procedures for a firm or one of its operating units are properly carried out. Generally applies only to activities for which qualitative standards can be specified. See *audit* and *internal audit.*

management by exception. A principle of management where attention is focused on performance only if it differs significantly from that expected.

management by objective. A management approach designed to focus on the definition and attainment of overall and individual objectives with the participation of all levels of management.

management discussion and analysis. A discussion of management's views of the company's performance required by the *SEC* since 1974 to be included in the *Form 10-K* and in the *annual report* to shareholders. The information typically contains discussion of such items as *liquidity*, results of *operations*, *segments*, and the effects of *inflation.*

management information system. A system designed to provide all levels of management with timely and reliable information required for planning, control, and evaluation of performance.

managerial (management) accounting. Reporting designed to enhance the ability of management to do its job of decision making, planning, and control; contrast with *financial accounting.*

manufacturing cost. Cost of producing goods, usually in a factory.

manufacturing expense. An imprecise, and generally incorrect, alternative title for *manufacturing overhead.*

manufacturing overhead. General manufacturing *costs* incurred in providing a capacity to carry on productive activities but that are not directly associated with identifiable units of product. *Fixed* manufacturing overhead costs are treated as a *product cost* under *absorption costing* but as an *expense* of the period under *direct costing.*

margin. *Revenue* less specified expenses. See *contribution margin*, *gross margin*, and *current margin*.

margin of safety. Excess of actual, or budgeted, sales over *breakeven* sales. Usually expressed in dollars; may be expressed in units of product.

marginal cost. The *incremental cost* or *differential cost* of the last unit added to production or the first unit subtracted from production. See *cost terminology*.

marginal costing. *Direct costing.*

marginal revenue. The increment in *revenue* from sale of one additional unit of product.

marginal tax rate. The tax imposed on the next dollar of taxable income generated; contrast with *average tax rate*.

markdown. See *markup* for definition and contrast.

markdown cancellation. See *markup* for definition and contrast.

market-based transfer price. A *transfer price* based on external market, rather than internal company, data.

market price. See *fair market price*.

market rate. The rate of *interest* a company must pay to borrow *funds* currently. See *effective rate*.

marketable equity securities. *Marketable securities* representing *owners' equity* interest in other companies, rather than *loans* to them.

marketable securities. *Stocks* and *bonds* of other companies held that can be readily sold on stock exchanges or over-the-counter markets and that the company plans to sell as cash if needed. Classified as *current assets* and as part of "cash" in preparing the *statement of cash flows*. The same securities held for *long-term* purposes would be classified as *noncurrent assets*. *SFAS No. 12* requires the *lower-of-cost-or-market* valuation basis for all marketable equity securities but different accounting treatments (with differing effect on income) depending upon whether the security is a *current* or a *noncurrent asset*.

markon. See *markup* for definition and contrast.

markup. When a retailer acquires items for *inventory*, the items are given a selling price. The difference between the original selling price and cost is most precisely called "markon," although many business people use the term "markup," and because of confusion of this use of "markup" with its precise definition (see below), "original markup" is sometimes used. If the originally established retail price is increased, the precise term for the amount of price increase is "markup," although "additional markup" is sometimes used. If a selling price is lowered, the terms "markdown" and "markup cancellation" are used. "Markup cancellation" refers to reduction in price following "additional markups" and can, by definition, be no more than the amount of the additional markup; "cancellation of additional markup," although not used, is descriptive. "Markdown" refers to price reductions from the original retail price. A price increase after a markdown is a "markdown cancellation." If original cost is $12 and original selling price is $20, then markon (original markup) is $8; if the price is later increased to $24, the $4 increase is markup (additional markup); if the price is later lowered to $21, the $3 reduction is markup cancellation; if price is lowered further to $17, the $4 reduction comprises $1 markup cancellation and $3 markdown; if price is later increased to $22, the $5 increase comprises $3 of markdown cancellation and $2 of markup (additional markup). Markup cancellations and markdowns are separately counted because the former are deducted (while the latter are not) in computing the selling prices of goods available for sale for the denominator of the *cost percentage* used in the conventional *retail inventory method*.

markup cancellation. See *markup* for definition and contrast.

markup percentage. *Markup* divided by (acquisition cost plus *markup*).

master budget. A *budget* projecting all *financial statements* and their components.

matching convention. The concept of recognizing cost expirations (*expenses*) in the same accounting period when the related *revenues* are recognized. Combining or simultaneously recognizing the revenues and expenses that jointly result from the same *transactions* or other events.

material. As an adjective, it means "relatively important." See *materiality*. Currently, no operational definition exists. As a noun, "*raw material*."

material variances. *Price* and *quantity variances* for *direct materials* in *standard cost systems*. Sometimes used to mean variances that are significant; see *materiality*.

materiality. The concept that accounting should disclose separately only those events that are relatively important (no operable definition yet exists) for the business or for understanding its statements. *SFAC No. 2* suggests that accounting information is material if "the judgment of a reasonable person relying on the information would have been changed or influenced by the omission or misstatement."

matrix. A rectangular array of numbers or mathematical symbols.

matrix inverse. For a given square *matrix* A, the square matrix inverse is the matrix, A^{-1}, such that $AA^{-1} = A^{-1}A = I$, the *identity matrix*. Not all square matrices have inverses. Those that do not are called "singular"; those that do are "nonsingular."

maturity. The date at which an obligation, such as the *principal* of a *bond* or a *note*, becomes due.

maturity value. The amount expected to be collected when a loan reaches *maturity*. Depending upon the context, the amount may be *principal* or principal and *interest*.

MBO. Abbrebreviation for *management by objective*.

measuring unit. See *attribute measured* for definition and contrast.

merchandise. *Finished goods* bought by a retailer or wholesaler for resale; contrast with finished goods of a manufacturing business.

merchandise turnover. *Inventory turnover* for merchandise; see *ratio*.

merchandising business. As opposed to a manufacturing or service business, one that purchases (rather than manufactures) *finished goods* for resale.

merger. The joining of two or more businesses into a single *economic entity*. See *holding company*.

minority interest. A *balance sheet account* on *consolidated statements* showing the *equity* in a less-than-100-percent-owned *subsidiary* company allocable to those who are not part of the controlling (majority) interest. May be classified either as *shareholders' equity* or as a liability of *indeterminate term* on the consolidated balance sheet. On the *income statement*, the minority's interest in current period's income of the less-than-100-percent-owned subsidiary must be subtracted to arrive at consolidated *net income* for the period.

minority investment. A holding of less than 50 percent of the *voting stock* in another corporation. Accounted for with the *equity method* when sufficient shares are owned so that the investor can exercise "significant influence," and with the *lower-of-cost-or-market* valuation otherwise. See *mutual fund*.

minutes book. A record of all actions authorized at corporate *board of director's* or shareholders' meetings.

MIS. Abbrebviation for *management information system*.

mix variance. Many *standard cost* systems specify combinations of inputs, for example, labor of a certain skill and materials of a certain quality grade. Sometimes combinations of inputs used differ from those contemplated by the standard. The mix variance attempts to report the cost change caused by changing the combination of inputs.

mixed cost. A *semifixed* or a *semivariable* cost.

modified accelerated cost recovery system. See *MACRS*.

modified cash basis. The *cash basis of accounting* with long-term assets accounted for with the *accrual basis of accounting*. Most uses of the term "cash basis of accounting" actually mean "modified cash basis."

monetary assets and liabilities. See *monetary items*.

monetary gain or loss. The *gain* or *loss* in *general purchasing power* as a result of holding *monetary assets* or liabilities during a period when the *general purchasing power of the dollar* changes. During periods of *inflation*, holders of net monetary assets lose, and holders of net monetary liabilities gain, general purchasing power. During periods of *deflation*, holders of net monetary assets gain, and holders of net monetary liabilities lose, general purchasing power. Explicitly reported in *constant dollar accounting*.

monetary items. Amounts fixed in terms of dollars by statute or contract. *Cash, accounts receivable, accounts payable*, and *debt*. The distinction between monetary and nonmonetary items is important for *constant dollar accounting* and for *foreign exchange gain* or *loss* computations. In the foreign exchange context, account amounts denominated in dollars are not monetary items, whereas amounts denominated in any other currency are monetary.

money. A word seldom used with precision in accounting, at least in part because economists have not yet agreed on its definition. Economists use the term to refer to both a medium of exchange and a unit of value. See *cash* and *monetary items*.

money purchase plan. A *pension plan* where the employer contributes a specified amount of cash each year to each employee's pension fund. Benefits ultimately received by the employee are not specifically defined but depend on the rate of return on the cash invested. Sometimes called a "defined-contribution" pension plan; contrast with *defined-benefit plan*. As of the early 1990s, most corporate pension plans were defined-benefit plans because both the law and *generally accepted accounting principles* for pensions made defined-benefit plans more attractive than money purchase plans. *ERISA* makes money purchase plans relatively more attractive than they had been. We expect the relative number of money purchase plans to increase.

mortality table. Data of life expectancies or probabilities of death for persons of specified ages and sex.

mortgage. A claim given by the borrower (mortgagor) to the lender (mortgagee) against the borrower's property in return for a loan.

moving average. An *average* computed on observations over time. As a new observation becomes available, the oldest one is dropped so that the average is always computed for the same number of observations and only the most recent ones. Sometimes, however, this term is used synonymously with *weighted average*.

moving average method. *Weighted-average method.*

multiple-step. Said of an *income statement* where various classes of *expenses* and *losses* are subtracted from *revenues* to show intermediate items such as *operating income*, income of the enterprise (operating income plus *interest* income), income to investors (income of the enterprise less *income taxes*), net income to shareholders (income to investors less interest charges), and income retained (income to shareholders less dividends). See *entity theory*.

municipal bond. A *bond* issued by a village, town, or city. *Interest* on such bonds is generally exempt from federal *income taxes* and from some state income taxes. Because bonds issued by state and county governments often have these characteristics, such bonds are often called "municipals" as well. Sometimes referred to as "tax exempts."

mutual fund. An investment company that issues its own stock to the public and uses the proceeds to invest in securities of other companies. A mutual fund usually owns less than five or ten percent of the stock of any one company and accounts for its investments using current *market values*; contrast with *holding company*.

mutually exclusive projects. Competing investment projects, where accepting one project eliminates the possibility of undertaking the remaining projects.

N

NAARS. *National Automated Accounting Research System.*

NASDAQ. National Association of Securities Dealers Automated Quotation System; a computerized system to provide brokers and dealers with price quotations for securities traded *over the counter* as well as for some *NYSE* securities.

National Association of Accountants. NAA. A national society generally open to all engaged in activities closely associated with *managerial accounting*. Oversees the administration of the *CMA* Examinations through the Institute of Certified Management Accountants.

National Automated Accounting Research System. NAARS. A computer-based information retrieval system containing, among other things, the complete text of most public corporate annual reports and *Forms 10-K*. The system is available to users through the *AICPA*.

natural business year. A 12-month period chosen as the reporting period so that the end of the period coincides with a low point in activity or inventories. See *ratio* for a discussion of analyses of financial statements of companies using a natural business year.

natural classification. Income statement reporting form in which expenses are classified by nature of items as acquired, that is, materials, wages, salaries, insurance, and taxes, as well as depreciation; contrast with *functional classification*.

natural resources. Timberland, oil and gas wells, ore deposits, and other products of nature that have economic value. The cost of natural resources is subject to *depletion*. Natural resources are "nonrenewable" (e.g., oil, coal, gas, ore deposits) or "renewable" (timberland, sod fields); the former are often called "wasting assets." See also *reserve recognition accounting* and *percentage depletion*.

negative confirmation. See *confirmation*.

negative goodwill. Refer to *goodwill*. When the purchase price of the company acquired is less than the sum of the *fair market value* of the *net assets* acquired, *APB Opinion No. 16* requires that the valuation of noncurrent assets (except *investments* in *marketable securities*) acquired be reduced until the purchase price equals the adjusted valuation of the fair market value of net assets acquired. If, after the adjusted valuation of noncurrent assets is reduced to zero, the purchase price is still less than the net assets acquired, then the difference appears as a credit balance in the balance sheet account negative goodwill and is amortized to income over a period not to exceed forty years. For negative goodwill to exist, someone must be willing to sell a company for less than the fair market value of net current assets and marketable securities. Because such a bargain purchase is rare, negative goodwill is rarely found in the financial statements; when it does appear, it generally signals unrecorded obligations, such as for *pensions* or contingent liability in a law suit.

negotiable. Legally capable of being transferred by endorsement. Usually said of *checks* and *notes* and sometimes of *stocks* and *bearer bonds*.

negotiated transfer price. A *transfer price* set jointly by the buying and selling divisions.

net. Reduced by all relevant deductions.

net assets. *Owners' equity;* total *assets* minus total *liabilities.*

net bank position. From a firm's point of view, *cash* in a specific bank less *loans* payable to that bank.

net current assets. *Working capital* = *current assets - current liabilities.*

net current asset value (per share). *Working capital* divided by the number of common shares outstanding. Many security analysts think that when a common share trades in the market for an amount less than net current asset value, then the shares are undervalued and should be purchased. We find this view naive because it ignores the efficiency of capital markets generally and, specifically, it ignores unrecorded obligations such as for some *pension plans,* not currently reported as liabilities in the *balance sheet* under *GAAP.*

net income. The excess of all *revenues* and *gains* for a period over all *expenses* and *losses* of the period. See *comprehensive income.*

net loss. The excess of all *expenses* and *losses* for a period over all *revenues* and *gains* of the period. Negative *net income.*

net markup. In the context of *retail inventory methods, markups* less *markup cancellations;* a figure that usually ignores *markdowns* and markdown cancellations.

net of tax method. A nonsanctioned method for dealing with the problem of *income tax allocation;* described in *APB Opinion No. 11.* Deferred tax items are subtracted from specific *asset* amounts rather than appearing as a deferred credit or *liability.*

net of tax reporting. Reporting, such as for *income from discontinued operations, extraordinary items,* and *prior-period adjustments,* where the amounts presented in *financial statements* have been adjusted for all income tax effects. For example, if an extraordinary loss amounted to $10,000 and the marginal tax rate were 40 percent, then the extraordinary item would be reported "net of taxes" as a $6,000 loss. Hence, all income taxes may not be reported on one line of the income statement. The taxes will be allocated to *income from continuing operations, income from discontinued operations, extraordinary items,* cumulative effects of *accounting changes,* and *prior-period adjustments.*

net operating profit. Income from *continuing operations.*

net present value. Discounted or *present value* of all cash inflows and outflows of a project or from an *investment* at a given *discount rate.*

net price method (of recording purchase or sales discounts). The *purchase* (or *sale*) is recorded at its *invoice* price less all *discounts* made available under the assumption that nearly all discounts will be taken. Discounts lapsed through failure to pay promptly are debited to an *expense* account. For purchases, management usually prefers to know about the amount of discounts lost because of inefficient operations, not the amounts taken, so that most managers prefer the net price method to the *gross price method.*

net realizable (sales) value. A method for *allocating joint costs* in proportion to *realizable values* of the joint products. For example, joint products A and B together cost $100 and A sells for $60 whereas B sells for $90. Then A would be allocated ($60/$150) x $100 = .40 x $100 = $40 of cost while B would be allocated ($90/$150) x $100 = $60 of cost.

net sales. Sales (at gross invoice amount) less *returns, allowances,* freight paid for customers, and *discounts* taken.

net working capital. *Working capital;* the "net" is redundant in accounting. Financial analysts sometimes mean *current assets* when they speak of working capital, so for them the "net" is not redundant.

net worth. A misleading term, to be avoided, that means the same as *owners' equity.*

network analysis. A method of planning and scheduling a project, usually displayed in diagrammatic form, in order to identify the interrelated sequences that must be accomplished to complete the project.

New York Stock Exchange. NYSE. A public market where various corporate *securities* are traded.

next-in, first-out. See *NIFO.*

NIFO. *Next-in, first-out.* In making decisions, many managers consider *replacement costs* (rather than *historical costs*) and refer to them as NIFO costs.

no par. Said of *stock* without a *par value.*

nominal accounts. *Temporary accounts,* such as *revenue* and *expense* accounts, as opposed to *balance sheet accounts.* All nominal accounts are *closed* at the end of each *accounting period.*

nominal amount (value). An amount stated in dollars, in contrast to an amount stated in *constant dollars.* Contrast with *real amount (value).*

nominal dollars. The measuring unit giving no consideration to differences in the *general purchasing power of the dollar* over time. The face amount of currency or coin, a *bond*, an *invoice*, a *receivable* is a nominal dollar amount. When that amount is adjusted for changes in *general purchasing power*, it is converted into a *constant dollar* amount.

nominal interest rate. A rate specified on a *debt* instrument, which usually differs from the market or *effective rate*. Also, a rate of *interest* quoted for a year. If the interest is compounded more often than annually, then the *effective interest rate* is higher than the nominal rate.

noncancelable. See *lease*.

nonconsolidated subsidiary. An *intercorporate investment* where more than 50 percent of the shares of the *subsidiary* are owned but the investment is accounted for with the *cost method* or *lower-of-cost-or-market method*.

noncontributory. Said of a *pension plan* where only the employer makes payments to a pension *fund*; contrast with *contributory*.

noncontrollable cost. A cost that is not *controllable* by a particular manager.

noncurrent. Due more than one year (or more than one *operating cycle*) hence.

nonexpendable fund. A governmental fund, whose *principal*, and sometimes earnings, may not be spent.

non-interest-bearing note. A *note* that bears no explicit interest. The *present value* of such a note at any time before *maturity* is less than the *face value* so long as *interest rates* are positive. *APB Opinion No. 21* requires that the present value, not face value, of long-term non-interest-bearing notes be reported as the *asset* or *liability* amount in financial statements. For this purpose, the *historical interest rate* is used. See *interest, imputed*.

nonmanufacturing costs. All *costs* incurred other than those to produce goods.

nonmonetary items. All items that are not monetary; see *monetary items*.

nonoperating. In the *income statement* context, said of revenues and expenses arising from transactions incidental to the company's main line(s) of business. In the *statement of cash flows* context, said of all sources or uses of cash other than cash provided by operations. See *operations*.

nonprofit corporation. An incorporated *entity*, such as a hospital, with owners who do not share in the earnings.

It usually emphasizes providing services rather than maximizing income.

nonrecurring. Said of an event that is not expected to happen often for a given firm. Under *APB Opinion No. 30*, the effects of such events should be disclosed separately, but as part of *ordinary* items unless the event is also unusual. See *extraordinary* item.

normal cost. Former name for *service cost*.

normal costing. Method of charging costs to products using actual *direct materials*, actual *direct labor*, and predetermined *factory overheard* rates.

normal costing system. *Costing* based on *actual material* and *labor* costs, but using *predetermined overhead* rates per unit of some *activity* basis (such as *direct labor hours* or machine hours) to apply overhead to production. This rate for overhead to be charged to production is decided at the start of the period. At the end of the period it is multiplied by the actual number of units of the base activity (such as actual direct labor hours worked or actual machine hours used during the period) to apply overhead to production.

normal spoilage. Costs incurred because of ordinary amounts of spoilage; such costs should be prorated to units produced as *product costs*; contrast with *abnormal spoilage*.

normal standard cost. normal standards. The *cost* expected to be incurred under reasonably efficient operating conditions with adequate provision for an average amount of rework, spoilage, and the like.

normal volume. The level of production over a time span, usually 1 year, that will satisfy demand by purchasers and provide for reasonable *inventory* levels.

note. An unconditional written promise by the maker (borrower) to pay a certain amount on demand or at a certain future time. See *footnotes* for another context.

note receivable discounted. A *note* assigned by the holder to another. The new holder of the note typically pays the old holder an amount less than the *face value* of the note; hence the word "discounted." But this word is used even if the payment by the new holder to the old is at or above face value. If the note is assigned with recourse, it is the *contingent liability* of the assignor until the debt is paid. See *factoring*.

NOW account. Negotiable order of withdrawal. A *savings account* on which orders to pay, much like *checks* but technically not checks, can be drawn and given to others who can redeem the order at the savings institution.

number of days sales in inventory (or receivables). Days of average inventory on hand (or average collection period for receivables). See *ratio*.

NYSE. *New York Stock Exchange.*

O

OASD(H)I. *Old Age, Survivors, Disability, and (Hospital) Insurance.*

objective. See *reporting objective* and *objectivity*.

objective function. In *linear programming*, the name of the profit or cost criterion to be optimized.

objectivity. The reporting policy implying that formal recognition will not be given to an event in financial statements until the magnitude of the events can be measured with reasonable accuracy and the event is subject to independent verification.

obsolescence. A decline in *market value* of an *asset* caused by improved alternatives becoming available that will be more *cost effective*; the decline in market value is unrelated to physical changes in the asset itself. See *partial obsolescence*.

Occupational Safety and Health Act. *OSHA.*

off-balance-sheet financing. A description often used for an obligation meeting all the tests to be a liability, except that the obligation arises from an *executory contract* and, hence, is not a *liability*. Consider the following example.

Miller Corporation desires to acquire land costing $25 million, on which it will build a shopping center. It could borrow the $25 million from its bank, paying interest at 12 percent, and buy the land outright from the seller. If so, both an asset and a liability will appear on the balance sheet. Instead, it borrows $5 million and purchases for $5 million from the seller an *option* to buy the land from the seller at any time within the next 6 years for a price of $20 million. The option costs Miller Corporation $5 million immediately and provides for continuing "option" payments of $2.4 million per year, which is just equal to Miller Corporation's borrowing rate multiplied by the remaining purchase price of the land: $2.4 million = .12 x $20 million. Although Miller Corporation need not continue payments and can let the option lapse at any time, it also has an obligation to begin developing on the site immediately. Because Miller Corporation has invested a substantial sum in the option, will invest more, and will begin immediately developing the land, Miller Corporation is almost certain to exercise its option before it expires. The seller of the land can take the option contract to the bank and borrow $20 million, paying interest at

Miller Corporation's borrowing rate, 12 percent per year. The continuing option payments from Miller Corporation will be sufficient to enable the seller to make its payments to the bank. *Generally accepted accounting principles* view Miller Corporation as having acquired an option for $5 million, rather than having acquired land costing $25 million in return for $5 million of "debt" off the balance sheet until it borrows more funds to exercise the option.

OHG; Offene Handelsgesellschaft. Germany. A general *partnership*. The partners have unlimited liability.

Old Age, Survivors, Disability, and (Hospital) Insurance. OASD(H)I. The technical name for Social Security under the Federal Insurance Contributions Act (*FICA*).

on (open) account. Said of a *purchase* or *sale* when payment is expected sometime after delivery and no *note* evidencing the *debt* is given or received. The purchaser has generally signed an agreement sometime in the past promising to pay for such purchases according to an agreed time schedule. When a sale (purchase) is made on open account, *Accounts Receivable (Payable)* is *debited (credited)*.

on consignment. Said of goods delivered by the owner (the consignor) to another (the consignee) to be sold by the consignee; the owner is entitled to the return of the property or payment of an amount agreed upon in advance. The goods are assets of the consignor. Such arrangements provide the consignor with better protection than an outright *sale on account* to the consignee in case the consignee becomes bankrupt. In event of *bankruptcy*, the consignor can reclaim the goods, without going through lengthy bankruptcy proceedings from which the consignor might recover only a small percentage of the amounts owed to it.

one-line consolidation. Said of an *intercorporate investment* accounted for with the *equity method*. The effects of this method on reported *income* and *balance sheet* total *assets* and *equities* are identical to those that would appear if the investee firm were consolidated, even though the income from the investment appears on a single line of the income statement, and the net investment appears on a single line in the assets section of the balance sheet.

one-write system. A system of bookkeeping that produces several records, including original documents, in one operation by the use of reproductive paper and special equipment that provides for proper alignment of the documents being processed.

open account. Any *account* with a nonzero *debit* or *credit balance*. See *on (open) account*.

operating. An adjective used to refer to *revenue* and *expense* items relating to the company's main line(s) of business. See *operations*.

operating accounts. *Revenue, expense,* and *production cost accounts;* contrast with *balance sheet accounts.*

operating activities. See *operations.* For purposes of the *statement of cash flows,* all *transactions* and *events* that are neither *financing activities* nor *investing activities.*

operating budget. A formal *budget* for the *operating cycle* or for a year.

operating cash flow. Financial statement analysts use this term to mean *cash flow - capital expenditures - dividends.*

operating cycle. *Earnings cycle.*

operating expenses. *Expenses* incurred in the course of *ordinary* activities of an *entity.* Frequently, a classification including only *selling, general,* and *administrative expenses,* thereby excluding *cost of goods sold, interest,* and *income tax* expenses. See *operations.*

operating lease. A *lease* accounted for by the *lessee* without showing an *asset* for the lease rights (*leasehold*) or a *liability* for the lease payment obligations. Rental payments of the *lessee* are merely shown as *expenses* of the period. The asset remains on the lessor's *books* where rental collections appear as *revenues;* contrast with *capital lease.*

operating leverage. Usually said of a firm with a large proportion of *fixed costs* in its *total costs.* Consider a book publisher or a railroad; the *incremental costs* of producing another book or transporting another freight car are much less than *average cost,* so the *gross margin* upon sale of the unit is relatively large. Contrast, for example, a grocery store, where the *contribution margin* is usually less than 5 percent of the selling price. For firms with equal profitability, however defined, the one with the larger percentage increase in income from a given percentage increase in unit sales is said to have the larger operating leverage. See *leverage* for contrast of this term with "financial leverage." See *cost terminology* for definition of terms involving the word "cost."

operating margin (based on current costs). *Revenues* from *sales* minus *current cost* of goods sold. A measure of operating efficiency that is independent of the *cost flow assumption* for *inventory.* Sometimes called "current (gross) margin." See *inventory profit* for illustrative computations.

operating ratio. See *ratio.*

operational control. See *control system.*

operations. A word not precisely defined in *accounting.* Generally, operating activities (producing and selling *goods* or *services*) are distinguished from financing activities (raising funds) and *investing activities.* Acquiring goods on account and then paying for them in one month, though generally classified as an operating activity, has the characteristics of a financing activity. Or consider the transaction of selling plant assets for a price in excess of book value. On the *income statement,* the gain is part of income from operations (continuing operations or discontinued operations, depending on the circumstances) but on the *statement of cash flows,* all of the funds received on disposition are reported below the "cash from operations" section, as a nonoperating source of cash, disposition of noncurrent assets. In income tax accounting, an "operating loss" results whenever deductions are greater than taxable revenues.

opinion. The *auditor's report* containing an attestation or lack thereof. Also, *APB Opinion.*

opinion paragraph. Section of *auditor's report,* generally following the *scope paragraph,* giving the auditor's conclusion that the *financial statements* are (rarely, are not) in accordance with *GAAP* and present fairly the *financial position,* changes in financial position, and the results of *operations.*

opportunity cost. The *present value* of the *income* (or *costs*) that could be earned (or saved) from using an *asset* in its best alternative use to the one being considered.

option. The legal right to buy something during a specified period at a specified price, called the *exercise* price. Employee stock options should not be confused with *put* and *call* options traded in various public markets.

ordinary annuity. An *annuity in arrears.*

ordinary income. For income tax purposes, reportable *income* not qualifying as *capital gains.*

organization costs. The *costs* incurred in planning and establishing an *entity;* example of an *intangible* asset. Often, since the amounts are not *material,* the costs are treated as *expenses* in the period incurred even though the *expenditures* clearly provide future benefits and meet the test to be *assets.*

original cost. *Acquisition cost.* In public utility accounting, the acquisition cost of the *entity* first devoting the asset to public use. See *aboriginal cost.*

original entry. Entry in a *journal.*

OSHA. Occupational Safety and Health Act. The federal law that governs working conditions in commerce and industry.

outlay. The amount of an *expenditure.*

outlier. Said of an observation (or data point) that appears to differ significantly in some regard from other observations (or data points) of supposedly the same phenomenon. Often used in describing the results of a *regression analysis* when an observation is not "near" the fitted regression equation.

out-of-pocket. Said of an *expenditure* usually paid for with cash. An *incremental* cost.

out-of-stock cost. The estimated decrease in future *profit* as a result of losing customers because insufficient quantities of *inventory* are currently on hand to meet customers' demands.

output. Physical quantity or monetary measurement of *goods* and *services* produced.

outside director. A member of a corporate board of directors who is not a company officer and who does not participate in the corporation's day-to-day management.

outstanding. Unpaid or uncollected. When said of *stock*, the shares issued less *treasury stock*. When said of checks, it means a check issued that did not clear the *drawer's* bank prior to the *bank statement* date.

over-and-short. Title for an *expense account* used to account for small differences between book balances of cash and actual cash and vouchers or receipts in *petty cash* or *change funds*.

overapplied (overabsorbed) overhead. An excess of costs applied, or *charged*, to product for a period over actual *overhead costs* during the period. A *credit balance* in an overhead account after overhead is assigned to product.

overdraft. A check written on a checking account that contains funds less than the amount of the check.

overhead costs. Any *cost* not directly associated with the production or sale of identifiable goods and services. Sometimes called "burden" or "indirect costs" and, in Britain, "oncosts." Frequently limited to manufacturing overhead. See *central corporate expenses* and *manufacturing overhead*.

overhead rate. Standard, or other predetermined rate at which *overhead costs* are applied to products or to services.

over-the-counter. Said of a *security* traded in a negotiated transaction, rather than in an auctioned one on an organized stock exchange, such as the *New York Stock Exchange*.

owners' equity. *Proprietorship; assets* minus *liabilities; paid-in capital* plus *retained earnings* of a corporation; partners' capital accounts in a *partnership*; owner's capital account in a *sole proprietorship*.

P

P & L. Profit and loss statement; *income statement*.

paid-in capital. Sum of balances in *capital stock* and *capital contributed in excess of par (or stated) value* accounts. Same as *contributed capital* (minus *donated capital*). Some use the term to mean only *capital contributed in excess of par (or stated value)*.

paid-in surplus. See *surplus*.

paper profit. A *gain* not yet realized through a *transaction*. An *unrealized holding gain*.

par. See *at par* and *face amount*. par value. *Face amount* of a *security*.

par value method. The method of accounting for *treasury stock* that *debits* a common stock account with the *par value* of the shares required and allocates the remaining debits between the *additional paid-in capital* and *retained earnings* accounts; contrast with *cost method*.

parent company. Company owning more than 50 percent of the voting shares of another company, called the *subsidiary*.

partial obsolescence. As technology improves, the economic value of existing *assets* declines. In many cases, however, it will not pay a firm to replace the existing asset with a new one even though the new type, rather than the old, would be acquired if a new acquisition were to be made currently. In these cases, the accountant should theoretically recognize a loss from partial obsolescence from the firm's owning an old, out-of-date asset, but *GAAP* does not permit recognition of partial obsolescence. The old asset will be carried at *cost* less *accumulated depreciation* until it is retired from service, so long as the *undiscounted* future *cash flows* from the asset exceed its book value. See *obsolescence*.

partially funded. Said of a *pension plan* where not all earned benefits have been funded. See *funded* for funding requirements.

partially vested. Said of a *pension plan* where not all employee benefits are *vested*. See *graded vesting*.

participating dividend. *Dividend* paid to preferred shareholders in addition to the minimum preferred dividends when the *preferred stock* contract allows such sharing in earnings. Usually applied after dividends on *common stock* have reached a certain level.

participating preferred stock. *Preferred stock* with rights to *participating dividends*.

partner's drawing. A payment to a partner to be charged against his or her share of income or capital. The name of a *temporary account* to record such payments.

partnership. Contractual arrangement between individuals to share resources and operations in a jointly run business. See *general* and *limited partner* and *Uniform Partnership Act*.

patent. A right granted for up to 17 years by the federal government to exclude others from manufacturing, using or selling a claimed design, product or plant (e.g., a new breed of rose) or from using a claimed process or method of manufacture. An asset if acquired by purchase. If developed internally, the development costs are *expensed* when incurred under current *GAAP*.

payable. Unpaid but not necessarily due or past due.

pay as you go. Said of an *income tax* scheme where periodic payments of income taxes are made during the period when the income to be taxed is being earned; in contrast to a scheme where no payments are due until the end of, or after, the period whose income is being taxed. (Called PAYE—pay as you earn—in Britain.) Sometimes used to describe an *unfunded pension plan*, where payments to pension plan beneficiaries are made from general corporate funds, not from cash previously contributed to a pension fund. Not acceptable as a method of accounting for pension plans under *SFAS No. 87* nor as a method of *funding* under *ERISA*.

payback period. Amount of time that must elapse before the cash inflows from a project equal the cash outflows.

payback reciprocal. One divided by the *payback period*. This number approximates the *internal rate of return* on a project when the project life is more than twice the payback period and the cash inflows are identical in every period after the initial period.

PAYE. See *pay as you go*.

payee. The person or entity to whom a cash payment is made or who will receive the stated amount of money on a check. See *draft*.

payout ratio. *Common stock dividends* declared for a year divided by net *income* to common stock for the year. A term used by financial analysts; contrast with *dividend yield*.

payroll taxes. Taxes levied because salaries or wages are paid; for example, *FICA* and unemployment compensation insurance taxes. Typically, the employer pays a portion and withholds part of the employee's wage fund.

P/E ratio. *Price-earnings ratio*.

PERT. Program Evaluation and Review Technique. A method of *network analysis* in which three time estimates are made for each activity—the optimistic time, the most likely time, and the pessimistic time—and which gives an expected completion date for the project within a probability range.

Pension Benefit Guarantee Corporation. PBGC. A federal corporation established under *ERISA* to guarantee basic pension benefits in covered pension plans by administering terminated pension plans and placing *liens* on corporate assets for certain unfunded pension liabilities.

pension fund. *Fund*, the assets of which are to be paid to retired ex-employees, usually as a *life annuity*. Usually held by an independent trustee and thus is not an *asset* of the employer.

pension plan. Details or provisions of employer's contract with employees for paying retirement *annuities* or other benefits. See *funded, vested, service cost, prior service cost, money purchase plan*, and *defined-benefit plan*.

per books. An expression used to refer to the *book value* of an item at a specific time.

percent. Any number, expressed as a decimal, multiplied by 100.

percentage depletion (allowance). Deductible *expense* allowed in some cases by the federal *income tax* regulations; computed as a percentage of gross income from a *natural resource* independent of the unamortized cost of the asset. Because the amount of the total deductions for tax purposes is usually greater than the cost of the asset being *depleted*, many people think the deduction is an unfair tax advantage or *loophole*.

percentage-of-completion method. Recognizing *revenues* and *expenses* on a job, order, or contract (a) in proportion to the *costs* incurred for the period divided by total costs expected to be incurred for the job or order ("cost to cost") or (b) in proportion to engineers' or architects' estimates of the incremental degree of completion of the job, order, or contract during the period. Contrast with *completed contract method*.

percentage statement. A statement containing, in addition to (or instead of) dollar amounts, ratios of dollar amounts to some base. In a percentage *income statement*, the base is usually either *net sales* or total *reve-*

nues and in a percentage *balance sheet*, the base is usually total *assets*.

period. *Accounting period.*

period cost. An inferior term for *period expense*.

period expense (charge). *Expenditure*, usually based upon the passage of time, charged to operations of the accounting period rather than *capitalized* as an asset; contrast with *product cost*.

periodic inventory. A method of recording *inventory* that uses data on beginning inventory, additions to inventories, and ending inventory to find the cost of withdrawals from inventory. Contrast with *perpetual inventory*.

periodic procedures. The process of making *adjusting entries, closing entries*, and preparing the *financial statements*, usually by use of *trial balances* and *work sheets*.

permanent account. An account which appears on the *balance sheet*; contrast with *temporary account*.

permanent difference. Difference between reported income and taxable income that will never be reversed and, hence, requires no entry in the *deferred income tax liability* account. An example is the difference between taxable and reportable income from interest earned on state and municipal bonds; contrast with *timing difference* and see *deferred income tax liability*.

permanent file. The file of working papers prepared by a public accountant containing information required for reference in successive professional engagements for a particular organization, as distinguished from working papers applicable only to a particular engagement.

perpetual annuity. *Perpetuity.*

perpetual inventory. Records on quantities and amounts of *inventory* that are changed or made current with each physical addition to or withdrawal from the stock of goods; an inventory so recorded. The records will show the physical quantities and, frequently, the dollar valuations that should be on hand at any time. Because *cost of goods sold* is explicitly computed, the *inventory equation* can be used to compute an amount for what *ending inventory* should be. The computed amount of ending inventory can be compared to the actual amount of ending inventory as a *control* device. Contrast with *periodic inventory*.

perpetuity. An *annuity* whose payments continue forever. The *present value* of a perpetuity in *arrears* is p/r where p is the periodic payment and r is the *interest rate* per period. If $100 is promised each year, in arrears, for-ever, and the interest rate is 8 percent per year, then the value of the perpetuity is $1,250 = $100/.08.

personal account. *Drawing account.*

petty cash fund. Currency and coins maintained for expenditures that are made with cash on hand.

physical units method. A method of allocating a *joint cost* to the *joint products* based on a physical measure of the joint products. For example, allocating the cost of a cow to sirloin steak and to hamburger, based on the weight of the meat. This method usually provides nonsensical (see *sterilized allocation*) results unless the physical units of the joint products tend to have the same value.

physical verification. *Verification*, by an *auditor*, performed by actually inspecting items in *inventory, plant assets*, and the like; may be based on statistical sampling procedures; in contrast to mere checking of written records.

planning and control process. General name for the techniques of management comprising the setting of organizational goals and *strategic plans, capital budgeting, operations* budgeting, comparison of plans with actual results, performance evaluation and corrective action, and revisions of goals, plans, and budgets.

plant. *Plant assets.*

plant assets. Assets used in the revenue production process. Plant assets include buildings, machinery, equipment, land, and natural resources. The phrase "property, plant and equipment" while often used as a balance sheet heading, is therefore a redundancy. In this context, "plant" used alone means buildings.

plant asset turnover. Number of dollars of *sales* generated per dollar of *plant assets*. Equal to sales divided by average *plant assets*.

PLC; Public Limited Company. United Kingdom. A publicly held *corporation*. Contrast with *Ltd*.

pledging. The borrower assigns *assets* as security or *collateral* for repayment of a loan.

pledging of receivables. The process of using expected collections on accounts receivable as *collateral* for a loan. The borrower remains responsible for collecting the receivable but promises to use the proceeds for repaying the debt.

plow back. To retain assets generated by earnings for continued investment in the business.

plug. For any *account*, beginning balance + additions - deductions = ending balance; if any three of the four items are known, the fourth can be found by plugging. In making a *journal entry*, often all *debits* are known, as are all but one of the *credits* (or vice versa). Because *double-entry* bookkeeping requires equal debits and credits, the unknown quantity can be computed by subtracting the sum of the known credits from the sum of all the debits (or vice versa). This process is also known as plugging. The unknown found is called the plug. For example, if a *discount* on *bonds payable* is being *amortized* with the *straight-line method*, then *interest expense* is a plug: interest expense = interest payable + discount amortization. See *trade-in transaction* for an example. The term sometimes has a bad connotation for accountants because plugging occurs in a slightly different context: In preparing a *pre-closing trial balance* (or balance sheet), often the sum of the debits does not equal the sum of the credits. Rather than find the error, some accountants are tempted to force equality by changing one of the amounts, with a plugged debit or credit to an account such as Other Expenses. There is really nothing wrong with this procedure if the amount of the error is very small compared to asset totals because it is not cost effective to spend tens or hundreds of dollars in bookkeeper's or accountant's time to find an error of a few dollars. Still, most accounting teachers and auditors gravely frown on the process.

pooling-of-interests method. Accounting for a *business combination* by merely adding together the *book value* of the *assets* and *equities* of the combined firms. Contrast with *purchase method*. Generally leads to a higher reported *net income* for the combined firms than would be reported had the business combination been accounted for as a purchase because the *market values* of the merged assets are generally larger than their book values. *APB Opinion No. 16* states the conditions that, when met, require the pooling-of-interests treatment.

population. The entire field of numbers or items which is to be the subject of sampling or other analysis.

positive confirmation. See *confirmation*.

post. To record entries in an *account* in a *ledger*; usually the entries are transferred from a *journal*.

post-closing trial balance. *Trial balance* taken after all *temporary accounts* have been closed.

post-statement events. Events with *material* impact that occur between the end of the *accounting period* and the formal publication of the *financial statements*. Such events must be disclosed in notes for the auditor to give a *clean opinion*, even though the events are subsequent to the period being reported on.

potentially dilutive. A *security* that may be converted into, or exchanged for, common stock and thereby reduce reported *earnings per share: options, warrants, convertible bonds*, and *convertible preferred stock*.

PPB. *Program budgeting*; the second "P" means "plan".

practical capacity. Maximum level at which the plant or department can operate efficiently.

precision. The degree of accuracy with which the estimate derived from sampling process is stated, usually expressed as a range of values around the estimate. A sample estimate may be expressed in the following terms: "Based on the sample, we are 95% sure [confidence level] that the true population value is within the range of X to Y [precision]". See *confidence level*.

preclosing trial balance. *Trial balance* taken at the end of the period before *closing entries*. In this sense, an *adjusted trial balance*. Sometimes taken before *adjusting entries* and then is synonymous with *unadjusted trial balance*.

predetermined (factory) overhead rate. Rate used in applying *overhead* to products or departments developed at the start of a period by dividing estimated overhead cost by the estimated number of units of the overhead allocation base (or *denominator volume*) activity. See *normal costing*.

preemptive right. The privilege of a *shareholder* to maintain a proportionate share of ownership by purchasing a proportionate share of any new stock issues. Most state corporation laws allow corporations to pay shareholders to waive their preemptive rights or state that preemptive rights exist only if the *corporation charter* explicitly grants them. In practice, then, preemptive rights are the exception, rather than the rule.

preference as to assets. The rights of *preferred shareholders* to receive certain payments in case of dissolution before common shareholders receive payments.

preferred shares. *Capital stock* with a claim to *income* or *assets* after *bondholders* but before *common shares*. Dividends on preferred shares are *income distributions*, not *expenses*. See *cumulative preferred stock*.

premium. The excess of issue (or market) price over *par value*. For a different context, see *insurance*.

premium on capital stock. Alternative but inferior title for *capital contributed in excess of (par) or stated value*.

prepaid expense. An *expenditure* that leads to a *deferred charge* or *prepayment*; strictly speaking, a contradiction in terms because an *expense* is a gone asset and this title refers to past *expenditures*, such as for rent or insurance premiums, that still have future benefits and thus are *assets*.

prepaid income. An inferior alternative title for *advances from customers*. An item should not be called *rev-*

enue or *income* until earned, when goods are delivered or services are rendered.

prepayments. *Deferred charges. Assets* representing *expenditures* for future benefits. Rent and insurance premiums paid in advance are usually classified as *current* prepayments.

present value. Value today (or at some specific date) of an amount or amounts to be paid or received later (or at other, different dates), discounted at some *interest* or *discount rate*.

price. The quantity of one *good* or *service*, usually *cash*, asked in return for a unit of another good or service. See *fair market price*.

price-earnings ratio. At a given time, the market value of a company's *common stock*, per share, divided by the *earnings per* common *share* for the past year. The denominator is usually based on *income from continuing operations* or, if the analyst thinks the current figure for that amount is not representative—such as when the number is negative—on some estimate of the number. See *ratio*.

price index. A series of numbers, one for each period, that purports to represent some *average* of prices for a series of periods, relative to a base period.

price level. The number from a *price index* series for a given period or date.

price level-adjusted statements. *Financial statements* expressed in terms of dollars of uniform purchasing power. *Nonmonetary* items are restated to reflect changes in general *price levels* since the time specific *assets* were acquired and *liabilities* were incurred. A *gain* or *loss* is recognized on *monetary items* as they are held over time periods when the general *price level changes*. Conventional financial statements show *historical costs* and ignore differences in purchasing power in different periods.

price variance. In accounting for *standard costs*, (actual cost per unit - standard cost per unit) × quantity purchased.

primary earnings per share. Net *income* to *common shareholders* plus *interest* (*net of tax* effects) or *dividends* paid on *common stock equivalents* divided by (weighted average of common share outstanding plus the net increase in the number of common shares that would become *outstanding* if all common stock equivalents were exchanged for common shares with cash proceeds, if any, used to retire common shares).

prime cost. Sum of *direct materials* plus *direct labor* costs assigned to product.

prime rate. The rate for loans charged by commercial banks to their creditworthy customers. Some customers pay even less than the prime rate and others, more. The *Federal Reserve Bulletin* is considered the authoritative source of information about historical prime rates.

principal. An amount in which *interest* is charged or earned. The *face amount* of a *loan*. Also, the absent owner (principal) who hires the manager (agent) in a "principal-agent" relationship.

principle. See *generally accepted accounting principles*.

prior-period adjustment. A *debit* or *credit* made directly to *retained earnings* (that does not affect *income* for the period) to adjust earnings as calculated for prior periods. Such adjustments are now extremely rare. Theory might suggest that corrections of errors in accounting estimates (such as the *depreciable life* or *salvage value* of an asset) should be treated as adjustments to retained earnings. But *GAAP* require that corrections of such estimates flow through current, and perhaps future, *income statements*. See *accounting changes* and *accounting errors*.

prior service cost. *Present value* at a given time of a *pension plan's* retroactive *benefits*. "Unrecognized prior service cost" refers to that portion of prior service cost not yet *debited* to *expense*. See *actuarial accrued liability* and *funded*; contrast with *normal cost*.

pro forma statements. Hypothetical statements. Financial statements as they would appear if some event, such as a *merger* or increased production and sales had occurred or were to occur. Pro forma is often, but incorrectly, spelled as one word.

proceeds. The *funds* received from disposition of assets or from the issue of securities.

process costing. A method of *cost accounting* based on average costs (total cost divided by the *equivalent units* of work done in a period). Typically used for assembly lines or for products that are produced in a series of steps that are more continuous than discrete.

product. *Goods* or *services* produced.

product cost. Any *manufacturing cost* that can be inventoried. See *flow of costs* for example and contrast with *period expenses*.

production cost. *Manufacturing cost*.

product(ion) cost account. A *temporary account* for accumulating *manufacturing costs* during a period.

production department. A department producing salable *goods* or *services*; contrast with *service department*.

production method (depreciation). The depreciable asset (e.g., a truck) is given a *depreciable life* measured, not in elapsed time, but in units of output (e.g., miles) or perhaps in units of time of expected use. Then the *depreciation* charge for a period is a portion of depreciable cost equal to a fraction computed by dividing the actual output produced during the period by the expected total output to be produced over the life of the asset. Sometimes called the "units-of-production (or output) method."

production method (revenue recognition). *Percentage-of-completion method* for recognizing *revenue*.

production volume variance. Standard fixed *overhead* rate per unit of normal *capacity* (or base activity) times (units of base activity budgeted or planned for a period minus actual units of base activity worked or assigned to product during the period). Often called a "volume variance."

productive capacity. In computing *current cost* of *long-term assets*, we are interested in the cost of reproducing the productive capacity (for example, the ability to manufacture one million units a year), not the cost of reproducing the actual physical assets currently used (see *reproduction cost*). Replacement cost of productive capacity will be the same as reproduction cost of assets only in the unusual case when there has been no technological improvement in production processes and the relative prices of goods and services used in production have remained approximately the same as when the currently used ones were acquired.

profit. Excess of *revenues* over *expenses* for a *transaction*; sometimes used synonymously with *net income* for the period.

profit and loss sharing ratio. The fraction of *net income* or loss allocable to a partner in a *partnership*. Need not be the same fraction as the partner's share of capital.

profit and loss statement. *Income statement*.

profit center. A unit of activity for which both *revenue* and *expenses* are accumulated; contrast with *cost center*.

profit margin. Sales minus all expenses as a single amount. Frequently used to mean ratio of sales minus all *operating* expenses divided by sales.

profit margin percentage. *Profit margin* divided by *net sales*.

profit maximization. The doctrine that a given set of operations should be accounted for so as to make reported *net income* as large as possible; contrast with *conservatism*. This concept in accounting is slightly different from the profit-maximizing concept in economics where the doctrine states that operations should be managed to max-

imize the present value of the firm's wealth, generally by equating *marginal costs* and *marginal revenues*.

profit sharing plan. A *defined contribution plan*, where the employer contributes amounts based on *net income*.

profit variance analysis. Analysis of the causes of the difference between *budgeted profit* in the *master budget* and the profits earned.

profit-volume analysis (equation). See *breakeven analysis*.

profit-volume graph. See *breakeven chart*.

profit-volume ratio. *Net income* divided by *net sales* in dollars.

profitability accounting. *Responsibility accounting*.

program budgeting. Specification and analysis of inputs, outputs, costs, and alternatives that link plans to *budgets*.

programmed costs. A *fixed cost* not essential for carrying out operations. Research and development and advertising designed to generate new business are controllable, but once a commitment is made to incur them, they become fixed costs. Sometimes called *managed costs* or *discretionary costs*; contrast with *capacity costs*.

progressive tax. Tax for which the rate increases as the taxed base, such as income, increases; contrast with *regressive tax*.

project financing arrangement. As defined by *SFAS No. 47*, the financing of an investment project in which the lender looks principally to the *cash flows* and *earnings* of the project as the source of funds for repayment and to the *assets* of the project as *collateral* for the loan. The general *credit* of the project entity is usually not a significant factor, either because the entity is a *corporation* without other assets or because the financing is without direct *recourse* to the entity's owners.

projected benefit obligation. The *actuarial present value* at a given date of all pension benefits attributed by a *defined-benefit pension* formula to employee service rendered before that date. The obligation is measured using assumptions as to future compensation levels if the formula incorporates future compensation, as happens, for example, when the eventual pension benefit is based on wages of the last several years of employees' work lives. Contrast to "accumulated benefit obligation," where the obligation is measured using employee compensation levels at the time of the measurement date of the obligation.

projected financial statement. *Pro forma* financial statement.

projection. See *financial projection* for definition and contrast.

promissory note. An unconditional written promise to pay a specified sum of money on demand or at a specified date.

proof of journal. The process of checking arithmetic accuracy of *journal entries* by testing for the equality of all *debits* with all *credits* since the last previous proof.

property dividend. A *dividend in kind*.

property, plant and equipment. See *plant assets*

proportionate consolidation. Canada. A presentation of the *financial statements* of any investor-investment relationship, whereby the investor's pro rata share of each *asset, liability, income* item, and *expense* item appears in the *financial statements* of the investor under the various *balance sheet and income statement* headings.

proprietary accounts. See *budgetary accounts* for definition and contrast in context of governmental accounting.

proprietorship. *Assets* minus *liabilities* of an *entity*; equals *contributed capital* plus *retained earnings*.

proprietorship theory. The view of the corporation that emphasizes the form of the *accounting equation* that says *assets - liabilities = owners' equity*; contrast with *entity theory*. The major implication of a choice between these theories deals with the treatment of *subsidiaries*. For example, the view that *minority interest* is an *indeterminate term liability* is based on the proprietorship theory. The proprietorship theory implies using a *single-step income statement*.

prorate. To *allocate* in proportion to some base; for example, allocate *service department* costs in proportion to hours of service used by the benefited department. Or, to allocate *manufacturing variances* to product sold and to product added to *ending inventory*.

prorating variances. See *prorate*.

prospectus. Formal written document describing *securities* to be issued. See *proxy*.

protest fee. Fee charged by banks or other financial agencies when items (such as checks) presented for collection cannot be collected.

provision. Often the exact amount of an *expense* is uncertain, but must, nevertheless, be recognized currently. The entry for the estimated expense, such as for *income taxes* or expected costs under *warranty*, is:

Expense (Estimated)	X	
Liability (Estimated)		X

In American usage, the term "provision" is often used in the expense account title of the above entry. Thus, Provision for Income Taxes is used to mean the estimate of income tax expense. (In British usage, the term "provision" is used in the title for the estimated liability of the above entry, so that Provision for Income Taxes is a balance sheet account.)

proxy. Written authorization given by one person to another so that the second person can act for the first, such as to vote shares of stock. Of particular significance to accountants because the *SEC* presumes that financial information is distributed by management along with its proxy solicitations.

public accountant. Generally, this term is synonymous with *certified public accountant*. In some jurisdictions, individuals have been licensed as public accountants without being CPAs.

public accounting. That portion of accounting primarily involving the *attest* function, culminating in the *auditor's report*.

PuPU. An acronym for *purchasing power unit* conceived by John C. Burton, former Chief Accountant of the SEC. Those who think *constant dollar accounting* not particularly useful poke fun at it by calling it "PuPU accounting."

purchase allowance. A reduction in sales *invoice price* usually granted because the *goods* received by the purchaser were not exactly as ordered. The goods are not returned to the seller, but are purchased at a price lower than originally agreed upon.

purchase discount. A reduction in purchase *invoice price* granted for prompt payment. See *sales discount* and *terms of sale*.

purchase investigation. An investigation of the financial affairs of a company for the purpose of disclosing matters that may influence the terms or conclusion of a potential acquisition.

purchase method. Accounting for a *business combination* by adding the acquired company's assets at the price paid for them to the acquiring company's assets. Contrast with *pooling-of-interests method*. The acquired assets are put on the books at current values, rather than original costs; the subsequent *amortization expenses* are usually larger (and reported income, smaller) than for the same business combination accounted for as a pooling of interests. The purchase method is required unless all the criteria in *APB Opinion No. 16* to be a pooling are met.

purchase order. Document authorizing a seller to deliver goods with payment to be made later.

purchasing power gain or loss. *Monetary gain or loss.*

push-down accounting. Assume that Company A purchases substantially all of the *common shares* of Company B but that Company B must still issue its own *financial statements*. The question arises, shall the *basis* for Company B's *assets* and *equities* be changed on its own books to the same updated amounts at which they are shown on Company A's *consolidated* statements. When Company B shows the new asset and equity bases reflecting Company A's purchase, Company B is using "push-down accounting," because the new bases are "pushed down" from Company A (where they are required in *GAAP* to Company B (where the new bases would not appear in *historical cost accounting*). Since 1983, the *SEC* has required push-down accounting under some circumstances.

put. An option to sell *shares* of a publicly traded corporation at a fixed price during a fixed time span. Contrast with *call.*

Q

qualified report (opinion). *Auditor's report* containing a statement that the auditor was unable to complete a satisfactory examination of all things considered relevant or that the auditor has doubts about the financial impact of some *material* item reported in the financial statements. See *except for* and *subject to.*

quantitative performance measure. A measure of output based on an objectively observable quantity, such as units produced or *direct costs* incurred, rather than on an unobservable quantity or one observable only non-objectively, such as quality of service provided.

quantity discount. A reduction in purchase price as quantity purchased increases; amount of the *discount* is constrained by law (Robinson-Patman Act). Not to be confused with *purchase discount.*

quantity variance. *Efficiency variance.* In *standard cost* systems, the standard price per unit times (actual quantity used minus standard quantity that should be used).

quasi-reorganization. A *reorganization* where no new company is formed or no court has intervened, as would happen in *bankruptcy*. The primary purpose is to absorb a *deficit* and get a "fresh start."

quick assets. *Assets* readily convertible into *cash*; includes cash, *current marketable securities*, and *current receivables.*

quick ratio. Sum of (*cash, current marketable securities,* and *receivables*) divided by *current liabilities.* Some non-liquid receivables may be excluded from the numerator. Often called the "acid test ratio." See *ratio.*

R

R^2. The proportion of the statistical variance of a *dependent variable* explained by the equation fit to *independent variable(s)* in a *regression analysis.*

R & D. See *research and development.*

Railroad Accounting Principles Board. RAPB. A board brought into existence by the Staggers Rail Act of 1980 to advise the Interstate Commerce Commission on matters of accounting affecting railroads.

random number sampling. A method of choosing a sample in which the items to be selected from the *population* are determined by use of a random number table or generator.

random sampling. A method of choosing a sample in which all items in the population have an equal chance of being selected. Compare *judgement(al) sampling.*

RAPB. *Railroad Accounting Principles Board.*

rate of return on assets. *Return on assets.*

rate of return on common stock equity. See *ratio.*

rate of return on shareholders' (owners') equity. See *ratio.*

rate of return (on total capital). See *ratio* and *rate of return on assets.*

rate variance. *Price variance,* usually for *direct labor costs.*

ratio. The number resulting when one number is divided by another. Ratios are generally used to assess aspects of profitability, solvency, and liquidity. The commonly used financial ratios are of three kinds: (1) those that summarize some aspect of *operations* for a period, usually a year; (2) those that summarize some aspect of *financial position* at a given moment—the moment for which a balance sheet has been prepared; and (3) those that relate some aspect of operations to some aspect of financial position.
The accompanying exhibit lists the most common financial ratios and shows separately both the numerator and denominator used to calculate each ratio.

Summary of Financial Statement Ratios

Ratio	Numerator	Denominator
Profitability Ratios		
Rate of Return on Assets . . .	Net Income + Interest Expense (net of tax effects)[a]	Average Total Assets During the Period[b]
Profit Margin Ratio (before interest effects)	Net Income + Interest Expense (net of tax effects)[a]	Revenues
Various Expense Ratios	Various Expenses	Revenues
Total Assets Turnover Ratio . .	Revenues	Average Total Assets During the Period
Accounts Receivable Turnover Ratio	Net Sales on Account	Average Accounts Receivable During the Period
Inventory Turnover Ratio	Cost of Goods Sold	Average Inventory During the Period
Plant Asset Turnover Ratio . .	Revenues	Average Plant Assets During the Period
Rate of Return on Common Shareholders' Equity	Net Income - Preferred Stock Dividends	Average Common Shareholders' Equity During the Period
Profit Margin Ratio (after interest expense and preferred dividends)	Net Income - Preferred Stock Dividends	Revenues
Leverage Ratio	Average Total Assets During the period	Average Common Shareholders' Equity During the Period
Earnings per Share of Stock[c] .	Net Income - Preferred Stock Dividends	Weighted-Average Number of Common Shares Outstanding During the Period
Short-Term Liquidity Ratios		
Current Ratio	Current Assets	Current Liabilities
Quick or Acid Test Ratio	Highly Liquid Assets (ordinarily, cash, marketable securities, and receivables)[d]	Current Liabilities

[a]If a consolidated subsidiary is not owned entirely by the parent corporation, the minority interest share of earnings must allso be added back to net income.

[b]Financial economists deduct the average of non-interest-bearing liabilities from the denominator. This deduction compensates for the implicit interest charges (such as for accounts payable) already subtracted in measuring net income.

[c]This calculation can be more complicated when there are convertible securities, options, or warrants outstanding.

[d]Receivables could conceivably be excluded for some firms and inventories included for others. Such refinements are seldom employed in practice.

Summary of Financial Statement Ratios

Ratio	Numerator	Denominator
Cash Flow from Operations to Current Liabilities Ratio	Cash Provided by Operations	Average Current Liabilities During the Period
Working Capital Turnover Ratio	Revenues	Average Working Capital During the Pefiod
Long-Term Liquidity Ratios		
Long-Term Debt Ratio	Total Long-Term Debt	Total Long-Term Debt Plus Shareholders'Equity
Debt-Equity Ratio	Total Liabilities	Total Equities (liabilities plus shareholders' equity)
Cash Flow from Operations to Total Liabilities Ratio	Cash Provided by Operations	Average Total Liabilities During the Period
Times Interest Charges Earned	Net Income Before Interest and Income Taxes	Interest Expense

For all ratios that require an average balance during the period, the average is most often derived as one half the sum of the beginning and ending balances. Sophisticated analysts recognize, however, that when companies use a fiscal year different from the calendar year, this averaging of beginning and ending balances may be misleading. Consider, for example, the *rate of return on assets* of Sears, Roebuck & Company whose fiscal year ends on January 31. Sears chooses a January 31 closing date at least in part because inventories are at a low level and are therefore easy to count—the Christmas merchandise has been sold and the Easter merchandise has not yet all been received. Furthermore, by January 31, most Christmas sales have been collected or returned, so receivable amounts are not unusually large. Thus at January 31, the amount of total assets is lower than at many other times during the year. Consequently, the denominator of the rate of return on assets, total assets, for Sears is more likely to represent the smallest amount of total assets on hand during the year than the average amount. The return on assets rate for Sears and other companies who choose a fiscal year-end to coincide with low points in the inventory cycle is likely to be larger than if a more accurate estimate of the average amounts of total assets were used.

raw material. Goods purchased for use in manufacturing a product.

reacquired stock. *Treasury stock.*

real accounts. *Balance sheet accounts*; as opposed to *nominal accounts.* See *permanent accounts.*

real amount (value). An amount stated in *constant dollars.* For example, if an investment costing $100 is sold for $130 after a period of 10 percent general *inflation,* the *nominal amount* of gain is $30 (= $130 - $100) but the real amount of gain is C$20 (= $130 - 1.10 x $100), where "C$" denotes constant dollars of purchasing power on the date of sale.

real estate. *Land* and its *improvements,* such as land-scaping and roads, but not buildings.

realizable value. *Market value* or, sometimes, *net realizable value.*

realization convention. The accounting practice of delaying the recognition of *gains* and *losses* from changes in the market price of *assets* until the assets are sold. However, unrealized losses on *inventory* and *marketable securities* classified as *current assets* are recognized prior to sale when the *lower-of-cost-or-market* valuation basis is used.

realize. To convert into *funds.* When applied to a *gain* or *loss,* implies that an *arm's-length transaction* has taken place. Contrast with *recognize*; a loss (as for example on *marketable equity securities*) may be recognized in the financial statements even though it has not yet been realized in a transaction.

realized gain (or loss) on marketable equity securities. An income statement account title for the difference between the proceeds of disposition and the *original cost* of *marketable equity securities.*

realized holding gain. See *inventory profit* for definition and an example.

rearrangement costs. Costs of re-installing assets perhaps in a different location. May be *capitalized* as part of the assets cost, just as is original installation cost.

recapitalization. *Reorganization.*

recapture. Various provisions of the *income tax* rules require refund by the taxpayer (recapture by the government) of various tax advantages under certain conditions. For example, the tax savings provided by the *investment credit* or by *accelerated depreciation* must be repaid if the item providing the tax savings is retired prematurely.

receipt. Acquisition of *cash*.

receivable. Any *collectible* whether or not it is currently due.

receivable turnover. See *ratio*.

reciprocal holdings. Company A owns stock of Company B and Company B owns stock of Company A.

recognize. To enter a transaction in the accounts. Not synonymous with *realize*.

reconciliation. A calculation that shows how one balance or figure is derived systematically from another, such as a *reconciliation of retained earnings* or a *bank reconciliation schedule*. See *articulate*.

record date. *Dividends* are paid on payment date to those who own the stock on the record date.

recourse. See *note receivable discounted*.

recovery of unrealized loss on marketable securities. An *income statement account title* for the *gain* during the current period on the *current asset* portfolio of *marketable equity securities*. This gain will be *recognized* only to the extent that net losses have been recognized in preceding periods in amounts no smaller than the current gain. (The Allowance for Declines in Marketable Equity Securities account can never have a *debit balance*.)

redemption. Retirement by the issuer, usually by a purchase or *call*, of *stocks* or *bonds*.

redemption premium. *Call premium.*

redemption value. The price to be paid by a corporation to retire *bonds* or *preferred stock* if called before *maturity*.

refinancing. An adjustment in the *capital structure* of a *corporation*, involving changes in the nature and amounts of the various classes of *debt* and, in some cases, *capital* as well as other components of *shareholders' equity*; asset carrying values in the accounts remain unchanged.

refunding bond issue. Said of a *bond* issue whose proceeds are used to retire bonds already *outstanding*.

register. Collection of consecutive entries, or other information, in chronological order, such as a check register or an insurance register, which lists all insurance policies owned. If entries are recorded, it may serve as a *journal*.

registered bond. *Principal* of such a *bond* and *interest*, if registered as to interest, is paid to the owner listed on the books of the issuer. As opposed to a bearer bond where the possessor of the bond is entitled to interest and principal.

registrar. An *agent*, usually a bank or trust company, appointed by a corporation to keep track of the names of shareholders and distributions of earnings.

registration statement. Statement required by the Securities Act of 1933 of most companies wishing to have their securities traded in public markets. The statement discloses financial data and other items of interest to potential investors.

regression analysis. A method of *cost estimation* based on statistical techniques for fitting a line (or its equivalent in higher mathematical dimensions) to an observed series of data points, usually by minimizing the sum of squared deviations of the observed data from the fitted line. The cost whose behavior is being explained is called the "dependent variable;" the variable(s) being used to estimate cost behavior is called "independent variable(s)." If there is more than one independent variable, the analysis is called "multiple regression analysis." See R^2, *standard error*, *t-value*.

regressive tax. Tax for which the rate decreases as the taxed base, such as income, increases. Contrast with *progressive tax*.

Regulation S-X. The *SEC's* regulation specifying the form and content of financial reports to the SEC.

rehabilitation. The improving of a used *asset* via an extensive repair. Ordinary *repairs* and *maintenance* restore or maintain expected *service potential* of an asset and are treated as *expenses*. A rehabilitation improves the asset beyond its current service potential, enhancing the service potential to significantly higher level than before the rehabilitation. Once rehabilitated, the asset may be better, but need not be, than it was when new. *Expenditures* for rehabilitation, like those for *betterment* and *improvements*, are *capitalized*.

reinvestment rate. In a *capital budgeting* context, the rate at which cash inflows from a project occurring before the project's completion are invested. Once such a rate is assumed, there will never be multiple *internal rates of return*. See *Descartes' rule of signs*.

relative performance evaluation. Setting performance targets and, sometimes, compensation in relation to performance of others, perhaps in different firms or divisions, facing a similar environment.

relevant cost. *Incremental cost. Opportunity cost.*

relevant range. Activity levels over which costs are linear or for which *flexible budget* estimates and *break-even charts* will remain valid.

relative sales value method. *Net realizable (sales) value method.*

remittance advice. Information on a *check stub*, or on a document attached to a check by the *drawer*, which tells the *payee* why a payment is being made.

rent. A charge for use of land, buildings, or other assets.

reorganization. A major change in the *capital structure* of a corporation that leads to changes in the rights, interests, and implied ownership of the various security owners. Usually results from a *merger* or agreement by senior security holders to take action to forestall *bankruptcy*.

repair. An *expenditure* to restore an *asset's* service potential after damage or after prolonged use. In the second sense, after prolonged use, the difference between repairs and maintenance is one of degree and not of kind. Treated as an *expense* of the period when incurred. Because repairs and maintenance are treated similarly in this regard, the distinction is not important. A repair helps to maintain capacity intact at levels planned when the *asset* was acquired; contrast with *improvement*.

replacement cost. For an asset, the current fair market price to purchase another, similar asset (with the same future benefit or service potential). *Current cost.* See *reproduction cost* and *productive capacity*. See also *distributable income* and *inventory profit*.

replacement cost method of depreciation. The original cost *depreciation* charge is augmented by an amount based upon a portion of the difference between the *current replacement cost* of the asset and its *original cost*.

replacement system of depreciation. See *retirement method of depreciation* for definition and contrast.

report. *Financial statement; auditor's report.*

report form. This form of *balance sheet* typically shows *assets* minus *liabilities* as one total. Then, below that appears the components of *owners' equity* summing to the same total. Often, the top section shows *current* assets less current liabilities before *noncurrent assets* less noncurrent liabilities. Contrast with *account form*.

reporting objectives (policies). The general purposes for which *financial statements* are prepared. The *FASB* has discussed these in *SFAC No. 1*.

representative item sampling. Sampling where the sample selected is believed to be typical of the entire population from which it is drawn. Compare *specific item sampling*.

reproduction cost. The *cost* necessary to acquire an *asset* similar in all physical respects to another asset for which a *current value* is wanted. See *replacement cost* and *productive capacity* for further contrast.

required rate of return. *Cost of capital.*

requisition. A formal written order or request, such as for withdrawal of supplies from the storeroom.

resale value. *Exit value. Net realizable value.*

research and development. Research is activity aimed at discovering new knowledge in hopes that such activity will be useful in creating a new product, process, or service or improving a present product, process, or service. Development is the translation of research findings or other knowledge into a new or improved product, process, or service. *SFAS No.2* requires that costs of such activities be *expensed* as incurred on the grounds that the future benefits are too uncertain to warrant *capitalization* as an asset. This treatment seems questionable to us because we wonder why firms would continue to undertake R&D if there were no expectation of future benefit; if future benefits exist, then their *costs* should be assets.

reserve. When properly used in accounting, the term refers to an account that appropriates *retained earnings* and restricts dividend declarations. Appropriating retained earnings is itself a poor and vanishing practice, so the word should seldom be used in accounting. In addition, used in the past to indicate an asset *contra account* (e.g., "reserve for depreciation") or an *estimated liability* (e.g., "reserve for warranty costs"). In any case, reserve accounts have *credit* balances and are not pools of *funds* as the unwary reader might infer. If a company has set aside a pool of *cash* (or *marketable securities*) to serve some specific purpose such as paying for a new factory, then that cash will be called a *fund*. No other word in accounting is so misunderstood and misused by laymen and "experts" who should know better. A leading unabridged dictionary defines "reserve" as "Cash, or assets readily convertible into cash, held aside, as by a corporation, bank, state or national government, etc., to meet expected or unexpected demands." This definition is absolutely wrong in accounting. Reserves are not funds. For example, a contingency fund of $10,000 is created by depositing cash in a fund and this entry is made:

Contingency Fund	10,000	
Cash		10,000

The following entry may accompany this entry, if retained earnings are to be appropriated:

Retained Earnings	10,000	
Reserve for Contingencies		10,000

The transaction leading to the first entry is an event of economic significance. The second entry has little economic impact for most firms. The problem with the word "reserve" arises because the second entry can be made without the first—a company can create a reserve, that is, appropriate retained earnings, without creating a fund. The problem is at least in part caused by the fact that in common usage, "reserve" means a pool of assets, as in the phrase "oil reserves." The *Internal Revenue Service* does not help in dispelling confusion about the term *reserves*. The federal *income tax* return for corporations uses the title "Reserve for Bad Debts" to mean "Allowance for Uncollectible Accounts" and speaks of the "Reserve Method" in referring to the *allowance method* for estimating *revenue* or *income* reductions from estimated *uncollectibles*.

reserve recognition accounting. In exploration for natural resources, there is the problem of what to do with the expenditures for exploration. Suppose that $10 million is spent to drill 10 holes ($1 million each), and that nine of them are dry whereas one is a gusher containing oil with a *net realizable value* of $40 million. Dry hole, or *successful efforts*, accounting would expense $9 million and *capitalize* $1 million to be *depleted* as the oil was lifted from the ground. *SFAS No. 19*, now suspended, required successful efforts accounting. Full costing would expense nothing, but capitalize the $10 million of drilling costs to be depleted as the oil is lifted from the single productive well. Reserve recognition accounting would capitalize $40 million to be depleted as the oil is lifted, with a $30 million *credit* to *income* or *contributed capital*. The *balance sheet* shows the *net realizable value* of proven oil and gas reserves. The *income statement* has three sorts of items: (1) current income resulting from production or "lifting profit," which is the *revenue* from sales of oil and gas less the expense based on the current valuation amount at which these items had been carried on the balance sheet; (2) profit or loss from exploration efforts where the current value of new discoveries is revenue and all the exploration cost is expense; and (3) gain or loss on changes in current value during the year, which is in other contexts called a *holding gain or loss*.

reset bond. A bond, typically a *junk bond*, which specifies that periodically the issuer will reset the coupon rate so that the bond sells at *par* in the market. Investment bankers created this type of instrument to make the purchasers of such bonds more sure of getting a fair rate of return, given the riskiness of the issuer. If the issuer gets into financial trouble, then its bonds will trade for less than par in the market. The issuer of a reset bond promises to raise the interest rate and preserve, in principle, the value of the bond. Ironically, the reset feature has often had just the opposite effect. The default risk of many issuers of reset bonds has deteriorated so much that the bonds have dropped to less than 50 percent of par. In order to raise the value to par, the issuer would have to raise the interest rate to more than 25 percent per year. That rate is so large that issuers have declared bankruptcy, rather than attempt to make the large new interest payments.

residual income. In an external reporting context, this term refers to *net income* to *common shares* (= net income less *preferred stock dividends*). In *managerial accounting*, this term refers to the excess of income for a *division* or *segment* of a company over the product of the *cost of capital* for the company multiplied by the average amount of capital invested in the division during the period over which the income was earned.

residual security. A *potentially dilutive security*. *Options, warrants, convertible bonds*, and *convertible preferred stock*.

residual value. At any time, the estimated or actual, *net realizable value* (that is, proceeds less removal costs) of an *asset*, usually a depreciable *plant asset*. In the context of depreciation accounting, this term is equivalent to *salvage value* and is preferable to *scrap value*, because the asset need not be scrapped. Sometimes used to mean net *book value*. In the context of a *noncancelable* lease, the estimated value of the leased asset at the end of the lease period. See *lease*.

responsibility accounting. Accounting for a business by considering various units as separate entities, or *profit centers*, giving management of each unit responsibility for the unit's *revenues* and *expenses*. Sometimes called "activity accounting." See *transfer price*.

responsibility center. Part or *segment* of an organization that is accountable for a specified set of activities. Also called "accountability center." See *cost center, investment center, profit center, revenue center*.

restricted assets. Governmental resources restricted by legal or contractual requirements for specific purpose.

restricted retained earnings. That part of *retained earnings* not legally available for *dividends*. See *retained earnings, appropriated*. Bond indentures and other loan contracts can curtail the legal ability of the corporation to declare dividends without formally requiring a retained earnings appropriation, but disclosure is required.

retail inventory method.   Ascertaining cost amounts of *ending inventory* as follows (assuming FIFO): cost of ending inventory = (selling price of *goods available for sale* - sales) x *cost percentage*. Cost of goods sold is then computed from the inventory equation; costs of beginning inventory, purchases and ending inventory are all known. (When *LIFO* is used, the method is similar to the *dollar-value LIFO method*). See *markup*.

retail terminology.   See *markup*.

retained earnings.   Net *income* over the life of a corporation less all *dividends* (including capitalization through *stock dividends*); *owners' equity* less *contributed capital*.

retained earnings, appropriated.   An *account* set up by crediting it and debiting *retained earnings*. Used to indicate that a portion of retained earnings is not available for dividends. The practice of appropriating retained earnings is misleading unless all capital is earmarked with its use, which is not practicable. Use of formal retained earnings appropriations is declining.

retained earnings statement.   *Generally accepted accounting principles* require that whenever *comparative balance sheets* and an *income statement* are presented, there must also be presented a *reconciliation* of the beginning and ending balances in the *retained earnings account*. This reconciliation can appear in a separate statement, in a combined statement of income and retained earnings, or in the balance sheet.

retirement method of depreciation.   No entry is recorded for *depreciation expense* until an *asset* is retired from service. Then, an entry is made *debiting* depreciation expense and *crediting* the asset account for the cost of the asset retired. If the retired asset has a *salvage value*, the amount of the debit to depreciation expense is reduced by the amount of salvage value with a corresponding debit to cash, receivables, or salvaged materials. The "replacement system of depreciation" is similar, except that the debit to depreciation expense equals the cost of the new asset less the salvage value, if any, of the old asset. These methods were used by some public utilities. For example, if ten telephone poles are acquired in Year 1 for $60 each and are replaced in Year 10 for $100 each when the salvage value of the old poles is $5 each, then the accounting would be as follows:

Retirement Method.

Plant Assets	600	
Cash		600
To acquire assets in Year 1.		

Depreciation Expense	550	
Salvage Receivable	50	
Plant Assets		600
To record retirement and depreciation in Year 10.		

Plant Assets	1,000	
Cash		1,000
To record acquisition of new assets in Year 10.		

Replacement Method.

Plant Assets	600	
Cash		600
To acquire assets in Year 1.		

Depreciation Expense	950	
Salvage Receivable	50	
Cash		1,000
To record depreciation on old asset in amount quantified by net cost of replacement asset in Year 10.		

The retirement method is like *FIFO* in that the cost of the first assets is recorded as depreciation and the cost of the second assets is put on the balance sheet. The replacement method is like *LIFO* in that the cost of the second assets determines the depreciation expense, and the cost of the first assets remains on the balance sheet.

retirement plan.   *Pension plan.*

retroactive benefits.   *Pension plan* benefits granted in initiating or amending a *defined-benefit* pension plan that are attributed by the benefit formula to employee services rendered in periods prior to the initiation or amendment. See *prior service costs*.

return.   A schedule of information required by governmental bodies, such as the tax return required by the *Internal Revenue Service*. Also the physical return of merchandise. See also *return on investment*.

return on assets.   *Net income* plus aftertax *interest charges* plus *minority interest* in income divided by average total *assets*. Perhaps the single most useful ratio for assessing management's overall operating performance. Most financial economists would subtract average non-interest bearing *liabilities* from the denominator. Economists realize that when liabilities do not provide for explicit interest charges, the creditor adjusts the terms of contract, such as setting a higher selling price or lower discount, to those who do not pay cash immediately. (To take an extreme example, consider how much higher salary a worker who receives salary once per year, rather than once per month, would demand.) This ratio requires in the numerator the income amount before the firm accrues any charges to suppliers of funds. We cannot measure the interest charges implicit in the non-interest bearing liabilities, because items such as cost of goods sold and salary expense are somewhat larger because of these charges. Subtracting their amount from the denominator adjusts for their implicit cost. Such subtraction assumes that assets financed with non-interest bearing liabilities have the same rate of return as all the other assets.

return on capital. *Return on assets.*

return on investment. *Return on assets.* Sometimes used to refer to the return on a particular subset of a firm's total assets, such as a group of assets acquired to carry out a particular project.

revenue. The increase in *owners' equity* caused by a service rendered or the sale of goods. The monetary measure of a service rendered. *Sales* of products, merchandise, and services, and earnings from *interest, dividends, rents,* and the like. The amount of revenue is the expected *net present value* of the net assets received. Do not confuse with *receipt of funds,* which may occur before, when, or after revenue is recognized. Contrast with *gain* and *income.* See also *holding gain.* Some writers use the term *gross income* synonymously with *revenue;* avoid such usage.

revenue center. A *responsibility center* within a firm that has control only over revenues generated; contrast with *cost center.* See *profit center.*

revenue expenditure. A phrase sometimes used to mean an *expense,* in contrast to a capital *expenditure* to acquire an *asset* or to discharge a *liability.* Avoid using this phrase; use *period expense* instead.

revenue received in advance. An inferior term for *advances from customers.*

reversal (reversing) entry. An *entry* in which all *debits* and *credits* are the credits and debits, respectively, of another entry, and in the same amounts. It is usually made on the first day of an *accounting period* to reverse a previous *adjusting entry,* usually an *accrual.* The purpose of such entries is to make the bookkeeper's tasks easier. Suppose that salaries are paid every other Friday, with paychecks compensating employees for the 2 weeks just ended. Total salaries accrue at the rate of $5,000 per 5-day work week. The bookkeeper is accustomed to making the following entry every other Friday:

(1) Salary Expense	10,000	
Cash		10,000

To record salary expense and salary payments.

If paychecks are delivered to employees on Friday, September 25, 1992, then the *adjusting entry* made on September 30 (or, perhaps, later) to record accrued salaries for September 28, 29, and 30 would be as follows:

(2) Salary Expense	3,000	
Salaries Payable		3,000

To charge November operations with all salaries earned in September.

The Salary Expense account would be closed as part of the September 30 closing entries. On the next pay day, October 9, the salary entry would have to be as follows:

(3) Salary Expense	7,000	
Salaries Payable	3,000	
Cash		10,000

To record salary payments split between expense for October (7 days) and liability carried over from September.

To make entry (3), the bookkeeper must look back into the records to see how much of the debit is to Salaries Payable accrued from the previous year so that total debits are properly split between third quarter expense and the liability carried over from the second quarter. Notice that this entry forces the bookkeeper both (a) to refer to balances in old accounts and (b) to make an entry different from the one customarily made, entry (1). The reversing entry, made just after the books have been closed for the second quarter, makes the salary entry for October 9, 1992, the same as that made on all other Friday pay days. The reversing entry merely *reverses* the adjusting entry (2):

(4) Salaries Payable	3,000	
Salary Expense		3,000

To reverse the adjusting entry.

This entry results in a zero balance in the Salaries Payable account and a credit balance in the Salary Expense account. If entry (4) is made just after the books are closed for September, then the entry on October 9 will be the customary entry (1). Entries (4) and (1) together have exactly the same effect as entry (3).

The procedure for using reversal entries is as follows: The required adjustment to record an accrual (*payable* or *receivable*) is made at the end of an *accounting period*; the closing entry is made as usual; as of the first day of the following period, an entry is made reversing the adjusting entry; when a payment is made (or received), the entry is recorded as though no adjusting entry had been recorded. Whether or not reversal entries are used affects the record-keeping procedures, but not the financial statements. Also used to describe the entry reversing an incorrect entry before recording the correct entry.

reverse stock split. A stock split in which the number of shares *outstanding* is decreased. See *stock split*.

revolving fund. A fund whose amounts are continually expended and then replenished; for example, a *petty cash fund*.

revolving loan. A *loan* that is expected to be renewed at *maturity*.

right. The privilege to subscribe to new *stock* issues or to purchase stock. Usually, rights are contained in securities called warrants and the *warrants* may be sold to others. See also *preemptive right*.

risk. A measure of the variability of the *return on investment*. For a given expected amount of return, most people prefer less risk to more risk. Therefore, in rational markets, investments with more risk usually promise, or are expected to yield, a higher rate of return than investments with lower risk. Most people use "risk" and "uncertainty" as synonyms. In technical language, however, these terms have different meanings. "Risk" is used when the probabilities attached to the various outcomes are known, such as the probabilities of heads or tails in the flip of a fair coin. "Uncertainty" refers to an event where the probabilities of the outcomes, such as winning or losing a lawsuit, can only be estimated.

risk adjusted discount rate. In a *capital budgeting* context, a decision maker compares projects by comparing their net *present values* for a given *interest* rate, usually the cost of capital. If a given project's outcome is considered to be much more or much less risky than the normal undertakings of the company, then the interest rate used in discounting will be increased (if the project is more risky) or decreased (if less risky) and the rate used is said to be "risk-adjusted."

risk premium. Extra compensation paid to an employee or extra *interest* paid to a lender, over amounts usually considered normal, in return for their undertaking to engage in activities more risky than normal.

ROA. *Return on assets*.

ROI. *Return on investment*, but usually used to refer to a single project and expressed as a ratio: *income* divided by average *cost* of *assets* devoted to the project.

royalty. Compensation for the use of property, usually a patent, copyrighted material, or natural resources. The amount is often expressed as a percentage of receipts from using the property or as an amount per unit produced.

RRA. See *Reserve recognition accounting*.

RRR. Required rate of return.

rule of 69. An amount of money invested at r percent per period will double in $69/r + .35$ periods. This approximation is accurate to one tenth of a period for interest rates between 1/4 and 100 percent per period. For example, at 10 percent per period, the rule says that a given sum will double in $69/10 + .35 = 7.25$ periods. At 10 percent per period, a given sum doubles in 7.27+ periods.

An Open Account, Ruled and Balanced
(Steps indicated in parentheses correspond to steps described in "ruling an account")

	Date 1990	Explanation	Ref.	Debit (1)		Date 1990	Explanation	Ref.	Credit (2)	
	Jan. 1	Balance	✓	100	00					
	Jan. 13		VR	121	37	Sept. 15		J		42
	Mar. 20		VR	56	42	Nov. 12		J	413	15
	June 5		J	1,138	09	Dec. 31	Balance	✓	1,050	59	(3)
	Aug. 18		J	1	21					
	Nov. 20		VR	38	43					
	Dec. 7		VR	8	64					
(4)			VR	1,464	16				1,464	16	(4)
(5)	Jan. 1	Balance	✓	1,050	59					

rule of 72. An amount of money invested at *r* percent per period will double in 72/*r* periods. A reasonable approximation but not nearly as accurate as the *rule of 69*. For example, at 10 percent per period, the rule says that a given sum will double in 72/10 = 7.2 periods.

rule of 78. The rule followed by many finance companies for allocating earnings on *loans* among the months of a year on the sum-of-the-months'-digits basis when equal monthly payments from the borrower are to be received. The sum of the digits from 1 through 12 is 78, so 12/78 of the year's earnings are allocated to the first month, 11/78 to the second month, and so on. See *sum-of-the-years'-digits depreciation*.

ruling (and balancing) an account. The process of summarizing a series of entries in an *account* by computing a new *balance* and drawing double lines to indicate the information above the double lines has been summarized in the new balance. The process is illustrated on the preceding page. The steps are as follows. (1) Compute the sum of all *debit* entries including opening debit balance, if any— $1,464.16. (2) Compute the sum of all credit entries including opening credit balance, if any—$413.57. (3) If the amount in (1) is larger than the amount in (2), then write the excess as a credit with a check mark—$1,464.16 - $413.57 = $1,050.59. (4) Add both debit and credit columns, which should both now sum to the same amount, and show that identical total at the foot of both columns. (5) Draw double lines under those numbers and write the excess of debits over credits as the new debit balance with a check mark. (6) If the amount in (2) is larger than the amount in (1), then write the excess as a debit with a check mark. (7) Do steps (4) and (5) except that the excess becomes the new credit balance. (8) If the amount in (1) is equal to the amount in (2), then the balance is zero, and only the totals with the double lines beneath them need be shown. This process is illustrated in the accompanying figure.

S

SA; Société anonyme. France. A *corporation*.

SAB. *Staff Accounting Bulletin* of the *SEC*.

safe-harbor lease. A form of *tax-transfer lease*.

salary. Compensation earned by managers, administrators, professionals, not based on an hourly rate. Contrast with *wage*.

sale. A *revenue* transaction where *goods* or *services* are delivered to a customer in return for cash or a contractual obligation to pay.

sale and leaseback. Describes a *financing* transaction where improved property is sold but is taken back for use on a long-term *lease*. Such transactions often have advantageous income tax effects, but usually have no effect on *financial statement income*.

sales allowance. A reduction in sales *invoice* price usually given because the *goods* received by the buyer are not exactly what was ordered. The amounts of such adjustments are often accumulated by the seller in a temporary *revenue contra account* having this, or a similar, title. See *sales discount*.

sales basis of revenue recognition. *Revenue* is recognized, not as goods are produced nor as orders are received, but only when the sale (delivery) has been consummated and cash or a *receivable* obtained. Most revenue is recognized on this basis. Compare with the *percentage-of-completion method* and the *installment method*. Identical with the *completed contract method* but this latter term is ordinarily used only for *long-term* construction projects.

sales contra, estimated uncollectibles. A title for the *contra-revenue account* to recognize estimated reductions in income caused by accounts receivable that will not be collected. See *bad debt expense*, *allowance for uncollectibles*, and *allowance method*.

sales discount. Reduction in sales *invoice* price usually offered for prompt payment. See *terms of sale* and *2/10, n/30*.

sales return. The physical return of merchandise; the amounts of such returns are often accumulated by the seller in a temporary *revenue contra account*.

sales value method. *Relative sales value method*.

sales volume variance. *Budgeted contribution margin* per unit times (planned sales volume minus actual sales volume).

salvage value. Actual or estimated selling price, net of removal or disposal costs, of a used *plant asset* to be sold or otherwise retired. See *residual value*.

SAR. *Summary annual report*.

SARL; Société à responsabilité limitée. France. A *corporation* with limited liability and a life of no more than 99 years. Must have at least two and no more than 50 *shareholders*.

SAS. *Statement on Auditing Standards* of the *AICPA*.

scale effect. See *discounted cash flow*.

scatter diagram. A graphic representation of the relationship between two or more variables within a population, achieved by plotting each magnitude or item against the co-ordinates provided.

schedule. A supporting set of calculations, with explanations, that show how figures in a *financial statement* or tax return are derived.

scientific method. *Effective interest method* of *amortizing bond discount* or *premium*.

scrap value. *Salvage value* assuming item is to be junked. A *net realizable value. Residual value.*

SEC. Securities and Exchange Commission, an agency authorized by the U.S. Congress to regulate, among other things, the financial reporting practices of most public corporations. The SEC has indicated that it will usually allow the *FASB* to set accounting principles but it often requires more disclosure than required by the FASB. The SEC's accounting requirements are stated in its *Accounting Series Releases (ASR), Financial Reporting Releases (FRR),* Accounting and Auditing Enforcement Releases, *Staff Accounting Bulletins,* and *Regulation S-X.* See also *registration statement* and *10-K.*

secret reserve. *Hidden reserve.*

Securities and Exchange Commission. *SEC.*

security. Document that indicates ownership or indebtedness or potential ownership, such as an *option* or *warrant.*

segment (of a business). As defined by *APB Opinion No. 30,* "a component of an *entity* whose activities represent a separate major line of business or class of customer. . . . [It may be] a *subsidiary,* a division, or a department, . . . provided that its *assets,* results of *operations,* and activities can be clearly distinguished, physically and operationally for financial reporting purposes, from the other assets, results of operations, and activities of the entity." In *SFAS No. 14* a segment is defined as "A component of an enterprise engaged in promoting a product or service or a group of related products and services primarily to unaffiliated customers . . . for a profit."

segment reporting. Reporting of *sales, income,* and *assets* by *segments of a business,* usually classified by nature of products sold but sometimes by geographical area where goods are produced or sold or by type of customers. Sometimes called "line of business reporting." *Central corporate expenses* are not allocated to the segments.

self balancing. A set of records with equal *debits* and *credits* such as the *ledger* (but not individual accounts), the *balance sheet,* and a *fund* in nonprofit accounting.

self-check(ing) digit. A digit forming part of an account or code number, normally the last digit of the number, which is mathematically derived from the other numbers of the code and is used to detect errors in transcribing the code number.

self insurance. See *insurance.*

self-sustaining foreign operation. A foreign operation that is financially and operationally independent of the reporting enterprise such that the exposure to exchange-rate changes is limited to the reporting enterprise's net investment in the foreign exchange.

selling and administrative expenses. *Expenses* not specifically identifiable with, nor assigned to, production.

semifixed costs. *Costs* that increase with activity as a step function.

semivariable costs. *Costs* that increase strictly linearly with activity but that are positive at zero activity level. Royalty fees of 2 percent of sales are variable; royalty fees of $1,000 per year plus 2 percent of sales are semivariable.

senior securities. *Bonds* as opposed to *preferred stock; preferred stock* as opposed to *common stock.* The senior security has a claim against *earnings* or *assets* that must be met before the claim of less senior securities.

sensitivity analysis. Most decision making requires the use of assumptions. Sensitivity analysis is the study of how the outcome of a decision making process changes as one or more of the assumptions change.

sequential access. Access to computer storage where information can be located only by a sequential search of the storage file. Compare *direct access.*

serial bonds. An *issue* of *bonds* that mature in part at one date, another part on another date, and so on; the various maturity dates usually are equally spaced; contrast them with *term bonds.*

service bureau. A commercial data center providing service to various customers.

service basis of depreciation. *Production method.*

service cost. (current) service cost. *Pension plan expenses incurred* during an *accounting period* for employment services performed during that period; contrast with *prior service cost* and see *funded.*

service department. A department, such as the personnel or computer department, that provides services to other departments, rather than direct work on a salable product; contrast with *production department.* Costs of service departments whose services benefit manufacturing operations must be *allocated* to as *product costs* under *absorption costing*.

service life. Period of expected usefulness of an asset; may not be the same as *depreciable life* for income tax purposes.

service potential. The future benefits embodied in an item that cause the item to be classified as an *asset*. Without service potential, there are no future benefits and the item should not be classified as an asset. *SFAS No. 6* suggests that the primary characteristic of service potential is the ability to generate future net cash inflows.

services. Useful work done by a person, a machine, or an organization. See *goods and services*.

setup. The time or costs required to prepare production equipment for doing a job.

SFAC. *Statement of Financial Accounting Concepts* of the *FASB*.

SFAS. *Statement of Financial Accounting Standards* of the *FASB*.

shadow price. One output of a *linear programming* analysis is the potential value of having available more of the scarce resources that constrain the production process; for example, the value of having more time available on a machine tool critical to the production of two products. This value is called a "shadow price" or the "dual value" of the scarce resource.

share. A unit of *stock* representing ownership in a corporation.

shareholders' equity. *Proprietorship* or *owners' equity* of a corporation. Because *stock* means inventory in Australian, British, and Canadian usage, the term "shareholders' equity" is usually used by Australian, British, and Canadian writers, who do not use the term "stockholders' equity."

short run. short term. The opposite of *long run* or *long term*. This pair of terms is equally imprecise.

short term. Current; ordinarily, due within one year.

short-term liquidity risk. The risk that an *entity* will not have enough *cash* in the *short run* to pay its *debts*.

shrinkage. An excess of *inventory* shown on the *books* over actual physical quantities on hand. Can result from theft or shoplifting as well as from evaporation or general wear and tear.

shutdown cost. A *fixed cost* that continues to be incurred after production has ceased. The costs of closing down a particular production facility.

sight draft. A demand for payment drawn by a person to whom money is owed. The *draft* is presented to the borrower's (the debtor's) bank in expectation that the borrower will authorize its bank to disburse the funds. Such drafts are often used when a seller sells goods to a new customer in a different city. The seller is not sure whether the buyer will pay the bill. The seller sends the *bill* of lading, or other evidence of ownership of the goods, along with a sight draft to the buyer's bank. Before the goods can be released to the buyer, the buyer must instruct its bank to honor the sight draft by withdrawing funds from the buyers' account. Once the sight draft is honored, the bill of lading or other document evidencing ownership is handed over to the buyer and the goods become the property of the buyer.

simple interest. *Interest* calculated on *principal* where interest earned during periods before maturity of the loan is neither added to the principal nor paid to the lender. *Interest = principal x interest rate x time*. Seldom used in economic calculations except for periods less than one year; contrast with *compound interest*.

single-entry accounting. Accounting that is neither *self-balancing* nor *articulated*; that is, it does not rely on equal *debits* and *credits*. *No journal entries* are made. *Plugging* is required to derive *owners' equity* for the *balance sheet*.

single proprietorship. *Sole proprietorship*.

single-step. Said of an *income statement* where *ordinary revenue* and *gain* items are shown first and totaled. Then all ordinary *expenses* and *losses* are totaled. Their difference, plus the effect of *income from discontinued operations* and *extraordinary items*, is shown as *net income*; contrast with *multiple-step* and see *proprietorship theory*.

sinking fund. *Assets* and their earnings earmarked for the retirement of bonds or other long-term obligations. Earnings of sinking fund investments are taxable income of the company.

sinking fund method of depreciation. The periodic charge is an amount so that when the charges are considered to be an *annuity*, the value of the annuity at the end of depreciable life is equal to the *acquisition cost* of the asset. In theory, the charge for a period ought also to include interest on the accumulated depreciation at the start of the period as well. A *fund* of cash is not necessarily, or even usually, accumulated. This method is rarely used.

skeleton account. *T-account*.

slide. The name of the error made by a bookkeeper in recording the digits of a number correctly with the decimal point misplaced; for example, recording $123.40 as $1,234.00 or as $12.34.

SMAC. The Society of Management Accountants of Canada. The national association of accountants whose provincial associations engage in industrial and governmental accounting. The association undertakes research and administers an educational program and comprehensive examinations; those who pass qualify to be designated as Registered Industrial Accountants.

SNC; Société en nom collectif. France. A *partnership*.

soak-up method. The *equity method*.

Social Security taxes. Taxes levied by the federal government on both employers and employees to provide *funds* to pay retired persons (or their survivors) who are entitled to receive such payments, either because they paid Social Security taxes themselves or because the Congress has declared them eligible. Unlike a *pension plan*, the Social Security system does not collect funds and invest them for many years. The tax collections in a given year are used primarily to pay benefits for that year. At any given time the system has a multitrillion-dollar-unfunded obligation to current workers for their eventual retirement benefits. See *Old Age, Survivors, Disability*, and *(Hospital) Insurance*.

software. The programming aids, such as compilers, sort and report programs, and generators, that extend the capabilities of and simplify the use of the computer, as well as certain operating systems and other control programs. Compare *hardware*.

sole proprietorship. All *owners' equity* belongs to one person.

solvent. Able to meet debts when due.

SOP. *Statement of Position* (of *AcSEC* of the *AICPA*).

sound value. A phrase used mainly in appraisals of *fixed assets* to mean *fair market value* or *replacement cost* in present condition.

source of funds. Any *transaction* that increases *cash* and *marketable securities* held as *current assets*.

sources and uses statement. *Statement of cash flows*.

SOYD. *Sum-of-the years'-digits depreciation*.

SP; Société en participation. France. A silent *partnership*, in which the managing partner acts for the partnership as an individual in transacting with others who need not know that the person represents a partnership.

special assessment. A compulsory levy made by a governmental unit on property to pay the costs of a specific improvement, or service, presumed not to benefit the general public but only the owners of the property so assessed. Accounted for in a special assessment fund.

special journal. A *journal*, such as a sales journal or cash disbursements journal, to record *transactions* of a similar nature that occur frequently.

special revenue debt. Debt of a governmental unit backed only by revenues from specific sources such as tolls from a bridge.

specific identification method. Method for valuing *ending inventory* and *cost of goods sold* by identifying actual units sold and in inventory and summing the actual costs of those individual units. Usually used for items with large unit value, such as precious jewelry, automobiles, and fur coats.

specific item sampling. Sampling where particular items are selected because of their nature, value, or method of recording. Compare *representative item sampling*.

specific price changes. Changes in the market prices of specific *goods and services*; contrast with *general price level changes*.

specific price index. A measure of the price of a specific good or service, or a small group of similar goods or services, at one time relative to the price during a base period; contrast with *general price index*. See *dollar-value LIFO method*.

spending variance. In *standard cost systems*, the *rate* or *price variance* for *overhead costs*.

split. *Stock split*. Sometimes called "splitup."

splitoff point. The point where all costs are no longer *joint costs* but can be identified with individual products or perhaps with a smaller number of *joint products*.

spoilage. See *abnormal spoilage* and *normal spoilage*.

spread sheet. A *work sheet* organized like a *matrix* that provides a two-way classification of accounting data. The rows and columns are both labeled with *account* titles. An entry in a row represents a *debit* whereas an entry in a column represents a *credit*. Thus, the number "100" in the "cash" row and the "accounts receivable" column records an entry debiting cash and crediting accounts receivable for $100. A given row total indicates all debit entries to the account represented by that row and a given column total indicates the sum of all credit entries to the account represented by the column.

squeeze. A term sometimes used for *plug*.

SSARS. See *Statement on Standards for Accounting and Review Services*.

stabilized accounting. *Constant dollar accounting*.

stable monetary unit assumption. In spite of *inflation* that appears to be a way of life, the assumption that underlies *historical cost/nominal dollar accounting*—namely that current dollars and dollars of previous years can be meaningfully added together. No specific recognition is given to changing values of the dollar in the usual *financial statements*. See *constant dollar accounting*.

Staff Accounting Bulletin. An interpretation issued by the Staff of the Chief Accountant of the *SEC* "suggesting" how the various *Accounting Series Releases* should be applied in practice. The suggestions are effectively part of *GAAP*.

standard cost. Anticipated *cost* of producing a unit of output; a predetermined cost to be assigned to products produced. Standard cost implies a norm: what costs should be. Budgeted cost implies a forecast, something likely, but not necessarily a "should," as implied by a norm. Standard costs are used as the benchmark for gauging good and bad performance. While a budget may similarly be used, it need not. A budget may simply be a planning document, subject to changes whenever plans change, whereas standard costs are usually changed annually or when technology significantly changes or costs of labor and materials significantly change.

standard costing. *Costing* based on *standard costs*.

standard costing system. *Product costing* using *standard costs* rather than actual costs. May be based on either *absorption* or *variable costing* principles.

standard error (of regression coefficients). A measure of the uncertainty about the magnitude of the estimated parameters of an equation fit with a *regression analysis*.

standard manufacturing overhead. *Overhead costs* expected to be incurred per unit of time and per unit produced.

standard price (rate). Unit price established for materials or labor used in *standard cost systems*.

standard quantity allowed. The quantity of direct material or direct labor (inputs) that should have been used if the units of output had been produced in accordance with preset *standards*.

standby costs. A type of *capacity cost*, such as property taxes, incurred even if operations are shut down completely. Contrast with *enabling costs*.

stated capital. Amount of capital contributed by shareholders. Sometimes used to mean *legal capital*.

stated value. A term sometimes used for the *face amount of capital stock*, when no *par value* is indicated. Where there is stated value per share, it may be set by the directors (in which case, capital *contributed in excess of stated value* may come into being).

statement of affairs. A *balance sheet* showing immediate *liquidation* amounts, rather than *historical costs*, usually prepared when *insolvency* or *bankruptcy* is imminent. The *going-concern assumption* is not used.

statement of cash flows. The *FASB* requires that all for-profit companies present a schedule of *cash receipts* and *payments*, classified by *investing, financing*, and *operating activities*. Operating activities may be reported with either the direct method (where only receipts and payments of cash appear) or the indirect method (which starts with *net income* and shows adjustments for *revenues* not currently producing cash and for *expenses* not currently using cash). "Cash" includes cash equivalents such as Treasury bills, commercial paper and *marketable securities* held as *current assets*. Sometimes called the "funds statement." Before 1987, the FASB required the presentation of a similar statement called the *statement of changes in financial position*, which tended to emphasize *working capital*, not cash. See *dual transactions assumption*.

statement of changes in financial position. As defined by *APB Opinion No. 19*, a statement that explains the changes in *working capital* (or cash) balances during a period and shows the changes in the working capital (or cash) accounts themselves. This statement has been replaced with the *statement of cash flows*.

statement of charge and discharge. A financial statement as to *capital* or *income*, drawn up by an executor or administrator to account for receipts and dispositions of cash or other assets in an estate or trust.

Statement of Financial Accounting Standards. SFAS. See *FASB*.

Statement of Financial Accounting Concepts. SFAC. One of a series of *FASB* publications in its *conceptual framework* for *financial accounting* and reporting. Such statements set forth objectives and fundamentals to be the basis for specific financial accounting and reporting standards.

statement of financial position. *Balance sheet. Statement of Position. SOP.* A recommendation on an emerging accounting problem issued by the *AcSEC* of the *AICPA*.

The AICPA's Code of Professional Ethics specifically states that *CPAs* need not treat *SOPs* as they do rules from the *FASB*, but a CPA would be wary of departing from the recommendations of a *SOP*.

statement of retained earnings (income). A statement that reconciles the beginning-of-period and end-of-period balances in the *retained earnings* account. It shows the effects of *earnings, dividend declarations,* and *prior-period adjustments.*

statement of significant accounting policies (principles). APB Opinion No. 22 requires that every *annual report* summarize the significant *accounting principles* used in compiling the annual report. This summary may be a separate exhibit or the first *note* to the financial statements.

Statement on Auditing Standards. SAS. *No. 1* of this series (1973) codifies all statements on auditing standards previously promulgated by the AICPA. Later numbers deal with specific auditing standards and procedures.

Statement on Standards for Accounting and Review Services. SSARS. Pronouncements issued by the AICPA on *unaudited financial statements* and unaudited financial information of nonpublic entities.

static budget. *Fixed budget.*

status quo. Events or costs incurrences that will happen or are expected to happen in the absence of taking some contemplated action.

statutory tax rate. The tax rate specified in the *income tax* law for each type of income (for example, *ordinary income, capital gain or loss*).

step allocation method. *Step-down method.*

step cost. *Semifixed cost.*

step-down method. The method for *allocating service department* costs that starts by allocating one service department's costs to *production departments* and to all other service departments. Then a second service department's costs, including costs allocated from the first, are allocated to production departments and to all other service departments except the first one. In this fashion, the costs of all service departments, including previous allocations, are allocated to production departments and to those service departments whose costs have not yet been allocated.

stepped cost. *Semifixed cost.*

sterilized allocation. Optimal decisions result from considering *incremental costs*, only. *Allocations* of *joint* or *common costs* are never required for optimal deci-

sions. An allocation of these costs that causes the optimal decision choice not to differ from the one that occurs when joint or common costs are unallocated is "sterilized" with respect to that decision. The term was first used in this context by Arthur L. Thomas. Because *absorption costing* requires that all manufacturing costs be allocated to product, and because some allocations can lead to bad decisions, Thomas (and we) advocate that the allocation scheme chosen lead to sterilized allocations that do not alter the otherwise optimal decision. There is, however, no single allocation scheme that is always sterilized with respect to all decisions. Thus, Thomas (and we) advocate that decisions be made on the basis of incremental costs before any allocations.

stewardship. The function of management to be accountable for an *entity's* resources, for their efficient use, and for protecting them, as well as is practicable, from adverse impact. Some theorists believe that a primary goal of *accounting* is to aid users of *financial statements* in their assessment of management's performance in stewardship.

stock. *Inventory. Capital stock.* A measure of the amount of something on hand at a specific time; in this sense, contrast with *flow.*

stock appreciation rights. The employer promises to pay to the employee an amount of *cash* on a certain future date. The amount of cash is the difference between the *market value* of a certain number of *shares* of *stock* in the employer's company on a given future date and some base price set on the date the rights are granted. This form of compensation is sometimes used because both changes in tax laws in recent years have made *stock options* relatively less attractive. *GAAP* computes compensation based on the difference between market value of the shares and the base price set at the time of the grant. *Expense* is recognized over time as the holder of the rights performs the services required for the rights to be exercised.

stock dividend. A so-called *dividend* where additional *shares* of *capital stock* are distributed, without cash payments, to existing shareholders. It results in a *debit* to *retained earnings* in the amount of the market value of the shares issued and a *credit* to *capital stock* accounts. It is ordinarily used to indicate that earnings retained have been permanently reinvested in the business; contrast with a *stock split*, which requires no entry in the capital stock accounts other than a notation that the *par* or *stated value* per share has been changed.

stock option. The right to purchase a specified number of shares of *stock* for a specified price at specified times, usually granted to employees; contrast with *warrant.*

stockout. A unit of *inventory* is needed in production or to sell to a customer but is unavailable.

stock out costs. *Contribution margin* or other measure of *profits* not earned because a seller has run out of *inventory* and is unable to fill a customer's order. May be an extra cost incurred because of delay in filling an order.

stock right. See *right*.

stock split. Increase in the number of common shares outstanding resulting from the issuance of additional shares to existing shareholders without additional capital contributions by them. Does not increase the total *par* (or *stated*) *value of common stock* outstanding because par (or stated) value per share is reduced in inverse proportion. A three-for-one stock split reduces par (or stated) value per share to one third of its former amount. Stock splits are usually limited to distributions that increase the number of shares outstanding by 20 percent or more; compare with *stock dividend*.

stock subscriptions. See *subscription* and *subscribed stock*.

stock warrant. See *warrant*.

stockholders' equity. See *shareholders' equity*.

stores. *Raw materials*, parts, and supplies.

straight-debt value. An estimate of what the *market value* of a *convertible bond* would be if the bond did not contain a conversion privilege.

straight line depreciation. If the *depreciable life* is *n* periods, then the periodic *depreciation* charge is $1/n$ of the *depreciable cost*. Results in equal periodic charges and is sometimes called "straight time depreciation."

strategic plan. A statement of the method for achieving an organization's goals.

stratified sampling. A method of choosing a *sample* in which the entire *population* is divided first into relatively homogeneous sub groups (strata), from which *random samples* are then selected.

street security. A stock certificate in immediately transferable form, most commonly because it is registered in the name of the broker and endorsed in blank.

Subchapter S Corporation. A firm legally organized as a *corporation* but taxed as if it were a *partnership*. The corporations paying their own income taxes are called "C Corporations."

subject to. Qualifications in an *auditor's report* usually caused by a *material* uncertainty in the valuation of an item, such as future promised payments from a foreign government or outcome of pending litigation.

subordinated. Said of *debt* whose claim on income or assets is junior to, or comes after, claims of other debt.

subscribed stock. A *shareholders' equity* account showing the capital that will be contributed as soon as the subscription price is collected. A subscription is a legal contract so that an entry is made *debiting* an *owners' equity contra account* and *crediting* subscribed stock as soon as the stock is subscribed.

subscription. Agreement to buy a *security*, or to purchase periodicals, such as magazines.

subsequent events. *Post-statement events*.

subsidiary. Said of a company more than 50 percent of whose voting stock is owned by another.

subsidiary (ledger) accounts. The *accounts* in a *subsidiary ledger*.

subsidiary ledger. The *ledger* that contains the detailed accounts whose total is shown in a *controlling account* of the *general ledger*.

successful efforts accounting. In petroleum accounting, the *capitalization* of the drilling costs of only those wells that contain gas or oil. See *reserve recognition accounting* for an example.

sum-of-the-years'-digits depreciation. SYD. SOYD. An *accelerated depreciation* method for an asset with *depreciable life* of *n* years where the charge in period *i* (*i* = 1, . . . , *n*) is the fraction $(n + 1 - i)/[n(n + 1)/2]$ of the *depreciable cost*. If an asset has a depreciable cost of $15,000 and a 5 year depreciable life, for example, the depreciation charges would be $5,000 (= 5/15 x $15,000) in the first year, $4,000 in the second, $3,000 in the third, $2,000 in the fourth, and $1,000 in the fifth. The name derives from the fact that the denominator in the fraction is the sum of the digits from 1 through *n*.

summary annual report. Condensed financial statements distributed in lieu of the usual *annual report*. Since 1987, the *SEC* has allowed firms to include such statements in the annual report to shareholders so long as the full, detailed statements appear in SEC filings and in *proxy* materials sent to shareholders.

summary of significant accounting principles. *APB Opinion No.* 22 requires that every *annual report* summarize the significant *accounting principles* used in compiling the annual report. This summary may be a separate exhibit or the first *note* to the financial statements.

sunk cost. *Costs* incurred in the past that cannot be affected by, and hence irrelevant for, current and future decisions, aside from *income tax* effects; contrast with *incremental costs* and *imputed costs*. For example, the *acquisition cost* of machinery is irrelevant to a decision of whether or not to scrap the machinery. The current *exit value* of the machine is the *opportunity cost* of continuing to own it and the cost of, say, electricity to run the machine is an incremental cost of its operation. Sunk costs become relevant for decision making when *income taxes* (*gain* or *loss* on disposal of asset) are taken into account because the cash payment for income taxes depends on the tax basis of the asset. The term should be avoided in careful writing because it is ambiguous. Consider, for example, a machine costing $100,000 with current *salvage* value of $20,000. Some (including us) would say that $100,000 is "sunk"; others would say that only $80,000 is "sunk."

supplementary statements (schedules). Statements (schedules) in addition to the four basic *financial statements* (including the *retained earnings* reconciliation as a basic statement).

surplus. A word once used but now considered poor terminology; prefaced by "earned" to mean *retained earnings* and prefaced by "capital" to mean *capital contributed in excess of par (or stated) value*.

surplus reserves. Of all the words in accounting, *reserve* is the most objectionable and *surplus* is the second most objectionable. This phrase, then, has nothing to recommend it. It means *appropriated retained earnings*.

suspense account. A *temporary account* used to record part of a transaction prior to final analysis of that transaction. For example, if a business regularly classifies all sales into a dozen or more different categories but wants to deposit the proceeds of cash sales every day, it may credit a sales suspense account pending detailed classification of all sales into sales, type 1; sales, type 2; and so on.

sustainable income. The part of *distributable income* (computed from *current cost* data) that the firm can be expected to earn in the next accounting period if operations are continued at the same levels as during the current period. *Income from discontinued operations*, for example, may be distributable but not sustainable.

S-X. See *Regulation S-X*.

SYD. *Sum-of-the-years'-digits depreciation. SOYD*.

T

T-account. Account form shaped like the letter T with the title above the horizontal line. *Debits* appear to the left of the vertical line, *credits* to the right.

take-home pay. The amount of a paycheck; earned wages or *salary* reduced by deductions for *income taxes, Social Security taxes*, contributions to fringe benefit plans, union dues, and so on. Take home pay might be as little as half of earned compensation.

take-or-pay contract. As defined by *SFAS No. 47*, an agreement between a purchaser and a seller that provides for the purchaser to pay specified amounts periodically in return for products or services. The purchaser must make specified minimum payments even if it does not take delivery of the contracted products or services.

taking a bath. To incur a large loss. See *big bath*.

tangible. Having physical form. Accounting has never satisfactorily defined the distinction between tangible and intangible assets. Typically, intangibles are defined by giving an exhaustive list and everything not on the list is defined as tangible. See *intangible asset* for such a list.

target cost. *Standard cost*.

tax. A nonpenal, but compulsory, charge levied by a government on income, consumption, wealth, or other basis, for the benefit of all those governed. The term does not include fines or specific charges for benefits accruing only to those paying the charges, such as licenses, permits, special assessments, admissions fees, and tolls.

tax allocation: interperiod. See *deferred income tax liability*.

tax allocation: intrastatement. The showing of income tax effects on *extraordinary items, income from discontinued operations*, and *prior-period adjustments* along with these items, separately from income taxes on other income. See *net-of-tax reporting*.

tax avoidance. See *tax shelter* and *loophole*.

tax credit. A subtraction from taxes otherwise payable, contrast with *tax deduction*.

tax deduction. A subtraction from *revenues* and *gains* to arrive at taxable income. Tax deductions are technically different from tax *exemptions*, but the effect of both is to reduce gross income in computing taxable income. Both are different from *tax credits*, which are subtracted from the computed tax itself in determining taxes payable. If the tax rate is the fraction t of pretax income, then a *tax credit* of $1 is worth $1/t$ of *tax deductions*.

tax evasion. The fraudulent understatement of taxable revenues or overstatement of deductions and expenses or both; contrast with *tax shelter* and *loophole*.

tax exempts. See *municipal bonds*.

tax shelter. The legal avoidance of, or reduction in, *income taxes* resulting from a careful reading of the complex income tax regulations and the subsequent rearrangement of financial affairs to take advantage of the regulations. Often the term is used pejoratively, but the courts have long held that an individual or corporation has no obligation to pay taxes any larger than the legal minimum. If the public concludes that a given tax shelter is "unfair," then the laws and regulations can be, and have been, changed. Sometimes used to refer to the investment that permits tax avoidance. See *loophole*.

tax shield. The amount of an *expense* that reduces taxable income but does not require *working capital*, such as *depreciation*. Sometimes this term is expanded to include expenses that reduce taxable income and use working capital. A depreciation deduction (or *R&D expense* in the expanded sense) of $10,000 provides a tax shield of $4,600 when the marginal tax rate is 46 percent.

taxable income. *Income* computed according to *IRS* regulations and subject to *income taxes*. Contrast with income, net income, income before taxes (in the *income statement*), and *comprehensive income* (a *financial reporting* concept). Use the term "pretax income" to refer to income before taxes on the income statement in financial reports.

tax-transfer lease. Congress has in the past provided business with an incentive to invest in qualifying *plant and equipment* by granting an *investment credit*, which although it occurs as a reduction in *income taxes* otherwise payable, is effectively a reduction in the purchase price of the assets. Similarly, Congress continues to grant an incentive to acquire such assets by allowing *Accelerated Cost Recovery* (*ACRS*, form of unusually *accelerated depreciation*). Accelerated depreciation for tax purposes allows a reduction of taxes paid in early years of an assets's life, which provides the firm with an increased *net present value* of *cash flows*. Both of these incentives are administered by the *IRS* through the income tax laws, rather than being granted as an outright cash payment by some other government agency. A business with no taxable income in many cases had difficulty reaping the benefits of the investment credit or of accelerated depreciation because Congress had not provided for tax refunds to those who acquire qualifying assets but who have no taxable income. In principle, a company without taxable income could lease from another firm with taxable income an asset that would otherwise have been purchased by the first company. The second firm acquires the asset, gets the tax reduction benefits from the acquisition, and becomes a lessor, leasing the asset (presumably at a lower price reflecting its own costs lowered by the tax reductions) to the unprofitable company. Such leases were discouraged by the tax laws prior to 1981. That is, although firms could enter into such leases, the tax benefits could not be legally transferred. Under certain restrictive conditions, the tax law allows a profitable firm to earn tax credits and take deductions while leasing to the firm without tax liability in such leases. These leases have sometimes been called "safe-harbor leases."

Technical Bulletin. The *FASB* has authorized its staff to issue bulletins to provide guidance on financial accounting and reporting problems. Although the FASB does not formally approve the contents of the bulletins, their contents are presumed to be part of *GAAP*.

technology. The sum of a firm's technical *trade secrets* and *know-how*, as distinct from its *patents*.

temporary account. *Account* that does not appear on the *balance sheet*. *Revenue* and *expense* accounts, their *adjuncts* and *contras*, production cost accounts, dividend distribution accounts, and purchases-related accounts (which are closed to the various inventories). Sometimes called a "nominal account."

temporary difference. Temporary differences include *timing differences* and differences between *taxable income* and pretax income caused by different cost bases for assets. For example, a plant asset might have a cost of $10,000 for financial reporting, but a basis of $7,000 for income tax purposes; this creates a temporary difference which is not a timing difference.

temporary investments. Investments in *marketable securities* that the owner intends to sell within a short time, usually one year, and hence classified as *current assets*.

10-K. The name of the annual report required by the *SEC* of nearly all publicly held corporations.

term bonds. A *bond issue* whose component bonds all mature at the same time; contrast with *serial bonds*.

term loan. A loan with a *maturity* date, as opposed to a demand loan which is due whenever the lender requests payment. In practice, bankers and auditors use this phrase only for loans for a year or more.

terms of sale. The conditions governing payment for a sale. For example, the terms *2/10, n(et)/30* mean that if payment is made within 10 days of the invoice date, a *discount* of 2 percent from *invoice* price can be taken; the invoice amount must be paid, in any event, within 30 days or it becomes overdue.

thin capitalization. A state of having a high *debt-equity ratio*. Under income tax legislation, the term has a special meaning.

throughput contract. As defined by *SFAS No. 47*, an agreement between a shipper (processor) and the owner of a transportation facility (such as an oil or natural gas pipeline or a ship) or a manufacturing facility that provides for the shipper (processor) to pay specified amounts periodically in return for the transportation (processing) of a product. The shipper (processor) is obligated to make cash payments even if it does not ship (process) the contracted quantities.

tickler file. A collection of *vouchers* or other memoranda arranged chronologically to remind the person in charge of certain duties to make payments (or to do other tasks) as scheduled.

time-adjusted rate of return. *Internal rate of return.*

time cost. *Period cost.*

time deposit. Cash in bank earning interest; contrast with *demand deposit.*

time-series analysis. See *cross-section analysis* for definition and contrast.

times-interest (charges) earned. Ratio of pretax *income* plus *interest* charges to interest charges. See *ratio.*

timing difference. The major type of *temporary difference.* A difference between taxable income and pretax income reported to shareholders that will be reversed in a subsequent period and requires an entry in the *deferred income tax* account. For example, the use of *accelerated depreciation* for tax returns and *straight line depreciation* for financial reporting. Contrast with *permanent difference.*

Toronto Stock Exchange (TSE). A public market where various corporate securities are traded.

total assets turnover. *Sales* divided by average total *assets.*

traceable cost. A *cost* that can be identified with or assigned to a specific product; in contrast to a *joint cost.*

trade acceptance. A *draft* drawn by a seller that is presented for signature (acceptance) to the buyer at the time goods are purchased and which then becomes the equivalent of a *note receivable* of the seller and the *note payable* of the buyer.

trade credit. One business allows another to buy from it in return for a promise to pay later. As contrasted with consumer credit, where a business extends the privilege of paying later to a retail customer.

trade discount. A *discount* from *list price* offered to all customers of a given type; contrast with a *discount* offered for prompt payment and *quantity discount.*

trade payables (receivables). *Payables (receivables)* arising in the ordinary course of business transactions. Most accounts payable (receivable) are of this kind.

trade secret. Technical or business information such as formulas, recipes, computer programs, and marketing data not generally known by competitors and maintained by the firm as a secret. A famous example is the secret formula for *Coca-Cola* (a registered *trademark* of the company). Compare with *know-how.* Theoretically capable of having an infinite life, this intangible asset is capitalized only if purchased and then amortized over a period not to exceed 40 years. If it is developed internally, then no asset will be shown.

trade-in. Acquiring a new *asset* in exchange for a used one and perhaps additional cash. See *boot* and *trade-in transaction.*

trade-in transaction. The accounting for a trade-in depends whether or not the asset received is "similar" to the asset traded in and whether the accounting is for *financial statements* or for *income tax* returns. Assume that an old asset cost $5,000, has $3,000 of *accumulated depreciation* (after recording depreciation to the date of the trade-in), and hence has a *book value* of $2,000. The old asset appears to have a market value of $1,500, according to price quotations in used asset markets. The old asset is traded in on a new asset with a list price of $10,000. The old asset and $5,500 cash (*boot*) are given for the new asset. The generic entry for the trade-in transaction is:

New Asset	A	
Accumulated Depreciation		
(Old Asset)	3,000	
Adjustment on Exchange of Asset . .	B or	B
Old Asset		5,000
Cash		5,500

(1) The *list price* method of accounting for trade-ins rests on the assumption that the list price of the new asset closely approximates its market value. The new asset is recorded at its list price (A = $10,000 in the example); B is a *plug* (= $2,500 credit in the example). If B requires a *debit* plug, the Adjustment on Exchange of Asset is a *loss*; if a *credit* plug is required (as in the example), the adjustment is a *gain.*

(2) Another theoretically sound method of accounting for trade-ins rests on the assumption that the price quotation from used-asset markets gives a more reliable measure of the market value of the old asset than is the list price a reliable measure of the market value of the new asset. This method uses the *fair market value* of the old asset, $1,500 in the example, to determine B (= $2,000 book value - $1,500 assumed proceeds on disposition = $500 debit or loss). The exchange results in a loss if the book value of the old asset exceeds its market value and in a gain if the market value exceeds the book value. The

new asset is recorded on the books by plugging for A (= $7,000 in the example).

(3) For income tax reporting, no gain or loss may be recognized on the trade in. Thus the new asset is recorded on the books by assuming B is zero and plugging for A (= $7,500 in the example). In practice, firms that wish to recognize the loss currently will sell the old asset directly, rather than trading it in, and acquire the new asset entirely for cash.

(4) *Generally accepted accounting principles (APB Opinion No. 29)* require a variant of these methods. The basic method is (1) or (2), depending on whether the list price of the new asset (1) or the quotation of the old asset's market value (2) is the more reliable indication of market value. If, when applying the basic method, a debit entry, or loss, is required for the Adjustment on Exchange of Asset, then the trade-in is recorded as described in (1) or (2) and the full amount of the loss is recognized currently. If, however, a credit entry, or gain, is required for the Adjustment on Exchange of Asset, then the amount of gain recognized currently depends on whether or not the old asset and the new asset are "similar." If the assets are not similar, then the entire gain is recognized currently. If the assets are similar and cash is not received by the party trading in, then no gain is recognized and the treatment is like that in (3); that is B = 0, plug for A. If the assets are similar and cash is received by the party trading in—a rare case—then a portion of the gain is recognized currently. The portion of the gain recognized currently is the fraction *cash received/fair market value of total consideration received.* (When the list price method, (1), is used, the market value of the old asset is assumed to be the list price of the new asset plus the amount of cash received by the party trading in.)

The accompanying exhibit summarizes the results of applying *GAAP* to the example.

Example for Trade-In Transaction

More Reliable Information As to Fair Market Value	Old Asset Compared with New Asset	
	Similar	Not Similar
New Asset List Price	A= $7,500 B= 0	A= $10,000 B= 2,500 gain
Old Asset Market Price	A= $7,500 B= 500 loss	A= $7,000 B= 500 loss

trademark. A distinctive word or symbol affixed to a product, its package or dispenser, which uniquely identifies the firm's products and services. See *trademark right.*

trademark right. The right to exclude competitors in sales or advertising from using words or symbols that may be confusingly similar to the firm's *trademarks.* Trademark rights last as long as the firm continues to use the trademarks in question. In the United States, trademark rights arise from use and not from government registration. They therefore have a legal life independent of the life of a registration. Registrations last 20 years and are renewable as long as the trademark is being used. Thus, as an asset, purchased trademark rights might, like land, not be subject to amortization if management believes that the life of the trademark is indefinite. In practice, accountants amortize a trademark right over some estimate of its life, not to exceed 40 years. Under *SFAS No. 2*, internally developed trademark rights must be *expensed.*

trading on the equity. Said of a firm engaging in *debt financing*; frequently said of a firm doing so to a degree considered abnormal for a firm of its kind. *Leverage.*

transaction. A *transfer* (of more than promises—see *executory contract*) between the accounting *entity* and another party, or parties.

transfer. *SFAC No. 6* distinguishes "reciprocal" and "nonreciprocal" transfers. In a reciprocal transfer, or "exchange," the entity both receives and sacrifices. In a nonreciprocal transfer the entity sacrifices but does not receive (examples include gifts, distributions to owners) or receives but does not sacrifice (investment by owner in entity). *SFAC No. 6* suggests that the term "internal transfer" is self-contradictory and that the term "internal event" be used instead.

transfer agent. Usually a bank or trust company designated by a corporation to make legal transfers of *stock (bonds)* and, perhaps, to pay *dividends (coupons).*

transfer price. A substitute for a *market,* or *arm's length, price* used in *profit,* or *responsibility center, accounting* when one segment of the business "sells" to another segment. Incentives of profit center managers will not coincide with the best interests of the entire business unless transfer prices are properly set.

transfer pricing problem. The problem of setting *transfer prices* so that both buyer and seller have *goal congruence* with respect to the parent organization's goals.

translation gain (or loss). *Foreign exchange gain (or loss).*

transportation-in. *Freight-in.*

transposition error. An error in record-keeping resulting from reversing the order of digits in a number, such as recording "32" for "23." If an error of this sort has been made in a number added in a total, then the incorrect total will always differ from the correct total by a number divisible by nine. Thus if *trial balance* sums differ by a number divisible by nine, one might search for a transposition error.

treasurer. The name sometimes given to the chief financial officer of a business.

treasury bond. A bond issued by a corporation and then reacquired; such bonds are treated as retired when reacquired and an *extraordinary gain or loss* on reacquisition is recognized. Also, a *bond* issued by the U.S. Treasury Department.

treasury shares. *Capital stock* issued and then reacquired by the corporation. Such reacquisitions result in a reduction of *shareholders' equity*, and are usually shown on the balance sheet as *contra* to shareholders' equity. Neither *gain* nor *loss* is recognized on transactions involving treasury stock. Any difference between the amounts paid and received for treasury stock transactions is debited (if positive) or credited (if negative) to *additional paid-in capital*. See *cost method* and *par value method*.

treasury stock. *Treasury shares.*

trial balance. A listing of *account balances*; all accounts with *debit* balances are totaled separately from accounts with *credit* balances. The two totals should be equal. Trial balances are taken as a partial check of the arithmetic accuracy of the entries previously made. See *adjusted, preclosing, post-closing, unadjusted trial balance, plug.*

troubled debt restructuring. As defined in *SFAS No. 15*, a concession (changing of the terms of a *debt*) granted by a *creditor* for economic or legal reasons related to the *debtor's* financial difficulty that the creditor would not otherwise consider.

TSE. *Toronto Stock Exchange.*

turnover. The number of times that *assets*, such as *inventory* or *accounts receivable*, are replaced on average during the period. Accounts receivable turnover, for example, is total sales on account for a period divided by average accounts receivable balance for the period. See *ratio*.

turnover of plant and equipment. See *ratio.*

t-value. In *regression analysis*, the ratio of an estimated regression coefficient divided by its *standard error*.

two T-account method. A method for computing either (1) *foreign exchange gains and losses* or (2) *monetary gains* or *losses* for *constant dollar accounting statements*. The left-hand *T-account* shows actual net balances of *monetary items* and the right-hand T-account shows implied *(common) dollar* amounts.

2/10, n(et)/30. See *terms of sale.*

U

unadjusted trial balance. *Trial balance* before *adjusting* and *closing entries* are made at the end of the period.

unappropriated retained earnings. *Retained earnings* not appropriated and therefore against which *dividends* can be charged in the absence of retained earnings restrictions. See *restricted retained earnings.*

unavoidable cost. A *cost* that is not an *avoidable cost.*

uncertainty. See *risk* for definition and contrast.

uncollectible account. An *account receivable* that will not be paid by the *debtor*. If the preferable *allowance method* is used, the entry on judging a specific account to be uncollectible is to *debit* the allowance for uncollectible accounts and to *credit* the specific account receivable. See *bad debt expense* and *sales contra, estimated uncollectibles.*

unconsolidated subsidiary. A *subsidiary* not consolidated and, hence, accounted for on the *equity method.*

uncontrollable cost. The opposite of *controllable cost.*

underapplied (underabsorbed) overhead. An excess of actual *overhead costs* for a period over costs applied, or charged, to products produced during the period. A *debit balance* remaining in an overhead account after overhead is assigned to product.

underlying document. The record, memorandum, *voucher*, or other signal that is the authority for making an *entry* into a *journal.*

underwriter. One who agrees to purchase an entire *security issue* for a specified price, usually for resale to others.

undistributed earnings. *Retained earnings*; typically, this term refers to that amount retained for a given year.

unearned income (revenue). *Advances from customers*; strictly speaking, a contradiction in terms.

unemployment tax. See *FUTA.*

unencumbered appropriation. In governmental accounting, portion of an *appropriation* not yet spent or *encumbered.*

unexpired cost. An *asset.*

unfavorable variance. In *standard cost* accounting, an excess of expected revenue over actual revenue or an excess of actual cost over standard cost.

unfunded. Not *funded.* An obligation or *liability,* usually for *pension costs,* exists but no *funds* have been set aside to discharge the obligation or liability.

Uniform Partnership Act. A model law, enacted by many states, to govern the relations between partners where the *partnership* agreement fails to specify the agreed-upon treatment.

unissued capital stock. *Stock* authorized but not yet issued.

units-of-production method. The *production method of depreciation.*

unlimited liability. The legal obligation of *general partners* or the sole proprietor for all debts of the *partnership* or *sole proprietorship.*

unqualified opinion. See *auditor's report.*

unrealized appreciation. An *unrealized holding gain;* frequently used in the context of *marketable securities.*

unrealized gross margin (profit). A *contra* account to *installment accounts receivable* used with the *installment method* of revenue recognition. Shows the amount of profit that will eventually be realized when the receivable is collected. Some accountants show this account as a *liability.*

unrealized holding gain. See *inventory profit* for definition and an example.

unrealized loss on marketable securities. An *income statement account* title for the amount of *loss* during the current period on the portfolio of *marketable securities* held as *current assets. SFAS No. 12* requires that losses caused by declines in price below market be *recognized* in the income statement, even though they have not been *realized.*

unrecovered cost. *Book value* of an *asset.*

usage variance. *Efficiency variance.*

use of funds. Any transaction that reduces funds (however funds is defined).

useful life. *Service life.*

V

valuation account. A *contra account* or *adjunct account.* When *marketable securities* are reported at *lower of cost or market,* any declines in market value below cost will be credited to a valuation account. In this way, the acquisition cost and the amount of price declines below cost can both be shown. *SFAC No. 6* says a valuation account is "a separate item that reduces and increases the carrying amount" of an asset (or liability). The accounts are part of the related assets (or liabilities) and are neither assets (nor liabilities) in their own right.

value. Monetary worth; the term is usually so subjective that it ought not to be used without a modifying adjective unless most people would agree on the amount; not to be confused with cost. See *fair market value, entry value, exit value.*

value added. *Cost* of a product or *work in process,* minus the cost of the material purchased for the product or work in process.

value variance. *Price variance.*

variable annuity. An *annuity* whose periodic payments depend on some uncertain outcome, such as stock market prices.

variable budget. *Flexible budget.*

variable costing. This method of allocating costs assigns only *variable manufacturing costs* to product and treats *fixed manufacturing costs* as *period expenses.* Contrast with *full absorption costing.*

variable costs. *Costs* that change as activity levels change. Strictly speaking, variable costs are zero when the activity level is zero. See *semivariable costs.* In accounting this term most often means the sum of *direct costs* and variable *overhead.*

variable overhead variance. Difference between actual and *standard variable overhead costs.*

variables sampling. The use of a sampling technique whereby a particular quantitative characteristic of an entire population is inferred from a sample, e.g., money value. See also *estimation sampling.* Compare *attribute(s) sampling.*

variance. Difference between actual and *standard costs* or between *budgeted* and actual *expenditures* or, sometimes, *expenses.* The word has completely different meanings in accounting and statistics, where it is a measure of dispersion of a distribution.

variance analysis (investigation). The investigation of the causes of *variances* in a *standard cost system.* This term has different meaning in statistics.

variation analysis. Analysis of the causes of changes in items of interest in financial statements such as net *income* or *gross margin.*

VAT. *Value added tax.*

vendor. A seller. Sometimes spelled, "vender."

verifiable. A qualitative *objective* of financial reporting specifying that items in *financial statements* can be checked by tracing back to *underlying documents*—supporting *invoices*, canceled *checks*, and other physical pieces of evidence.

verification. The auditor's act of reviewing or checking items in *financial statements* by tracing back to *underlying documents*—supporting *invoices*, canceled *checks*, and other business documents—or sending out *confirmations* to be returned. Compare with *physical verification.*

vertical analysis. Analysis of the financial statements of a single firm or across several firms for a particular time, as opposed to *horizontal* or time-series analysis where items are compared over time for a single firm or across firms.

vertical integration. The extension of activity by an organization into business directly related to the production or distribution of the organization's end products. Although products may be sold to others at various stages, a substantial portion of the output at each stage is devoted to the production of the end products. Compare *horizontal integration.*

vested. Said of an employee's *pension plan* benefits that are not contingent on the employee's continuing to work for the employer.

visual curve fitting method. Sometimes, when only rough approximations to the amounts of *fixed* and *variable costs* are required, one need not engage in a formal *regression analysis*, but need merely plot the data and draw in a line by hand that seems to fit the data, using the parameters of that line for the rough approximations.

volume variance. *Production volume variance.* Less often, used to mean *sales volume variance.*

voucher. A document that signals recognition of a *liability* and authorizes the disbursement of cash. Sometimes used to refer to the written evidence documenting an *accounting entry*, as in the term *journal voucher.*

voucher system. A method for controlling *cash* that requires each *check* to be authorized with an approved

voucher. No *disbursements* of currency or coins are made except from *petty cash funds.*

W

wage. Compensation of employees based on time worked or output of product for manual labor. But see *take-home pay.*

warrant. A certificate entitling the owner to buy a specified number of shares at a specified time(s) for a specified price. Differs from a *stock option* only in that options are granted to employees and warrants are issued to the public. See *right.*

warranty. A promise by a seller to correct deficiencies in products sold. When warranties are given, proper accounting practice recognizes an estimate of warranty *expense* and an *estimated liability* at the time of sale. See *guarantee* for contrast in proper usage.

wash sale. The sale and purchase of the same or similar *asset* within a short time period. For *income tax* purposes, *losses* on a sale of stock may not be recognized if equivalent stock is purchased within 30 days before or 30 days after the date of sale.

waste. Residue of material from manufacturing operations with no sale value. Frequently, it has negative value because additional costs must be incurred for disposal.

wasting asset. A *natural resource* having a limited *useful life* and, hence, subject to *amortization*, called *depletion.* Examples are timberland, oil and gas wells, and ore deposits.

watered stock. Shares issued for *assets* with *fair market value* less than *par* or *stated value.* The assets are put onto the books at the overstated values. In the law, for shares to be considered watered, the *board of directors* must have acted in bad faith or fraudulently in issuing the shares under these circumstances. The term originated from a former practice of cattlemen who fed cattle ("stock") large quantities of salt to make them thirsty. The cattle then drank a lot of water before being taken to market. This was done to make the cattle appear heavier and more valuable than otherwise.

weighted average. An average computed by counting each occurrence of each value, not merely a single occurrence of each value. For example, if one unit is purchased for $1 and two units are purchased for $2 each, then the simple average of the purchase prices is $1.50 but the weighted average price per unit is $5/3 = $1.67. Contrast with *moving average.*

weighted-average inventory method. Valuing either *withdrawals* or *ending inventory* at the *weighted-average* purchase price of all units on hand at the time of withdrawal or of computing ending inventory. The *inventory equation* is used to calculate the other quantity. If the *perpetual inventory* method is in use, often called the "moving average method."

where-got, where-gone statement. A term used by W. M. Cole for a statement much like the *statement of cash flows*.

wind up. To bring to an end, such as the life of a corporation. The later is accomplished either by following the winding-up provisions of applicable statutes, surrendering the charter or following bankruptcy proceedings. See also *liquidation*.

window dressing. The attempt to make financial statements show *operating* results, or *financial position*, more favorable than would be otherwise shown.

with recourse. See *note receivable discounted*.

withdrawals. *Assets* distributed to an owner. *Partner's drawings*. See *inventory equation* for another context.

withholding. Deductions from *salaries* or *wages*, usually for *income taxes*, to be remitted by the employer, in the employee's name, to the taxing authority.

without recourse. See *note receivable discounted*.

work in process (inventory account). Partially completed product; an asset that is classified as *inventory*.

work sheet (program). A computer program that is designed to combine explanations and calculations. This type of program is useful in preparing *financial statements, schedules,* and *worksheets*. It is a tabular schedule for convenient summary of *adjusting* and *closing entries*. The work sheet usually begins with an *unadjusted trial balance*. Adjusting entries are shown in the next two columns, one for *debts* and one for *credits*. The horizontal sum of each line is then carried to the right into either the *income statement or balance sheet* column, as appropriate. The *plug* to equate the income statement column totals is the income, if a debit plug is required, or loss, if a credit plug is required, for the period. That income will be closed to retained earnings on the balance sheet. The income statement credit columns are the revenues for the period and the debit columns are the expenses (and revenue *contras*) to be shown on the income statement. Work sheet is also used to refer to *schedules* for determining other items appearing on the *financial statements* that require adjustment or compilation.

working capital. *Current assets* minus *current liabilities*.

working papers. The schedules and analyses prepared by the *auditor* in carrying out investigations prior to issuing an *opinion* on *financial statements*.

worth. *Value.* See *net worth*.

worth-debt ratio. Reciprocal of the *debt-equity ratio*. See *ratio*.

write down. *Write off*, except that not all the assets' cost is charged to expense or *loss*. Generally used for nonrecurring items.

write off. *Charge* an *asset* to *expense* or *loss*; that is, *debit* expense (or loss) and *credit* asset.

write-off method. A method for treating *uncollectible accounts* that charges *bad debt expense* and credits accounts receivable of specific customers as uncollectible amounts are identified. May not be used when uncollectible amounts are significant and can be estimated. See *bad debt expense, sales contra, estimated uncollectibles* and the *allowance method* for contrast.

write up. To increase the recorded *cost* of an *asset* with no corresponding *disbursement* of *funds*; that is, *debit* asset and *credit revenue*, or perhaps, *owners' equity*. Seldom done because currently accepted accounting principles are based on actual transactions. When a portfolio of *marketable equity securities* increases in market value subsequent to a previously recognized decrease, the *book value* of the portfolio is written up—the debit is to the *contra account*.

Y

yield. *Internal rate of return* of a stream of cash flows. Cash yield is cash flow divided by book value. See also *dividend yield*.

yield to maturity. At a given time, the *internal rate of return* of a series of cash flows, usually said of a *bond*. Sometimes called the "effective rate."

yield variance. The portion of an *efficiency variance* that is not the *mix variance*.

Z

zero-base(d) budgeting. ZBB. In preparing an ordinary *budget* for the next period, a manager starts with the budget for the current period and makes adjustments as seem necessary, because of changed conditions for the next period. Because most managers like to increase the scope of the activities managed and since most prices increase most of the time, amounts in budgets prepared in the ordinary, incremental way seem to increase period after period. The authority approving the budget assumes operations will be carried out in the same way as in the past and that next period's expenditures will have to be at least as large as the current period's. Thus, this authority tends to study only the increments to the current period's budget. In ZBB, the authority questions the process for carrying out a program and the entire budget for next period. Every dollar in the budget is studied, not just the dollars incremental to the previous period's amounts. The advocates of ZBB claim that in this way: (1) programs or divisions of marginal benefit to the business or governmental unit will more likely be deleted from the program, rather than being continued with costs at least as large as the present ones and (2) alternative, more cost-effective, ways of carrying out programs are more likely to be discovered and implemented. ZBB implies questioning the existence of programs, and the fundamental nature of the way they are carried out, not merely the amounts used to fund them. Experts appear to be evenly divided as to whether the middle word should be "base" or "based."

GENERAL ELECTRIC
1989 Annual Report

Authors' Introduction

This section excerpts from General Electric's Annual Report. GE's Annual Reports are consistently among the best we see. The first twenty-four pages of the annual report, which we have not reproduced, give general information about the company, illustrations, and highlights of the year's operations. We comment on various aspects of the financial statements in numbered comments keyed to the GE Annual Report. We leave the page numbers of the original report intact and references, both in the report and in our comments, use these numbers.

Our comments appear on a page near the page of the annual report we comment on. Our comments begin at the bottom of this page. We have inserted circled numbers—referred to as callouts—in the annual report to refer to the comments. The Glossary explains all accounting terms we use in our comments.

We can think of no better way to learn financial accounting than to try to understand all that appears in GE's statements. (The GE corporate symbol—known as "the meatball" at GE—as it appears above is a trademark of General Electric Company. It is, perhaps, the single most valuable asset of the Company. In accordance with generally accepted accounting principles, this asset does not appear in the financial statements.)

Authors' Comments on General Electric Annual Report

① This is the first of our numbered comments. These paragraphs indicate management's taking responsibility for the preparation of the financial statements. We have deleted two paragraphs from the original letter, which appears on page 44 of the annual report.

② The paragraphs here comprise the auditors' report. This particular report is both nonqualified ("clean") and in standard format. The first two paragraphs of the auditors' report describe the work done. The third paragraph gives the opinion. The fourth paragraph describes a change in accounting principles to alert the reader to an inconsistency across time. See GE's income statement near the callout for our comment 8. The auditors' report appears in the published annual report on page 45, but we reproduce it here for convenience.

③ This is the income statement.

Management's Discusion of ① Financial Responsibility

The financial information in this report, including the audited financial statements, has been prepared by management. Preparation of financial statements and related data involves estimates and the use of judgment. Accounting principles used in preparing the financial statements are those that are generally accepted in the United States. These principles are consistent in most important respects with standards issued to date by the International Accounting Standards Committee. Where there is no single specified accounting principle or standard, management makes a choice from reasonable, accepted alternatives, using methods that it believes are prudent for General Electric Company and its consolidated affiliates.

KPMG Peat Marwick provide an objective, independent review of management's discharge of its obligations relating to the fairness of reported operating results and financial condition. Their report for 1989 appears on the opposite page.

The Audit Committee of the Board (consisting solely of Directors from outside GE) maintains an ongoing appraisal — on behalf of share owners — of the effectiveness of the independent auditors, the Company's staff of corporate auditors and management, with respect to the financial reporting process, and of the adequacy of internal financial controls. The committee also reviews the Company's accounting policies, compliance with key policies, and the Annual Report and proxy material.

John F. Welch, Jr.

John F. Welch, Jr.
Chairman of the Board and
Chief Executive Officer

Dennis D. Dammerman

Dennis D. Dammerman
Senior Vice President
Finance

February 16, 1990

Independent Auditors' Report ②

To Share Owners and Board of Directors of General Electric Company

We have audited the accompanying statement of financial position of General Electric Company and consolidated affiliates as of December 31, 1989 and 1988 and the related statements of earnings and cash flows for each of the years in the three-year period ended December 31, 1989. These consolidated financial statements are the responsibility of the Company's management. Our responsibility is to express an opinion on these consolidated financial statements based on our audits.

We conducted our audits in accordance with generally accepted auditing standards. Those standards require that we plan and perform the audit to obtain reasonable assurance about whether the financial statements are free of material misstatement. An audit includes examining, on a test basis, evidence supporting the amounts and disclosures in the financial statements. An audit also includes assessing the accounting principles used and significant estimates made by management, as well as evaluating the overall financial statement presentation. We believe that our audits provide a reasonable basis for our opinion.

In our opinion, the aforementioned financial statements appearing on pages 26-31 and 46-68 present fairly, in all material respects, the financial position of General Electric Company and consolidated affiliates at December 31, 1989 and 1988, and the results of their operations and their cash flows for each of the years in the three-year period ended December 31, 1989, in conformity with generally accepted accounting principles.

As discussed in note 1 to the consolidated financial statements, in 1987 the Company changed its methods of accounting for income taxes and overhead recorded in inventory. We concur with these accounting changes.

KPMG Peat Marwick

KPMG Peat Marwick
Stamford, Connecticut

February 16, 1990

Statement of Earnings ③

For the years ended December 31 (In millions)	General Electric Company and consolidated affiliates		
	1989	1988	1987
Revenues			
Sales of goods	$31,314	$28,953	$29,937
Sales of services	9,673	9,840	9,370
Other income (note 3)	690	675	655
Earnings of GEFS	—	—	—
GEFS revenues from operations (note 4)	12,897	10,621	8,196
Total revenues	54,574	50,089	48,158
Costs and expenses (note 5)			
Cost of goods sold	22,827	21,155	22,359
Cost of services sold	6,873	7,676	7,290
Interest and other financial charges (note 7)	6,591	4,817	3,912
Insurance policy holder losses and benefits	1,614	1,501	1,560
Provision for losses on financing receivables (note 8)	527	434	290
Other costs and expenses	10,355	9,724	8,406
Unusual expenses, including provisions for business restructurings (note 9)	—	—	1,118
Minority interest in net earnings (loss) of consolidated affiliates	84	61	(4)
Total costs and expenses	48,871	45,368	44,931
Earnings before income taxes, extraordinary item and cumulative effect of accounting changes	5,703	4,721	3,227
Provision for income taxes (note 10)	(1,764)	(1,335)	(1,108)
Earnings before extraordinary item and cumulative effect of accounting changes	3,939	3,386	2,119
Extraordinary item (note 25)	—	—	(62)
Cumulative effect to January 1, 1987 of accounting changes			
Initial application of Statement of Financial Accounting Standards No. 96 — "Accounting for Income Taxes" (note 1)	—	—	577
Change in overhead recorded in inventory (note 1)	—	—	281
Net earnings	$ 3,939	$ 3,386	$ 2,915
Net earnings per share (in dollars)			
Before extraordinary item and cumulative effect of accounting changes	$ 4.36	$ 3.75	$ 2.33
Extraordinary item (note 25)	—	—	(.07)
Cumulative effect to January 1, 1987 of accounting changes			
Initial application of Statement of Financial Accounting Standards No. 96 — "Accounting for Income Taxes" (note 1)	—	—	.63
Change in overhead recorded in inventory (note 1)	—	—	.31
Net earnings per share	$ 4.36	$ 3.75	$ 3.20
Dividends declared per share (in dollars)	$ 1.70	$ 1.46	$ 1.32

The notes to consolidated financial statements on pages 46-68 are an integral part of this statement.

	GE			GEFS	
1989	1988	1987	1989	1988	1987
$31,326	$28,958	$29,937	$ —	$ —	$ —
9,693	9,866	9,378	—	—	—
704	680	649	—	—	—
927	788	552	—	—	—
—	—	—	12,945	10,655	8,225
42,650	40,292	40,516	12,945	10,655	8,225
22,839	21,160	22,359	—	—	—
6,893	7,702	7,298	—	—	—
726	669	645	5,912	4,177	3,277
—	—	—	1,614	1,501	1,560
—	—	—	527	434	290
6,662	6,250	5,979	3,708	3,484	2,440
—	—	1,027	—	—	91
38	29	1	46	32	(5)
37,158	35,810	37,309	11,807	9,628	7,653
5,492	4,482	3,207	1,138	1,027	572
(1,553)	(1,096)	(1,088)	(211)	(239)	(20)
3,939	3,386	2,119	927	788	552
—	—	(62)	—	—	(62)
—	—	577	—	—	518
—	—	281	—	—	—
$ 3,939	$ 3,386	$ 2,915	$ 927	$ 788	$ 1,008

In the supplemental consolidating data on this page, "GE" means the pre-1988 basis of consolidation as described in note 1 to the consolidated financial statements; "GEFS" means General Electric Financial Services, Inc. and all of its affiliates and associated companies. Transactions between GE and GEFS have been eliminated from the "General Electric Company and consolidated affiliates" columns on the preceding page. Eliminations are shown on page 47.

④ GE presents income statements for three economic entities. See GE's discussion in its note 1 on page 46. GE presents the first set of columns because GAAP require them. GE prefers the presentation in the other columns, for reasons it explains in its own notes.

⑤ SEC *Staff Accounting Bulletin 67* requires separate disclosure of gains and losses from restructuring of a business. These items appear among income from continuing operations. A firm must report separately results of operations it plans to discontinue. To be included in "Discontinued operations" on the income statement, a firm must discontinue an entire line of business. If a firm remains in a line of business but restructures or sells or abandons part of the assets of the business, it does not include the gains or losses in "Discontinued operations" but classifies them separately, as GE does here, with other income from continuing operations.

⑥ GE does not own all the shares in all of its consolidated subsidiaries. Some of the shares belong to outsiders, called the *minority interest*.
Refer to the data for 1988 and 1989, where GE adds amounts for this item. The minority interest's share of the earnings of the subsidiary companies does not belong to GE's shareholders. Hence, in deriving income to GE's shareholders, GE subtracts the minority interest's share in earnings from the earnings of the consolidated group of companies. GE accomplishes the subtraction by adding the amount to the "costs and expenses."
Note that this reduction in income uses no cash so that there is an adjustment on the Statement of Cash Flows for this charge against income. The item is too small, however, to appear separately in the Statement.
For 1987, the less-than-100-percent-owned consolidated subsidiaries apparently had a loss for the year—negative net income. GE's shareholders do not bear all of that loss, so it adds the minority interest's share of the loss to the earnings of the consolidated group (subtracted from "costs and expenses") in deriving GE's shareholders' net income.

⑦ Provision usually means "estimated expense" in this country; see the Glossary at *provision* for the contrast in this word's meanings in the U.S. and the U.K.

⑧ GE explains the large increase in 1987 income; see its notes about income taxes on page 47, right column. That note also explains that firms have an option to adopt *SFAS No. 96* early. GE adopted those rules in 1987. Survey of data for other firms indicates that most of the early adopters, like GE, show increased reported income from the early adoption.

⑨ GE's note 1 on pages 47-48 explains that it now charges to inventory accounts costs it previously charged to expense. This results in delaying the reporting of expense. Ultimately, GE reports the item as expense when it sells the goods.

⑩ This is primary earnings per share, as called for by APB *Opinion No. 15*. Firms need not separately show fully diluted earnings per share if it is within 3 percent of primary earnings per share.

⑪ GE uses the completed contract method of recognizing revenue from long term construction contracts; see GE's Summary of Significant Accounting Policies on GE page 47 at "Sales" and our comment 32. As GE incurs costs on these contracts it makes journal entries such as:

Work in Process Inventory for Long Term Contracts X
    Various Assets and Liabilities   X
To record cost of construction activity.

Some of GE's long term construction contracts provide that the customer shall make progress payments to GE as GE does the work. GE does not recognize revenue until it completes the work, so the journal entry GE makes at the time it receives cash is one such as:

Cash . . . .   Y
   Advances from Customers on Long Term Contracts . . . .   Y
To record cash received and to set up the corresponding liability.

When GE prepares the balance sheet, it nets the amounts in the inventory accounts, X (debit balance), against the amounts in the liability accounts, Y (credit balance). If there is a net credit balance, as here, with Y greater than X, then GE records the difference, Y - X, as a liability. GE shows this liability under the title "Progress collections." On contracts where the amounts in the inventory account exceed the cash collections, then the difference, X - Y, appears as an asset under a title such as "Costs Incurred on Long term Contracts in Excess of Billings." ARB *No. 45* requires this netting of costs incurred against cash collections and the separate showing of the excesses. On many of its contracts, the only cash GE collects before completion of construction is for engineering costs incurred in preparation to undertake construction. GE expenses these engineering costs, rather than accumulating them in Work in Process inventory accounts. Thus, there is no asset account to net against the liability. The "Progress collections" title is appropriate because it tends to represent gross "advances from customers," rather than a netting of work in process inventory against advances from customers. The "price adjustments accrued" represent amounts that GE expects to have to pay in the future but which it will not specifically collect from the buyer under the contract.

⑫ (Refer to our comment 6 for a description of "minority interest" on the income statement.) This account represents the equity of the minority shareholders in the consolidated affiliates. From the point of view of GE's shareholders, this equity belonging to the minority is a liability. From the point of view of an outsider, such as a government regulator or labor union negotiator, the minority shareholders' interest is part of total owners' equity. Whether one believes that minority interest is a liability or an item of owners' equity depends upon whether one views the financial statements as being prepared for the shareholders of GE (the proprietorship theory) or for all potential readers (the entity theory). Note that GE avoids the issue by not classifying "minority interest" either with liabilities or with owners' equity.

⑬ GE uses the cost method of accounting for treasury stock and shows the cost of its own shares acquired on the market as contra to all of owners' equity. Refer to our comment 93.

⑭ In its preferred financial statement presentation—the second pair of columns here, GE uses the equity method for General Electric Financial Services (GEFS). Because GE has owned 100 percent of GEFS since it was organized, GE's investment (asset) account for GEFS mirrors GEFS's owners' equity accounts. Consider the possible transactions. GE makes an investment in GEFS by sending it cash: GE debits the investment account; GEFS credits a contributed capital account. GEFS earns income: GEFS credits retained earnings and GE, using the equity method, debits the investment account. GEFS declares a dividend: GEFS debits retained earnings; GE, using the equity method, credits the investment account. GE's investment account in GEFS equals GEFS's total owners' equity.

⑮ The FASB requires GE (and other firms) to consolidate all majority-owned and controlled subsidiaries. GE consolidates GEFS in its first pair of columns in the balance sheet presentation. After consolidation, all GEFS's assets and liabilities appear on GE's balance sheet. GE's consolidated retained earnings do not differ, however, because the equity method records income of unconsolidated subsidiaries as earned. In consolidation, GE adds $6,069 (= $90,928 - $84,141 - $718) million of net assets to its balance sheet and eliminates the account "Investments in GEFS."

Statement of Financial Position

At December 31 (In millions)	General Electric Company and consolidated affiliates	
	1989	1988
Assets		
Cash and equivalents (note 11)	$ 2,258	$ 2,456
Marketable securities carried at cost (note 12)	6,799	5,510
Marketable securities carried at market (note 13)	8,488	5,089
Securities purchased under agreements to resell	16,020	13,811
Current receivables (note 14)	6,976	6,780
Inventories (note 15)	6,655	6,486
GEFS financing receivables (investment in time sales, loans and financing leases) — net (note 16)	41,779	35,832
Other GEFS receivables (note 17)	5,476	4,699
Property, plant and equipment (including equipment leased to others) — net (note 18)	15,646	13,611
Investment in GEFS	—	—
Intangible assets (note 19)	8,822	8,552
All other assets (note 20)	9,425	8,039
Total assets	**$128,344**	**$110,865**
Liabilities and equity		
Short-term borrowings (note 21)	$ 37,200	$ 30,422
Accounts payable (note 22)	6,666	6,004
Securities sold under agreements to repurchase	16,555	13,864
Securities sold but not yet purchased, at market (note 23)	4,090	2,088
Progress collections and price adjustments accrued ⑪	3,315	3,504
Dividends payable	426	369
All other GE current costs and expenses accrued (note 24)	5,650	5,549
Long-term borrowings (note 25)	16,110	15,082
Reserves of insurance affiliates	5,032	4,177
All other liabilities (notes 17 and 26)	7,866	6,986
Deferred income taxes (note 27)	3,543	3,373
Total liabilities	106,453	91,418
Minority interest in equity of consolidated affiliates (note 28) ⑫	1,001	981
Common stock (926,564,000 shares issued)	584	584
Other capital	826	823
Retained earnings	20,352	17,950
Less common stock held in treasury ⑬	(872)	(891)
Total share owners' equity (notes 29 and 30)	20,890	18,466
Total liabilities and equity	**$128,344**	**$110,865**
Commitments and contingent liabilities (note 31)		

The notes to consolidated financial statements on pages 46-68 are an integral part of this statement.

	GE		⑮ GEFS	
	1989	1988	1989	1988
	$ 1,749	$ 1,823	$ 509	$ 633
	49	80	6,750	5,430
	—	—	8,488	5,089
	—	—	16,020	13,811
	7,218	7,110	—	—
	6,655	6,486	—	—
	—	—	41,779	35,939
	—	—	5,856	4,806
	9,666	9,360	5,980	4,251
⑭	6,069	4,819	—	—
	7,048	6,984	1,774	1,568
	5,653	4,621	3,772	3,418
	$ 44,107	$ 41,283	$ 90,928	$ 74,945
	$ 1,696	$ 1,861	$ 35,740	$ 28,731
	2,901	2,136	4,144	4,132
	—	—	16,555	13,864
	—	—	4,090	2,088
	3,315	3,504	—	—
	426	369	—	—
	5,650	5,549	—	—
	3,947	4,330	12,165	10,862
	—	—	5,032	4,177
	5,635	5,481	2,236	1,505
	(636)	(641)	4,179	4,014
	22,934	22,589	84,141	69,373
	283	228	718	753
	584	584	1	1
	826	823	1,702	1,379
	20,352	17,950	4,366	3,439
	(872)	(891)	—	—
	20,890	18,466	⑭ 6,069	4,819
	$ 44,107	$ 41,283	$ 90,928	$ 74,945

In the supplemental consolidating data on this page, "GE" means the pre-1988 basis of consolidation as described in note 1 to the consolidated financial statements; "GEFS" means General Electric Financial Services, Inc. and all of its affiliates and associated companies. Transactions between GE and GEFS have been eliminated from the "General Electric Company and consolidated affiliates" columns on the preceding page. Eliminations are shown on page 47.

The consolidation policy with respect to GEFS affects the appearance of the financial statements. Below, we show two key financial ratios, as they would be calculated from year-end account balances.

GENERAL ELECTRIC AND GE FINANCIAL SERVICES, INC., 1989
(For Authors' comment 15)

Using Equity Method for GEFS (from second set of columns)	Consolidating GEFS (as reported) (from first set of columns)

Rate of Return on Assets:

$$\frac{\$3,939 + \$38^a + (.66 \times \$726^b)}{\$34,591 \quad 44,107} \qquad\qquad \frac{\$3,939 + \$84^a + (.66 \times \$6,591^b)}{\$128,334}$$

$$= \frac{\$\,4,456}{\$44,107} = 10.1\% \qquad\qquad\qquad = \frac{\$\,8,373}{\$128,334} = 6.5\%$$

Debt-Equity Ratio:

$$\frac{\$22,934}{\$44,107} = 52\% \qquad\qquad\qquad \frac{\$106,453}{\$128,334} = 83\%$$

a. Minority interest in net income from income statement.
b. Interest expense. Multiply by .66 (= 1.00 - .34 federal tax rate) to state on after-tax basis.

---

⑯ This statement starts with net income as shown in the income statement on pages 26 and 27. The next four lines show subtractions for revenues and other credits to income that did not produce cash and additions for expenses and other charges against income that did not use cash. The next six lines show the uses of cash for increases in working capital and sources of cash from decreases in working capital.

The Statement of Cash Flows Position classifies sources and uses of cash into three types: operating activities, financing activities, and investment activities. The accountant must classify cash used to increase the other working capital items (or cash provided from decreases in the other working capital items) as one of these three. The FASB requires that these items appear as operating items. One could argue that using cash to acquire inventory is an investing item, just as is acquiring plant. Similarly, one could argue that saving cash by letting accounts payable increase is a financing item, just as is borrowing from a bank.

Total funds produced by operations appears after these adjustments to income. This presentation is known as the "indirect method" because we derive cash indirectly, from income with adjustments. An acceptable alternative format, the "direct method," shows only those revenues that produce cash and subtracts only those expenses that use cash in deriving cash provided by operations.

⑰ Depreciation expense reduces net income without using cash currently. Hence, its amount increases the amount of net income in deriving funds provided by operations. The firm used cash some time in the past when it acquired the depreciable assets; see "Additions to property, plant, and equipment," at our comment 23, below.

(18) GE includes all earnings of GEFS, which were $927 million in 1989, in income under the equity method. GEFS declared no dividends in 1989; note that GEFS's Retained earnings account increased by $927, from $3,439 to $4,366, during 1989. This amount equals GEFS's earnings, so GEFS declared no dividends. The $927 million income, therefore, provided no cash to GE (the income produced a larger investment balance on GE's balance sheet) and GE must subtract it from net income to derive its cash from operations.

(19) For GE consolidated (first set of columns), income tax expense for each of the three the years exceeded the amount of income taxes payable. See the discussion at GE's note 10 and our comments there. Because GE used less cash for income taxes than it reported as income tax expense, it must add back the amount of expense not using cash in deriving cash from operations.

(20) Increases in accounts receivables use funds, just as increases in property and plant use funds. Conversely, decreases in accounts receivable provide funds.

(21) Increases in inventories use funds, just as increases in property and plant use funds. Conversely, decreases in inventories provide funds.

(22) Increases in accounts payable provide funds, just as increases in long-term debt provide funds. Conversely, decreases in accounts payable use funds.

(23) The primary use of funds for most companies most of the time is the acquisition of new property, plant, and equipment to replace the old as it wears out and to grow. The amounts here will appear on the income statement in future periods as depreciation charges. GE uses funds when it acquires assets. GE's income decreases in later periods when it uses the assets.

(24) Because of GE's triple presentation, discussed in our comment 4, GE uses an unclassified balance sheet which does not distinguish current assets and liabilities from noncurrent ones. If GE were to classify its balance sheet items as current or noncurrent, then this item would report a change in a current liability and it would necessarily appear in the operating section. The largest single equity of GEFS are these short-term borrowings (see the balance sheet on page 29). GE, correctly in our opinion, views this item as financing, not as operating. GAAP would allow GE to show the item as operating.

(25) As is preferable, GE shows separately cash provided by new long-term borrowings and cash used to reduce old long-term borrowings. Some companies show only the net effect, as GE does on the line above for "less than 90-day maturities," either as a source or use of cash; they provide no information about the amount of actual borrowings and repayments during the period.

(26) GE demonstrates that the net uses of cash ($198 million in 1989) exactly explains the change in the Cash and equivalents account on the balance sheet.

(27) APB *Opinion No. 22* requires that all annual reports include a summary of significant accounting policies used so that the reader can know which accounting alternatives have been chosen by the company.

(28) Before 1988 a parent, such as GE, usually consolidated a subsidiary which met all three of the following criteria:

   (i)   The parent owned more than 50 percent of the voting shares of the subsidiary.

   (ii) There were no important restrictions on the ability of the parent to exercise control of the subsidiary.

   (iii) The asset and equity structure of the subsidiary did not significantly differ from that of the parent.

In 1988, the FASB eliminated the third criterion above, requiring consolidation when the parent/subsidiary relations meet the first two. GE believes that the financial statements make more sense if it does not consolidate GEFS; hence, it presents three sets of financial statements.

(29) In this presentation, GE consolidates all "majority owned" (greater than 50 percent) and "controlled" companies except the finance companies which are not similar to the others in the consolidated group. Instead, GE accounts for the finance affiliates using the equity method. As

Statement of Cash Flow

For the years ended December 31 (In millions)		General Electric Company and consolidated affiliates		
		1989	1988	1987
Cash flows from operating activities				
Net earnings	(16)	$ 3,939	$ 3,386	$ 2,915
Adjustments to reconcile net earnings to cash provided from operating activities				
Extraordinary item and cumulative effect of changes in accounting principles		—	—	(796)
Depreciation, depletion and amortization	(17)	2,256	2,266	1,913
Earnings retained by GEFS	(18)	—	—	—
Deferred income taxes	(19)	281	124	37
Decrease (increase) in GE current receivables	(20)	(100)	123	138
Decrease (increase) in GE inventories	(21)	(167)	(209)	375
Increase (decrease) in accounts payable	(22)	503	303	149
Increase in insurance reserves		486	315	669
Provision for losses on financing receivables		527	434	290
Net change in certain broker-dealer accounts		(872)	(573)	(103)
All other operating activities		(230)	933	252
Cash provided from operating activities		6,623	7,102	5,839
Cash flows from investing activities				
Property, plant and equipment including equipment leased to others				
Additions	(23)	(5,474)	(3,681)	(2,277)
Dispositions		1,294	470	890
Net increase in GEFS financing receivables		(6,649)	(6,057)	(4,575)
Payments for principal businesses purchased, net of cash acquired		(1,860)	(3,504)	(555)
Proceeds from principal business dispositions		—	880	646
All other investing activities		(400)	(1,620)	(1,097)
Cash used for investing activities		(13,089)	(13,512)	(6,968)
Cash flows from financing activities				
Net change in borrowings (less than 90-day maturities)	(24)	7,360	3,868	2,519
Debt having maturities more than 90 days				
Newly issued	(25)	8,078	11,324	8,219
Repayments and other reductions		(7,710)	(8,801)	(6,883)
Sale of preferred stock by GE Capital		—	600	—
Disposition of GE shares from treasury (mainly for employee plans)		509	356	361
Purchase of GE shares for treasury		(490)	(387)	(846)
Dividends paid to GE share owners		(1,479)	(1,263)	(1,177)
Cash provided from (used for) financing activities		6,268	5,697	2,193
Increase (decrease) in cash and equivalents during year	(26)	(198)	(713)	1,064
Cash and equivalents at beginning of year		2,456	3,169	2,105
Cash and equivalents at end of year		$ 2,258	$ 2,456	$ 3,169

The notes to consolidated financial statements on pages 46-68 are an integral part of this statement.

	GE			GEFS	
1989	1988	1987	1989	1988	1987
$ 3,939	$ 3,386	$ 2,915	⑱ $ 927	$ 788	$ 1,008
—	—	(796)	—	—	(456)
1,524	1,522	1,544	732	744	369
⑱ (927)	(788)	(552)	—	—	—
178	(215)	(158)	103	339	195
(12)	(170)	111	—	—	—
(167)	(209)	375	—	—	—
693	(342)	21	(75)	693	48
—	—	—	486	315	669
—	—	—	527	434	290
—	—	—	(872)	(573)	(103)
(468)	440	413	256	751	159
4,760	3,624	3,873	2,084	3,491	2,179
(2,217)	(1,884)	(1,698)	(3,257)	(1,797)	(579)
205	118	410	1,089	352	480
—	—	—	(6,542)	(5,943)	(4,627)
(759)	(2,963)	—	(1,101)	(541)	(555)
—	880	646	—	—	—
115	444	(6)	(801)	(2,007)	(1,282)
(2,656)	(3,405)	(648)	(10,612)	(9,936)	(6,563)
850	(466)	(961)	6,576	4,249	3,515
204	934	396	7,874	10,291	7,818
(1,772)	(30)	(238)	(6,046)	(8,771)	(6,645)
—	—	—	—	600	—
509	356	361	—	—	—
(490)	(387)	(846)	—	—	—
(1,479)	(1,263)	(1,177)	—	—	—
(2,178)	(856)	(2,465)	8,404	6,369	4,688
(74)	(637)	760	(124)	(76)	304
1,823	2,460	1,700	633	709	405
$ 1,749	$ 1,823	$ 2,460	$ 509	$ 633	$ 709

In the supplemental consolidating data on this page, "GE" means the pre-1988 basis of consolidation as described in note 1 to the consolidated financial statements; "GEFS" means General Electric Financial Services, Inc. and all of its affiliates and associated companies. Transactions between GE and GEFS have been eliminated from the "General Electric Company and consolidated affiliates" columns on the preceding page. Eliminations are shown on page 47.

Notes to Consolidated Financial Statements

Index

Subject	Page
Accounting Policies (note 1)	46
Accounts Payable (note 22)	60
Acquisitions (note 2)	49
Allowance for Losses on Financing Receivables (note 8)	53
Borrowings — Long-Term (note 25)	60
Borrowings — Short-Term (note 21)	59
Cash and Equivalents (note 11)	55
Cash Flows — Supplemental Information (note 32)	63
Commitments and Contingent Liabilities (note 31)	63
Income Taxes — Deferred (note 27)	61
Income Taxes — Provision for (note 10)	54
Intangible Assets (note 19)	58
Interest and Other Financial Charges (note 7)	53
Inventories (note 15)	55
Marketable Securities Carried at Cost (note 12)	55
Marketable Securities Carried at Market — GEFS (note 13)	55
Minority Interest in Equity (note 28)	61
Other Assets (note 20)	58
Other Costs and Expenses Accrued — GE (note 24)	60
Other Income (note 3)	50
Other Liabilities (note 26)	61
Pensions and Other Retiree Benefits (note 6)	52
Property, Plant and Equipment (note 18)	57
Quarterly Information [unaudited] (note 35)	68
Receivables and Payables — Brokers and Dealers (note 17)	57
Receivables — Current — GE (note 14)	55
Receivables — Financing — GEFS (note 16)	56
Revenues from Operations — GEFS (note 4)	51
Securities Sold but Not Yet Purchased (note 23)	60
Segments — Geographic (note 34)	68
Segments — Industry (note 33)	64
Share Owners' Equity (note 29)	62
Stock-Related Information — Other (note 30)	62
Supplemental Cost Details (note 5)	51
Unusual Expenses (note 9)	53

Note 1 Summary of Significant Accounting Policies

Consolidation and financial statement presentation

Consolidation. The consolidated financial statements represent the adding together of all companies in which General Electric Company directly or indirectly has a majority ownership or otherwise controls ("affiliated companies"). Prior to 1988, results of financial services affiliates — the principal one being General Electric Financial Services, Inc. (GEFS or GE Financial Services) and its affiliated companies — were included on the equity basis as one line in total earnings and net assets. This was permissible under accounting rules in effect before 1988. Because financial services operations are so different in nature from and essentially unrelated to operations of other GE businesses, management believed that financial statements were more understandable if GEFS' statements were shown separately. It should be emphasized that, under both current and prior procedures, consolidated net earnings and share owners' equity are the same for all periods presented. However, substantially more detail is required under the current standard than under rules previously in effect. Also as a result of this change, the Company adopted an unclassified consolidated statement of financial position.

Management believes it is important to preserve as much as possible the identity of the principal financial data and related measurements to which share owners and others have become accustomed over the years. Accordingly, consolidated financial statements and notes now are generally presented in a format that includes data grouped basically as follows.

- *GE* — this is essentially the pre-1988 basis of consolidation except that it includes some very small financial services affiliates previously not consolidated. The effect of transactions among companies within this group has been eliminated. Where appropriate for clarification or emphasis, particularly in the notes, this group of entities also is referred to as "GE except GEFS."

- *GEFS* — this affiliate owns all of the common stock of General Electric Capital Corporation (GECC or GE Capital) and of Employers Reinsurance Corporation (ERC), and 80% of the stock of Kidder, Peabody Group Inc. (Kidder, Peabody). These affiliates and their respective affiliates are consolidated in the GEFS columns with the effect of transactions among them eliminated before the consolidated presentation.

(30) ▪ **Consolidated** — these columns represent the adding together of GE and GEFS. However, it is necessary to remove the effect of transactions between GE except GEFS and GEFS to arrive at a consolidated total. The "eliminations" used to arrive at these consolidated totals are summarized below.

Eliminations
(In millions)

	1989	1988	1987
Statement of Earnings			
Sales of goods	$ (12)	$ (5)	$ —
Sales of services	(20)	(26)	(8)
Other income	(14)	(5)	6
Earnings of GEFS	(927)	(788)	(552)
GEFS revenues from operations	(48)	(34)	(29)
Total revenues	(1,021)	(858)	(583)
Cost of goods sold	(12)	(5)	—
Cost of services sold	(20)	(26)	(8)
Interest and other financial charges	(47)	(29)	(10)
Other costs and expenses	(15)	(10)	(13)
Total costs and expenses	(94)	(70)	(31)
Earnings before income taxes, extraordinary item and cumulative effect of accounting changes	(927)	(788)	(552)
Extraordinary item	—	—	62
Income tax accounting change	—	—	(518)
Net earnings	$ (927)	$ (788)	$(1,008)
Statement of Financial Position			
GE current receivables	$ (242)	$ (330)	
GEFS financing receivables	—	(107)	
Other GEFS receivables	(380)	(107)	
Investment in GEFS	(6,069)	(4,819)	
Total assets	$(6,691)	$(5,363)	
Short-term borrowings	$ (236)	$ (170)	
Accounts payable	(379)	(264)	
Long-term borrowings	(2)	(110)	
All other liabilities	(5)	—	
Total liabilities	(622)	(544)	
GEFS equity	(6,069)	(4,819)	
Total liabilities and equity	$(6,691)	$(5,363)	
Statement of Cash Flows			
Net earnings (operating activities)	$ (221)	$ (13)	$ (213)
Investing activities	179	(171)	243
Financing activities	42	184	(30)
Total	$ —	$ —	$ —

Results of companies in which GE or GEFS owns between 20% and 50% ("associated companies") are (31) included in the financial statements on a "one-line" basis.

Cash flows. During 1989, the definition of "cash and equivalents" for GE except GEFS was modified to exclude marketable securities having original maturities between 90 and 365 days. GEFS' cash and equivalents, which includes only cash and very short-term (only a few days' maturities), is not affected by this modification.

Pensions and other retirement benefits. Accounting policies for pensions and other retirement benefits are discussed in note 6.

Income taxes. SFAS No. 96 — "Accounting for Income Taxes" was issued by the Financial Accounting Standards Board in December 1987. A requirement of SFAS No. 96 is that deferred tax liabilities or assets at the end of each period be determined using the tax rate expected to be in effect when taxes are actually paid or recovered. Accordingly, under SFAS No. 96 rules, income tax expense provisions will increase or decrease in the same period in which a change in tax rates is enacted. Previous rules required providing deferred taxes using rates in effect when the tax asset or liability was first recorded without subsequent adjustment solely for tax-rate changes (except with respect to leveraged leases).

In conformity with SFAS No. 96 transition rules, the Company elected to adopt the new income tax accounting during 1987. The cumulative effect to January 1, 1987 ($577 million, including $518 million for GEFS) of the change is shown in the 1987 columns of the Statement of Earnings.

GE accounting policies

(32) **Sales.** A sale is recorded when title passes to the customer or when services are performed in accordance with contracts.

(33) **Investment tax credit (ITC).** The ITC was repealed, with some transitional exceptions, effective January 1, 1986. However, for financial reporting purposes, GE has deferred recognition of the ITC each year and continues to amortize ITC as a reduction of the provision for income taxes over the lives of the facilities to which the credit applies.

(34) (35) **Inventories.** The values of most inventories are determined on a last-in first-out, or LIFO, basis and do not exceed realizable values. Effective January 1, 1987, GE changed its accounting procedures to include in inventory certain manufacturing overhead costs previously charged directly to expense. The more significant types of manufacturing overhead included in inventory as a result of the change are: depreciation of plant and equipment; pension and other benefits of manufacturing employees; and certain product-related engineering expenses. The Company believes this change was preferable because it provides a better matching of production costs with related revenues

in reporting operating results. In accordance with generally accepted accounting principles, the cumulative effect of this change for periods prior to January 1, 1987 ($281 million after providing for taxes of $215 million) is shown separately in 1987 in the Statement of Earnings on page 26. There was virtually no effect from this change on 1987 results after recording the cumulative effect.

Depreciation, depletion and amortization. The cost of most manufacturing plant and equipment is depreciated using an accelerated method based primarily on a sum-of-the-years digits formula. If manufacturing plant and equipment is subject to abnormal economic conditions or obsolescence, additional depreciation is provided.

GEFS accounting policies

Methods of recording revenues ("earned income"). Income on all loans is earned on the interest method. For loan contracts on which finance charges are precomputed, finance charges are deferred at the time of contract acquisition. For loan contracts on which finance charges are not precomputed but are billed to customers, income is recorded when earned. Accrual of interest income is suspended when collection of an account becomes doubtful, generally after the account becomes 90 days delinquent.

Financing lease income that includes related investment tax credits and residual values is recorded on the interest method so as to produce a level yield on funds not yet recovered. Unguaranteed residual values included in lease income are based primarily on independent appraisals of the values of leased assets remaining at expiration of the lease terms.

Origination, commitment and other nonrefundable fees related to fundings are deferred and recorded in earned income on the interest method. Commitment fees related to loans not expected to be funded and line-of-credit fees are deferred and recorded in earned income on a straight-line basis over the period to which the fees relate. Syndication fees are recorded in earned income at the time the related services are performed unless significant contingencies exist.

Kidder, Peabody's proprietary securities and commodities transactions are recorded on a trade-date basis. Trading and investment securities are valued at market or estimated fair value. Unrealized gains and losses on open contractual commitments, principally financial futures, when-issued securities and forward contracts on U.S. government and federal agency securities, are reflected in the Statement of Earnings on a trade-date basis. Customers' transactions and the related revenues and expenses are reflected in the financial statements on a settlement-date basis. Revenues and expenses on a trade-date basis are not materially different. Investment banking revenues from management fees, sales concessions and underwriting fees are recorded on settlement date. Advisory fee revenue is recorded when services are substantially completed and the revenue is reasonably determinable.

See "insurance affiliates" on page 49 for information with respect to earned income of these businesses.

Allowance for losses on financing receivables. GE Capital maintains an allowance for losses on financing receivables at an amount that it believes is sufficient to provide adequate protection against future losses in the portfolio. For small-balance and certain large-balance receivables, the allowance for losses is determined principally on the basis of actual experience during the preceding three years. Further allowances also are provided to reflect management's judgment of additional loss potential. For other receivables, principally the larger loans and leases, the allowance for losses is determined primarily on the basis of management's judgment of net loss potential, including specific allowances for known troubled accounts.

All accounts or portions thereof deemed to be uncollectible or to require an excessive collection cost are written off to the allowance for losses. Small-balance accounts are progressively written down (from 10% when more than three months delinquent to 100% when more than 12 months delinquent) to record the balances at estimated realizable value. However, if at any time during that period an account is judged to be uncollectible, such as in the case of a bankruptcy, the remaining balance is written off. Larger-balance accounts are reviewed at least quarterly, and those accounts that are more than three months delinquent are written down, if necessary, to record the balances at estimated realizable value.

Marketable securities. Marketable securities of Kidder, Peabody are carried at market value with the difference between cost and market value included in operations. Marketable debt securities held by all other GEFS affiliates are carried at amortized cost. Marketable equity securities of insurance affiliates are carried at market value, and unrealized gains or losses, less applicable deferred income taxes, are recognized in equity.

Securities purchased under agreements to resell (reverse repurchase agreements) and securities sold under agreements to repurchase (repurchase agreements). Repurchase and reverse repurchase agreements are treated as financing transactions and are carried at the contract amount at which the securities subsequently will be resold or reacquired. Repurchase agreements relate either to marketable securities, which are carried at market value, or to securities obtained pursuant to reverse repurchase agreements. It is GEFS' policy to take possession of securities subject to reverse repurchase agreements. GEFS monitors the market value of the underlying securities in relation to the related receivable, including accrued interest, and requests additional collateral if appropriate.

Depreciation and amortization. The cost of equipment leased to others on operating leases is amortized, principally on a straight-line basis, to estimated net salvage value over the lease term or over the estimated economic life of the equipment. Depreciation of property and equipment for GEFS' own use is recorded on either a sum-of-the-years digits or a straight-line basis over the lives of the assets.

Investment tax credit (ITC). ITC associated with equipment on operating leases and with buildings and equipment is deferred and amortized over the lives of the underlying assets.

Insurance affiliates. Premiums on short-duration insurance contracts are reported as earned income over the terms of the related reinsurance treaties or insurance policies. In general, earned premiums are calculated on a pro-rata basis or are determined based on reports received from reinsureds. Premium adjustments under retrospectively rated reinsurance contracts are recorded based on estimated losses and loss expenses, including both case and incurred-but-not-reported (IBNR) reserves. Revenues on long-duration contracts are reported as earned when due.

Deferred insurance acquisition costs are amortized as the related premiums are earned for property and casualty business. Deferred insurance acquisition costs for the life insurance business are amortized over the premium-paying periods of the contracts in proportion either to anticipated premium income or to gross profit, as appropriate. Deferred insurance acquisition costs are reviewed for recoverability, and for short-duration contracts, anticipated investment income is considered in making recoverability evaluations.

The estimated liability for outstanding losses and loss expenses consists of case reserves based on reports and estimates of losses and an IBNR reserve based primarily on experience. Where experience is not sufficient, industry averages for the particular insurance products are used. Estimated amounts of salvage and subrogation recoverable on paid and unpaid losses are deducted from outstanding losses. The liability for future policy benefits of the life insurance affiliates has been computed mainly by a net-level-premium method based on assumptions for investment yields, mortality and terminations that were appropriate at date of purchase or at the time the policies were developed, including provisions for adverse deviations.

Note *2* Acquisitions and Related Matters

GE

Although there were a number of acquisitions and dispositions during 1989, the larger transactions involved completion of arrangements for several joint ventures. These included the combining of interests in European appliances and electrical controls with General Electric plc, (GEC), an unrelated corporation in the United Kingdom. (GE also acquired GEC's medical systems sales and service in the United Kingdom.) Besides the businesses and resources contributed by the parties in these transactions, GE paid cash of $570 million to GEC in the second quarter of 1989. Other new joint ventures included an arrangement with Ericsson of Sweden (mobile communications businesses). Legal form and percentage ownerships in these alliances vary.

During 1988, GE completed a number of acquisitions. The largest of these were:

Roper Corporation, acquired in April for $507 million cash. Roper's principal businesses were the manufacture and sale of gas and electric ranges and outdoor power garden equipment. In December, GE sold Roper's garden equipment business for $295 million cash. Roper's kitchen appliance business prior to acquisition had annual sales of about $375 million.

Borg-Warner's chemicals businesses, acquired in September for $2.3 billion cash. These businesses (annual sales of about $1.6 billion prior to acquisition) manufacture and sell products complementary to GE's plastics businesses.

Both of these acquisitions were accounted for as purchases with the excess of purchase price over the estimate of fair values of net assets acquired recorded as goodwill. See note 19.

Business dispositions during 1988 included most of the GE Solid State (semiconductor) business; seven of NBC's eight radio stations; RCA Global Communications, Inc. (a provider of international communications services); and Sadelmi-Cogepi, a foreign construction firm. Cash proceeds from these transactions aggregated about $700 million. Aggregate annual sales of these businesses were about $900 million.

On December 31, 1987, GE and a French electronics company, Thomson, S.A., completed a transaction in which GE acquired Thomson's medical equipment business (CGR) and Thomson acquired most of GE's consumer electronics business. The total transaction included cash received by GE of about $560 million. CGR's 1987 sales of about $800 million came mainly from digital x-ray, mammography, computed tomography, ultrasound, and related sales and service in Europe and Latin America. GE's consumer electronics business included mainly GE and RCA brand television sets, VCRs and audio products with sales of about $3 billion annually. GE will continue for some time to receive royalty income from patents related to consumer electronics products. Other related closings, principally for offshore consumer electronics operations, took place in 1988.

Also during 1987, activities involving a "new products" division and NBC's radio networks were sold for cash aggregating about $90 million and a note for $3 million. In addition, GE donated RCA's David Sarnoff Research Center to a not-for-profit organization in 1987.

There was no material effect on GE's operating results or financial position from the above transactions in the year when they occurred.

GEFS

During 1989, GE Capital acquired for $407 million cash the remaining 62% of the common stock it had not previously owned in FGIC Corporation (FGIC), a company principally engaged in providing financial guarantee insurance on selected securities. FGIC, which had annual revenues prior to acquisition of about $125 million, is now consolidated with GE Capital. The aggregate effect of this acquisition and a number of asset acquisitions from other financial services businesses during 1989 was not material.

In June 1988, as part of the management-led acquisition of Montgomery Ward & Co., Incorporated (Montgomery Ward) from Mobil Corporation, GE Capital acquired Montgomery Ward's credit operations comprising Montgomery Ward Credit Corporation (MW Credit) and certain related assets (collectively with MW Credit, MW Credit Operations) for a cash purchase price of $718 million. GE Capital and Kidder, Peabody acquired 40% and 10%, respectively, of Montgomery Ward's common stock for a cash purchase price of $4 million and $1 million, respectively. In addition, GE Capital and Kidder, Peabody paid cash of $82 million and $8 million, respectively, for preferred stock in Montgomery Ward. The management-led acquisition of Montgomery Ward was partially financed by GE Capital in the form of a $275 million subordinated loan.

The acquisition of the MW Credit Operations was accounted for as a purchase, and, accordingly, the purchase price was allocated to the assets and liabilities of MW Credit Operations based on estimates of fair value. The excess purchase price over estimated fair value of net assets acquired (goodwill) is being amortized on a straight-line basis over 20 years.

If the preceding 1988 transactions had occurred on January 1, 1988 or January 1, 1987, management estimates that GEFS results of operations for the years ended December 31, 1988 and 1987 would have been as follows.

(In millions)	1988	1987
Revenues	$10,889	$8,702
Earnings before extraordinary item and cumulative effect of change in accounting principle	784	579
Net earnings	784	1,035

The above unaudited pro forma information has been (41) prepared based on assumptions that management deems appropriate, but the results are not necessarily indicative of those that might have occurred had the acquisitions taken place at the beginnings of the respective years. The results of MW Credit Operations have been consolidated with GEFS since the date of acquisition. There would not have been any significant pro forma effect on consolidated net earnings per share from this transaction.

In July and December 1987, GE Capital acquired the outstanding capital stock of D&K Financial Corporation (D&K) and Gelco Corporation (Gelco), respectively, for an aggregate purchase price of approximately $535 million. Both entities are in the business of leasing vehicle fleets and other equipment. The acquisitions were accounted for as purchases. Results of operations of the acquired corporations have been included in GE Capital since their respective dates of acquisition and are not material.

Note 3　GE Other Income

Other income of GE except GEFS is summarized in the table below.

(In millions)	1989	1988	1987
Royalty and technical agreements	$359	$359	$283
Marketable securities and bank deposits	106	155	133
Associated companies	14	62	61
Customer financing (42)	30	38	52
Other investments			
Interest	11	13	15
Dividends	2	8	4
Other sundry items	182	45	101
	$704	$680	$649

you can see in GEFS's balance sheet on page 29, much (70 percent at year-end 1989) of the its assets are receivables (including amounts receivables for securities in its brokerage business) and most (over 90 percent) of its equities are debt, rather than owner's equity. In this sense, the operations of the finance affiliates "are not similar to those of the consolidated group." As our comment 15 points out, nonconsolidation of the finance company makes GE's balance sheet differ substantially from its appearance under consolidation.

(30) Consolidated financial statements present information about a group of affiliated companies as if the group were one economic entity. Consequently, GE must eliminate from reported financial statements the gains or losses on sales of assets between companies in the consolidated group. GE postpones recognizing such gains or losses until one company of the consolidated group sells the assets to a buyer outside of the consolidated group.

(31) The "one-line basis" is the equity method.

(32) GE uses the completed contract method of recognizing revenue on long-term construction projects. We know this, not because the language here is perfectly clear, but because we have asked GE about these words. See our comment 11.

(33) See our comment 61 for a discussion of the investment credit.

(34) Most foreign governments do not allow LIFO for tax purposes.

(35) GE tells us it will not show an item of inventory on the balance sheet at an amount greater than net realizable value; we can deduce that it must be using a lower-of-cost-or-market valuation basis.

(36) GE is unusual among U.S. corporations in using accelerated depreciation for financial reporting. Most corporations use accelerated depreciation for tax reporting but less conservative methods in financial reporting.

(37) See "effective interest method" in the Glossary.

(38) See "allowance method" in the Glossary.

(39) Purchase accounting contrasts with pooling of interests accounting, under which the assets acquired would appear at lower, old book values, rather than at current market values at the time of acquisition. As a result of purchase accounting, net income in the future will be lower than it would have been under pooling. The acquiring firm does not have a choice of accounting methods once it sets the form of the acquisition. Some acquisition structures require pooling of interests accounting.

(40) GE explains in its note 19 that it amortizes this goodwill over 40 years, the longest period allowed under APB *Opinion No. 17.*

(41) See "pro forma statements" in the Glossary.

(42) "Customer financing" is interest on receivables held by GE arising from some of its sales.

㊸ See "capital lease" and "operating lease" in the Glossary.

㊹ Although GE has an assured right to receive these payments and has already put the equipment in the hands of the users, it will not recognize revenue until it receives cash. Accounting views such operating leases as executory contracts, not yet having generated revenue.

㊺ Contrast "functional classification" and "natural classification" in the Glossary. This is a natural classification of expenses.

㊻ *SFAS No. 2* requires the expensing of research and development costs, and the disclosure, such as GE's here, of the costs incurred during the year for R & D. *SFAS No. 2* allows the capitalizing of R & D costs that a firm incurs under contract and that the buyer will reimburse. GE is making clear that these costs ($1,334 million in 1989) do not qualify for capitalization by stating that they are Company funded.

㊼ That is, these are *defined benefit plans*, in contrast to *defined contribution plans*; see the Glossary.

㊽ The projected benefit method contrasts with the accumulated benefit method, which bases calculations on salaries earned to date, rather than on projections of future salaries. See the Glossary at *projected benefit obligation*.

㊾ This cost, sometimes called current service benefits, arises solely because employees have worked for a year while covered by the pension plan. *SFAS No. 87* requires the firm to charge all this cost to expense for the current year.

㊿ At any time, a defined benefit pension plan has an obligation to employees and ex-employees for work performed before that time. As time passes, the obligation grows in amount because of interest accumulation. This amount is the interest on the obligation to the beneficiaries at the start of the year.

(51) This amortization includes the benefit (expense reduction) to GE arising from the fact that at its adoption of *SFAS No. 87*, GE's pension plan had market value of assets larger than the present value of the benefits projected to be payable.

(52) The pension plan invests the assets; these are the earnings for the year, which exceed the amounts GE projected to be earned; see our next comment.

(53) Because the projected return on the assets (of 8.5 percent; see GE's comment two paragraphs above) was less than the actual return, there is extra income (or less expense) to be recognized. GE recognizes that extra income over future periods, in accordance with *SFAS No. 87*. Thus, GE does not recognize all of the pension plan's income in the current year.

(54) The amount of this liability appears on GE's balance sheet, probably included in the amount called "All other liabilities." See GE's note 26.

(55) GE shows here the annual cost of its post-employment benefits other than pensions. The FASB does not yet require disclosure of the present value of the benefits already earned by current and ex-employees nor does the FASB require a firm to count these as accounting liabilities. The amounts can be significant. The FASB is proposing to require firms to account for these other post-employment benefits.

(56) SFAS No. 34 requires separate disclosure of amounts of interest capitalized into plant under construction.

Note 4 GEFS Revenues from Operations

GEFS revenues from operations (earned income) are summarized in the table below.

(In millions)	1989	1988	1987
Time sales, loan, investment and other income ㊸	$ 8,113	$ 5,986	$ 4,475
Financing leases	1,078	870	738
Operating lease rentals	1,426	1,372	536
Premium and commission income of insurance affiliates	1,810	1,802	1,748
Commissions and fees of securities broker-dealer	518	625	728
	$12,945	$10,655	$ 8,225

Details of certain items included in earned income from financing leases are shown below.

(In millions)	1989	1988	1987
Deferred investment tax credit amortized			
Direct financing leases	$16	$20	$31
Leveraged leases	21	3	16
Total financing leases	$37	$23	$47
Gains on sale of residual values at lease completion			
Direct financing leases	$38	$39	$44
Leveraged leases	12	29	4
Total financing leases	$50	$68	$48

㊹ Noncancelable future rentals due from customers for equipment on operating leases as of December 31, 1989 totaled $2,354 million and are due as follows: 1990 — $734 million; 1991 — $484 million; 1992 — $353 million; 1993 — $254 million; 1994 — $164 million; and $365 million thereafter.

Note 5 Supplemental Cost Details (excluding unusual expenses) ㊺

Supplemental cost details are shown in the table below.

Supplemental cost details (In millions)	1989			1988			1987		
	GE	GEFS	Total	GE	GEFS	Total	GE	GEFS	Total
Employee compensation, including Social Security taxes and other benefits	$11,960	$1,103	$13,063	$11,690	$1,052	$12,742	$12,139	$959	$13,098
Selling, general and administrative expense	6,662	—	6,662	6,250	—	6,250	5,979	—	5,979
Company-funded research and development ㊻	1,334	—	1,334	1,155	—	1,155	1,194	—	1,194
Maintenance and repairs	821	—	821	839	—	839	840	—	840
Rental expense	709	176	885	700	160	860	657	123	780
Advertising	415	75	490	413	66	479	495	51	546
Taxes, except payroll and income taxes	298	110	408	374	77	451	289	82	371

Total employee compensation data include Social Security taxes of $804 million in 1989, $819 million in 1988 and $796 million in 1987.

1994

Note 6   Pensions and Other Retiree Benefits

GE and its affiliates sponsor a number of pension and other retiree benefit plans. This note summarizes important financial aspects of GE's obligations for these plans. Measurements of obligations and costs are based on actuarial calculations involving various assumptions as to future events.

Principal pension plans

The principal pension plans are the GE Pension Plan (GE Plan) and the GE Supplementary Pension Plan (Supplementary Plan). The RCA Retirement Plan (RCA Plan) was merged with the GE Pension Plan at the end of 1988. Amounts and comments about the GE Plan in this note include the RCA Plan for all periods shown. Other pension plans are sponsored by domestic and foreign affiliates, but these are not considered to be significant individually or in the aggregate to the consolidated financial position.

The GE Plan covers substantially all employees in the United States, including approximately 50% of GEFS employees. Generally, benefits are based on the greater of a formula recognizing career earnings or a formula recognizing length of service and final average earnings. Benefits are funded through the GE Pension Trust. At the end of 1989, approximately 208,900 employees were covered, approximately 122,900 former employees with vested rights were entitled to future benefits and approximately 154,500 retirees or beneficiaries were receiving benefits.

The Supplementary Plan is an unfunded plan providing supplementary retirement benefits primarily to higher-level, longer-service management and professional employees in the United States. At the end of 1989, about 3,400 employees were eligible for this plan, and about 4,100 retirees or beneficiaries were receiving benefits.

Statement of Financial Accounting Standards (SFAS) No. 87 requires use of the projected unit credit cost method to determine the projected benefit obligation and plan cost. The projected benefit obligation is the actuarial present value of the portion of projected future benefits that is attributed to employee service to date. The benefit cost for service during the year is the portion of the projected benefit obligation that is attributed to employee service during the year. This cost method recognizes the effect of future compensation and service in projecting the future benefits.

In addition, SFAS No. 87 establishes a "transition gain." This is the excess at January 1, 1986 (when the Company adopted SFAS No. 87) of the current fair market value of plan assets over the plan's projected benefit obligation. This transition gain is being amortized over 15 years except that such excess for the RCA Plan was recognized as an asset in accounting for the RCA acquisition in 1986.

Gains and losses that occur because actual experience differs from that assumed are amortized over the average future service period of employees. Prior-service cost for changes in pension benefits that are allocable to previous periods of service are amortized in the same manner.

Actuarial assumptions for the principal pension plans include 8.5% for both the assumed discount rate used to determine the present value of future benefits and the expected long-term rate of return on plan assets. The assumed rate of average future increases in pension benefit compensation is 6.5%.

Employer costs for the principal pension plans in 1989 and 1988 recognized the impact of continued favorable investment performance. Benefit costs for service during the year recognize plan design changes in 1988. For example, beginning in 1989, employee contributions no longer reduce pension costs because such contributions are used to provide additional pension benefits. Details of cost for the principal pension plans follow.

Cost for principal pension plans

(In millions)	1989	1988	1987
Benefit cost for service during the year — net of employee contributions	$ 413	$ 300	$ 385
Interest cost on projected benefit obligation	1,259	1,232	1,187
Recognized return on plan assets	(1,574)	(1,460)	(1,293)
Net amortization	(339)	(299)	(254)
Net pension cost	$ (241)	$ (227)	$ 25
Details of return on plan assets			
Actual return on plan assets	$ 4,026	$ 2,261	$ 1,237
Recognized return on plan assets	(1,574)	(1,460)	(1,293)
Unrecognized return on plan assets	$ 2,452	$ 801	$ (56)

Recognized return on plan assets is determined by applying the expected long-term rate of return to the market-related value of assets.

Funding policy for the GE Plan is to contribute amounts sufficient to meet minimum funding requirements set forth in U.S. employee benefit and tax laws plus such additional amounts as GE may determine to be appropriate from time to time. GE made no contribution for 1989 and 1988 because the funding status of the GE Plan precluded current tax deduction and a contribution would have generated an excise tax.

The funding status of an ongoing plan may be measured by comparing the market-related value of assets with the projected benefit obligation. The market-related value of assets is based on amortized cost plus recognition of market appreciation and depreciation in the portfolio over five years. GE believes the market-related value of assets is a more realistic measure than current fair market value because the market-related value reduces the impact of short-term market fluctuations. The funding status for the principal pension plans follows.

Funding status for principal pension plans

December 31 (In millions)	1989	1988
Market-related value of assets	$20,794	$19,308
Projected benefit obligation	16,057	15,473

A schedule reconciling the projected benefit obligation for principal pension plans with GE's recorded pension liability is shown below.

Reconciliation of projected benefit obligation with pension liability for principal pension plans

December 31 (In millions)	1989	1988
Projected benefit obligation	$16,057	$15,473
Less current fair market value of trust assets	(24,211)	(21,502)
Unrecognized SFAS No. 87 transition gain	1,693	1,847
Other unrecognized net experience gains	5,333	3,303
Unrecognized prior-service cost	90	114
Recorded prepaid pension assets	1,469	1,177
Recorded pension liability �54	$ 431	$ 412

The portion of the projected benefit obligation representing the accumulated benefit obligation amounted to $14,940 million and $14,073 million at the ends of 1989 and 1988, respectively. The vested benefit obligation was $14,721 million and $13,895 million at the ends of 1989 and 1988, respectively. These amounts are based on compensation and service to date.

Trust assets consist mainly of common stock and fixed income investments. Trust assets included GE common stock valued at $201 million at year-end 1989 ($139 million at year-end 1988) mainly held in connection with an indexed portfolio.

Other unrecognized net experience gains resulted principally from favorable investment performance.

Principal retiree health care and life insurance plans

�55 GE and its affiliates sponsor a number of plans providing retiree health care and life insurance benefits. GE's aggregate cost for the principal plans, which cover substantially all employees in the United States, was $283 million in 1989, $302 million in 1988 and $278 million in 1987.

Generally, employees who retire after qualifying for optional early retirement under the GE Plan are eligible to participate in retiree health care and life insurance plans. Health care benefits for eligible retirees under age 65 and eligible dependents are included in costs as covered expenses are actually incurred. For eligible retirees and spouses over age 65, the present value of future health care benefits is funded or accrued and is included in costs in the year the retiree becomes eligible for benefits. The present value of future life insurance benefits for eligible retirees is funded and is included in costs in the year of retirement.

Most retirees outside the United States are covered by government health care programs, and GE's cost is not significant.

Note 7 Interest and Other Financial Charges

GE. Interest capitalized, principally on major property, plant and equipment projects, was $48 million in 1989, $11 million in 1988 and $23 million in 1987. �56

GEFS. GEFS interest and discount expense reported in the Statement of Earnings is net of interest income on temporary investments of excess funds ($160 million, $285 million and $165 million in 1989, 1988 and 1987, respectively) and capitalized interest of $13 million, $16 million and $4 million, respectively, for 1989, 1988 and 1987.

Note 8 GEFS Allowance for Losses on Financing Receivables

GEFS allowance for losses on financing receivables represented 2.63% of total financing receivables at both year-ends 1989 and 1988. The table below shows the activity in the allowance for losses on financing receivables during each of the last three years.

(In millions)	1989	1988	1987
Balance at January 1	$ 972	$ 743	$ 603
Additions charged to operations	527	434	290
Net transfers related to companies acquired and sold	48	89	21
Amounts written off	(420)	(294)	(171)
Balance at December 31	$1,127	$ 972	$ 743

Amounts written off in 1989 were approximately 0.98% of average financing receivables outstanding during the year, compared with 0.81% and 0.62% of average financing receivables outstanding during 1988 and 1987, respectively.

Note 9 Unusual Expenses

GE. Unusual expenses in 1987 were provisions for corporate restructurings. These were for the expenses of refocusing a wide variety of business and marketing activities and reducing foreign and domestic risk exposures. These provisions included costs of rationalizing and improving a large number of production facilities; rearranging production activities among a number of existing plants; and reorganizing, phasing out or otherwise concluding other activities no longer considered essential to the conduct of the Company's business.

GEFS. GEFS unusual expenses in 1987 included amounts related to insider trading charges and business restructuring activities of Kidder, Peabody.

Note 10 Provision for Income Taxes (excluding 1987 extraordinary item and cumulative effect of changes in accounting principles)

Provision for income taxes ⑤⑦ (In millions)	1989 GE	GEFS	Total	1988 GE	GEFS	Total	1987 GE	GEFS	Total
Estimated amounts payable (recoverable)	$1,375	$ 48	$1,423	$1,311	$ (32)	$1,279	$1,246	$ (212)	$1,034
Deferred tax expense (benefit) from "temporary differences" ⑤⑧	242	144	386	(152)	274	122	(71)	231	160
Investment credit deferred (amortized) — net ⑤⑨	(64)	19	(45)	(63)	(3)	(66)	(87)	1	(86)
Expense	$1,553	$ 211	$1,764	$1,096	$ 239	$1,335	$1,088	$ 20	$1,108

"Estimated amounts payable" includes amounts applicable to foreign jurisdictions of $272 million, $344 million and $197 million in 1989, 1988 and 1987, respectively.

General Electric Company files a consolidated U.S. federal income tax return that includes GEFS. GEFS' provision for estimated taxes recoverable (payable) includes its effect on the consolidated tax return. The amount reported by GEFS has been reduced to the extent of consolidated investment tax credit carryforwards of $168 million at December 31, 1987. Investment tax credit carryforwards of $168 million and $107 million realized in 1988 and 1987, respectively, were reflected as reinstatements of deferred tax balances.

Deferred income taxes reflect the impact of "temporary differences" between the amount of assets and liabilities for financial reporting purposes and such amounts as measured by tax laws and regulations. See note 27 for details of the balances in deferred income taxes at the ends of 1989 and 1988.

The U.S. investment tax credit (ITC) was repealed, with some transitional exceptions, effective January 1, 1986. However, because of its use of the deferral method of accounting for the ITC, GE has an unamortized balance remaining. As a result of the accounting change in 1987, unamortized ITC is treated as a temporary difference for deferred tax accounting. GE's remaining unamortized ITC balance was $112 million, net of deferred tax at year-end 1989, and will be added to income in future years.

The U.S. federal statutory tax rate on corporations was 34% in 1989 and 1988, down from 40% in 1987. Data about "effective tax rates," i.e., provision for income taxes as a percentage of earnings before income taxes, extraordinary item and cumulative effect of accounting changes, follow.

Effective tax rates (before extraordinary item and cumulative effect of accounting changes)

	1989	1988	1987
GE	28.3%	24.5%	33.9%
GEFS	18.6	23.3	3.5
Consolidated ⑥②	30.9	28.3	34.3

31.1

A reconciliation from the consolidated provision for income taxes that would have resulted using the U.S. federal statutory rate to the actual provision is shown below.

Differences between expected U.S. federal statutory ⑥③ tax-rate provision and actual tax provision

(In millions)	1989	1988	1987
Expected consolidated tax provision at statutory rates	$1,939	$1,605	$1,291
Increase (reduction) in taxes resulting from GE			
Inclusion of GEFS earnings (before extraordinary item and cumulative effect of accounting change in 1987) in before-tax income on an after-tax basis ⑥④	(315)	(268)	(221)
Varying tax rates of other affiliates (principally foreign) ⑥⑤	(60)	(76)	(117)
Amortization of investment tax credit ⑥⑥	(64)	(70)	(88)
Current-year effect of income tax accounting change	—	—	133
All other — net	125	(14)	98
	(314)	(428)	(195)
Increase (reduction) in taxes resulting from GEFS			
Amortization of investment tax credit on financing and operating leases	(22)	(17)	(27)
Dividends received which are not fully taxable ⑥⑦	(27)	(17)	(13)
Income from tax-exempt marketable securities ⑥⑧	(131)	(104)	(112)
Income taxes at capital gains rate ⑥⑨	—	—	(14)
Adjustment of tax-deductible claim reserves of insurance affiliates	(21)	(22)	—
Change in tax-rate assumptions for leveraged leases	(23)	(14)	(31)
All other — net	48	64	(12)
	(176)	(110)	(209)
Eliminations	315	268	221
Actual consolidated tax provision	$1,764	$1,335	$1,108

Provision has been made for substantially all U.S. federal income tax liabilities applicable to undistributed earnings of affiliates and associated companies.

57. This first schedule shows the details of income tax expense, which GE calls a "provision." The bottom line of the first schedule is the total expense reported on the statement of earnings. It is the sum of U.S. federal, foreign, and other income tax expenses. GE derives the U.S. federal and foreign income tax expense amounts in essentially two steps: first appears the amount of taxes payable; then there is an adjustment for temporary differences; GE also shows the effect of the investment credit, which we discuss in our comment 61.

58. In 1989, GE's (excluding GEFS's) ~~U.S. federal~~ income taxes payable ~~exceeded~~ *was less than* income tax expense because of ~~timing~~ *temporary* differences. In ~~1988 and 1987,~~ GE's ~~U.S. federal~~ income tax expense exceeded income taxes payable because of *temporary differences*. See the Glossary for an explanation of temporary differences. The details of the deferred income tax balance sheet accounts appear in GE's note ~~27.~~ 23.

59. GE uses the deferral method of accounting for the investment credit; see our comment 61.

60. The SEC requires disclosure of the disaggregation of pretax income into domestic and foreign sources. (See the last paragraph of GE's note 10, on page ~~55~~.) The analyst can thereby compute an effective foreign tax rate for ~~1989 of~~ 35.2 percent (= $272/$773). ~~Compare this rate to that appearing at the bottom of the left column on page 54.~~ 187/634

61. Before Congress changed the tax laws, GE earned investment credits in the year it acquired new qualifying assets. GE has used the deferral method of accounting for the investment credit, rather than the less conservative flow-through method. The deferral method recognizes the tax-reducing (income-increasing) effects of the investment credit over the lives of the assets producing the credit. (Most U.S. corporations use the flow through method.) GE and GEFS recognized ($45) million of investment credits during (1989). If GE had used the flow-through method, income tax expense would have been lower in some earlier years and larger in 1989 by $45 million. Under the flow-through method, retained earnings at the end of 1989 would have been $112 million larger.

62. The 30.9 percent figure for 1989 results from dividing income tax expense of $1,764 million by the pretax income of the enterprise. Pretax income of the enterprise is $5,703 million, the sum of $1,764 million (income tax expense) + $3,939 million (net earnings).

63. Most readers of financial statements are aware that the U.S. federal tax rate on most corporate income was 34 percent of pretax income in 1989. The SEC requires that companies explain why the reported income tax expense rate differs from the statutory rate, 34 percent in 1989. The preceding comment derives GE's 1989 consolidated pretax income of $5,703 million; 34 percent of that amount is $1,939 million. Thus, this schedule starts with the $1,939 million "expected" income tax expense and shows the additions and subtractions to derive the actual $1,764 million income tax expense.

64. GE reports income of $927 million from GEFS in 1989 using the equity method. That income amount is after taxes. Yet it appears in GE's income statement before the income tax calculation. GE need pay no further taxes on the income from GEFS; this accounts for part of the difference between GE's effective tax rate on "pretax income."

65. See the Glossary at *DISC* and *FSC*; some of the income of such an entities is not currently taxed or is taxed at rates different from usual rates.

66. GE's using the deferral method for the investment credit reduces income tax expense otherwise reportable; this accounts for part of the difference between the effective rate and the statutory rate.

67. See "double taxation" in the Glossary. In order to reduce the negative incentives created by taxing dividends paid by one corporation to another, Congress exempts 80 percent of intercorporate dividends from income tax. This permanent difference reduces the effective corporate income tax rate on inter-company dividends.

⑥⑧ See "permanent difference" in the Glossary. Such income appears in full on the income statement but the U.S. does not tax such income. This reduces the effective rate.

⑥⑨ The U.S. excludes a portion of capital gains from taxable income, creating another permanent difference. Thus the effective tax rate declines to the extent that pretax income includes capital gains.

⑦⓪ APB *Opinion No. 11* says that a parent need not provide for income taxes on income of affiliates the parent expects to reinvest indefinitely. If the parent expects to receive dividends from the affiliate in the foreseeable future, then the parent must make an income tax provision. In one of its most controversial moves, the FASB has proposed to require parents to provide for income taxes for all such income of affiliates, even when the parent expects to reinvest indefinitely.

As this book goes to press, the FASB has not indicated whether it will change the reporting rules.

⑦① See our comment 60.

⑦② See *compensating balance* in the Glossary. Compensating balances increase the stated cost of borrowing; accordingly, the SEC requires disclosure of such amounts, if they are significant. GE states that its compensating balances are not significant.

⑦③ *SFAS No. 12* requires disclosure of aggregate cost and aggregate market value of marketable securities held as current assets. From these disclosures, we can compute that GEFS earned a $95 million unrealized holding gain on these securities during the year 1989. At the end of the year the market value of the securities was $6,952 million; their cost was $6,750 million (see GEFS balance sheet on page 29). Thus, the unrealized holding gain at the end of the year was $202 (= $6,952 - $6,750) million. At the beginning of the year, the unrealized holding gain was $107 (= $5,537 - $5,430) million. The unrealized holding gain increased by $95 (= $202 - $107) million during the year.

⑦④ This note tell us that if management of GEFS wished to do so, it could selectively sell securities from its portfolio to generate pretax income of $32 million or to generate pretax losses of $37 million. SFAS No. 12 requires disclosure of the unrealized holding gains on securities with gains and of the unrealized losses on securities with losses. This disclosure provides some indication of the latitude management has to manipulate reported income by selecting securities to hold or to sell.

⑦⑤ GE uses a LIFO cost flow assumption for inventories, but manages its inventories, as most sensible businesses do, on FIFO, using the older materials and finished goods before the newer. It keeps its records internally on a FIFO basis. The FIFO cost of 1989 year-end inventories is $8,844 [$6,382] million. GE makes an adjustment at year-end to convert the internal records to LIFO. The adjustment involves a debit to Cost of Goods Sold (or Work in Process Inventory) and a credit to Ending Inventory for the $2,189 [1,508] million. The numbers given for "Less revaluation to LIFO" allow the computation of pretax income had GE used FIFO, rather than LIFO. See our next comment. Some business analysts call this amount the "LIFO reserve," but we prefer GE's more descriptive caption.

⑦⑥ GE provides information that allows us to calculate its operating income if it had used a FIFO cost flow assumption. The IRS does not allow companies using LIFO for tax purposes to disclose hypothetical FIFO income in the financial statements. But the SEC requires the disclosure of beginning and ending inventories as they would have been under FIFO, if these amounts differ significantly from the LIFO amounts. The SEC's required disclosure of FIFO beginning and ending inventories allows the reader to compute the LIFO/FIFO income difference. As of December 31, 1989, cumulative pretax income is $2,189 million less than it would have been under FIFO. As of January 1, 1989, cumulative pretax income is $2,226 million less than it would have been under FIFO. This difference decreased by $37 (= $2,226 - $2,189) million during the year 1989. Hence 1989 pretax income would have been $37 million smaller if GE had used FIFO. You may see this calculation more clearly in the accompanying exhibit. Generally, FIFO leads to larger income than does LIFO. Because of the dips into old LIFO layers, however, LIFO cost of goods sold is smaller than would have been FIFO cost of goods sold. See the next comment.

Based on the location (not tax jurisdiction) of the business providing goods or services, consolidated domestic income before taxes, extraordinary item and cumulative effect of changes in accounting principles was $4,930 million in 1989, $3,936 million in 1988 and $2,710 million in 1987. The corresponding amounts for foreign-based operations were $773 million, $785 million and $517 million in each of those years, respectively.

⑦

Note *11* Cash and Equivalents

⑦ Deposits restricted as to usage and withdrawal or used as partial compensation for short-term borrowing arrangements were not material for either GE except GEFS or GEFS. See note 21 for related information about credit lines and compensating balances.

Note *12* Marketable Securities Carried at Cost

Carrying value of marketable securities for GE except GEFS was substantially the same as market value at year-ends 1989 and 1988. Market value of GEFS' securities carried at amortized cost was $6,952 million and $5,537 ⑦ million at December 31, 1989 and 1988, respectively.

Note *13* GEFS Marketable Securities Carried at Market

December 31 (In millions)	1989	1988
U.S. government and federal agency securities	$4,399	$2,433
State and municipal securities	191	215
Corporate stocks, bonds and foreign securities	3,898	2,441
	$8,488	$5,089

At December 31, 1989, the carrying value of equity securities carried at market value included unrealized gains and unrealized losses of approximately $32 million ⑦ and $37 million, respectively.

A significant portion of securities carried at market value at December 31, 1989 was pledged as collateral for bank loans and repurchase agreements.

Note *14* GE Current Receivables

December 31 (In millions)	1989	1988
Receivable from:		
Customers	$5,298	$5,289
Associated companies	190	160
Others	1,897	1,857
	7,385	7,306
Less allowance for losses	(167)	(196)
	$7,218	$7,110

Note *15* GE Inventories

December 31 (In millions)		1989	1988
Raw materials and work in process		$ 5,492	$ 5,603
Finished goods		3,103	2,863
Unbilled shipments		249	246
		8,844	8,712
Less revaluation to LIFO	⑦	(2,189)	(2,226)
LIFO value of inventories	⑦	$ 6,655	$ 6,486

LIFO revaluations decreased $37 million in 1989 compared with an increase of $150 million in 1988. LIFO revaluations increased $324 million in 1987, mostly related to the accounting change described in note 1. Included in these changes were decreases of $68 million, $23 million ⑦ and $22 million (1989, 1988 and 1987, respectively) due lower inventory levels. In each of the last three years, there was a current-year expense for price increases.

Inventory Data from Financial Statements and Footnotes (For Authors' comment 76. Amounts shown in boldface appear in General Electric Company's financial statements. We compute other amounts as indicated.)

	(Dollar Amounts in Millions)		
	LIFO Cost-Flow Assumption + (Actually Used)	Excess of FIFO over = LIFO Amount	FIFO Cost-Flow Assumption (Hypothetical)
Beginning Inventory	$ 6,486 *5,321*	$ 2,226 *2,012*	$ 8,712 *7,333*
Purchases	22,996[a] *21,360*	0	22,996 *21,360*
Cost of Goods Available for Sale	$29,482 *26,681*	$ 2,226 *2,012*	$31,708 *28,693*
Less Ending Inventory	6,655 *4,574*	2,189 *1,808*	8,844 *6,382*
Cost of Goods Sold	$22,827 *22,107*	$ 37 *204*	$22,864 *22,311*
Sale of Goods	$31,314 *29,575*	$ 0	31,314 *29,575*
Less Cost of Goods Sold ...	$22,827 *22,107*	372	2,864
Gross Margin on Sales	$ 8,487 *7,468*	($ 37) *($204)*	$ 8,450 *7,264*

[a]Computation of Purchases not presented in GE's financial statements:

Purchases = Cost of Goods Sold + Ending Inventory - Beginning Inventory
$22,996 = $22,827 + $6,655 - $6,486
21,360   22,107   +   4,574 — 5,321

(77) See the Glossary at *LIFO inventory layer*, particularly the last sentence. When the layers assumed sold cost less than current purchases would have cost, cost of goods sold declines and income for the period increases. GE tells us that 1989 pretax income is $68 million larger because of the dips into old LIFO layers, "lower inventory levels."

(78) We omit GE notes 16 and 17 which contain a page and a half of details about GEFS receivables.

(79) Assume a firm depreciates an asset costing $1,000 on a straight-line basis in the amount of $100 per year and that accumulated depreciation is $400 at year-end. At year-end, the asset must be four (= $400/$100) years old. GE's Statement of Cash Flows on page 31 indicates 1989 depreciation charges of $1,524 million. If GE used straight-line depreciation for financial reporting, then the analogous computation indicates the dollars used by GE to acquire Property, plant, and equipment were spent, on average, 7.1 (= $10,756/$1,524) years prior to the end of 1989. GE uses accelerated depreciation for some of its depreciable assets (see page 48 of the GE Annual Report). Thus, accumulated depreciation builds up at a faster rate than under straight-line depreciation. We can conclude that GE spent dollars for plant on average less than 7.1 years prior to the end of 1989. GE has a relatively young plant compared to some: U.S. Steel (now called USX), for example, spent its dollars for plant, on average, more than 10 years before the end of 1989.

[handwritten margin notes: 1992, 1483, 12,046, 12,346/1483]

(80) Both the SEC and the FASB (*SFAS No. 13*) require disclosure of material commitments under long-term noncancelable leases.

(81) Firms need not amortize intangibles acquired before October 1970. APB *Opinion No. 17* requires firms to amortize licenses and intangibles acquired after October 1970 over a period not to exceed 40 years.

Note *18* Property, Plant and Equipment (including equipment leased to others)
(78)

December 31 (In millions)	1989	1988
Original cost		
GE		
Land and improvements	$ 266	$ 260
Buildings, structures and related equipment	4,600	4,250
Machinery and equipment	13,756	12,957
Leasehold costs and manufacturing plant under construction	1,051	1,126
Oil and gas properties	749	764
	20,422	19,357
GEFS		
Buildings and equipment	1,206	745
Equipment leased to others		
Vehicles	2,076	1,564
Railroad rolling stock	1,347	1,038
Marine shipping containers	816	857
Aircraft	1,324	618
Data processing equipment	461	355
Other	816	634
	8,046	5,811
	$28,468	$25,168
Accumulated depreciation, depletion and amortization		
GE (79)	$10,756	$ 9,997
GEFS		
Equipment leased to others	1,745	1,321
Buildings and equipment	321	239
	$12,822	$11,557

GEFS' increase in buildings and equipment includes the effect of the transfer of GE Americom from GE at year-end 1989. Current-year amortization of GEFS' equipment on lease to others was $647 million, $665 million and $316 million in 1989, 1988 and 1987, respectively.

(80) At December 31, 1989, GE except GEFS had minimum rental commitments under noncancelable operating leases aggregating $3,069 million. Amounts payable over the next five years are: 1990 — $537 million; 1991 — $480 million; 1992 — $394 million; 1993 — $338 million; and 1994 — $308 million.

At December 31, 1989, GEFS had minimum rental commitments under noncancelable operating leases aggregating $942 million. Amounts payable over the next five years are: 1990 — $168 million; 1991 — $143 million; 1992 — $106 million; 1993 — $65 million; and 1994 — $68 million.

Note *19* Intangible Assets

December 31 (In millions)	1989	1988
GE		
Goodwill	$6,517	$6,423
Other intangibles	531	561
	7,048	6,984
GEFS		
Goodwill	1,587	1,364
Other intangibles	187	204
	1,774	1,568
	$8,822	$8,552

Accumulated amortization of GE's goodwill was $484 million and $318 million at December 31, 1989 and 1988, respectively. Accumulated amortization of other intangibles for GE was $474 million and $455 million at December 31, 1989 and 1988, respectively. The largest GE goodwill and other intangibles were from the RCA acquisition, for which goodwill is being amortized on a straight-line basis over 40 years. Other amounts of goodwill being amortized over 40 years arose from a number of acquisi- (81) tions in 1987 and 1988. All other GE intangibles and goodwill are being amortized over shorter periods as appropriate, ranging from one year to 20 years.

Accumulated amortization of GEFS' goodwill was $181 million and $133 million at December 31, 1989 and 1988, respectively. Accumulated amortization of GEFS' other intangibles was $90 million and $73 million at December 31, 1989 and 1988, respectively. The principal sources of GEFS goodwill include acquisitions of FGIC Corporation; Gelco; MW Credit Operations; Kidder, Peabody; ERC; and a number of auto auctions. Amortization is being recorded over various periods, none more than 30 years. GEFS' other intangibles represent principally the value of insurance-in-force related to ERC's property and casualty reinsurance business, which is being amortized on a straight-line basis over its estimated life of approximately 16 years.

Note 20 All Other Assets

December 31 (In millions)		1989	1988
GE			
Investments			
Associated companies			
(including advances of $54 million			
and $29 million)		$1,448	$ 647
Miscellaneous investments			
Government and government-			
guaranteed securities		144	202
Other		167	175
Marketable equity securities		54	72
Less allowance for losses	⑧②	(113)	(100)
		1,700	996
Prepaid pension assets		1,469	1,177
Recoverable engineering costs on			
government contracts		782	752
Long-term receivables		608	675
Television program costs		410	352
Deferred charges		372	318
Real estate development projects		31	73
Customer financing		62	73
Other		219	205
		5,653	4,621
GEFS			
Investment in associated companies			
(including advances of $277 million			
and $389 million)		1,045	1,145
Miscellaneous investments		1,539	1,034
Broker-dealer cash and securities			
segregated by regulation		134	383
Deferred insurance acquisition costs		410	262
Deferred charges		274	225
Real estate properties		151	122
Other		219	247
		3,772	3,418
		$9,425	$8,039

For GE, aggregate market value of marketable equity securities, which are carried at cost, was $67 million and $72 million at year-ends 1989 and 1988, respectively. Gross ⑧③ unrealized gains and losses were $19 million and $6 million, respectively, at December 31, 1989.

The National Broadcasting Company (NBC, an affiliate of GE) capitalizes program costs (including rights to broadcast) when paid or when a program is ready for broadcast, if earlier. These costs are amortized based upon projected revenues or expensed when a program is determined to have no value.

At year-end 1989, NBC had approximately $1.70 billion ⑧④ of commitments to acquire broadcast material or the rights to broadcast television programs that require payments over the next six years.

For GEFS, miscellaneous investments included $1.149 billion and $641 million at December 31, 1989 and 1988, respectively, of items at estimated realizable values previously included in financing receivables.

Note 21 Short-Term Borrowings

Amount and average rate at December 31

	1989		1988	
(In millions)	Amount	Rate	Amount	Rate
GE				
Commercial paper	$ 597	8.5%	$ —	
Notes with trust				
departments	313	8.2	337	8.5%
Affiliate bank borrowings				
(principally foreign)	436	18.8	261	25.7
Current portion of				
long-term borrowings	150		1,233	
Other	200		30	
	1,696		1,861	
GEFS				
Commercial paper	30,452	8.80	24,591	9.32
Banks	2,702	8.58	1,987	9.34
Current portion of				
long-term borrowings	1,365		790	
Notes with trust				
departments	847	8.29	990	8.48
Passbooks and				
investment certificates	374		373	
	35,740		28,731	
Eliminations	(236)		(170)	
	$37,200		$30,422	

The average balance of short-term borrowings for GE except GEFS, excluding the current portion of long-term borrowings, was $2,284 million in 1989 compared with an average balance of $1,416 million in 1988. (Except for commercial paper, the average balance is calculated by averaging month-end balances for the year; commercial paper average borrowings are based on daily balances for the year.) The maximum balances in these calculations were $2,791 million at the end of June 1989 and $2,444 million at the end of September 1988. The average worldwide effective interest rate for the year 1989 was 11%; for 1988, it was 15%. These average rates represent total short-term interest incurred divided by the average balance outstanding. Although the total unused credit available to GE through banks and commercial credit markets is not readily quantifiable, confirmed credit lines of about $1.3 billion had been extended by 47 banks at year-end 1989. Substantially all of these lines also are available for use by GE Capital and GEFS in addition to their own credit lines.

(82) See our comment 83.

(83) *SFAS No. 12* requires that firms value their portfolios of marketable equity securities at lower of aggregate cost or market and separately disclose the total amounts of unrealized gains and losses on individual holdings in their portfolios.

The aggregate market value of these securities at year-end 1989 is $67 million. Their cost is $54 million; see the data at callout for our comment 82. Thus, the unrealized holding gain at the end of 1989 is $13 (= $67 - $54) million. The $13 million consists of unrealized holding gains of $19 million offset by $6 million of holding losses. At year-end 1988, the unrealized holding gain was zero because the cost and market value of the portfolio were both $72 million. Thus, the unrealized holding loss during the year 1989 was $13 million.

(84) Firms must disclose material amounts of commitments under executory contracts.

(85) The borrower can repay these long-term borrowings at any time and the lender can demand repayment at specified "option" times. At the option date, the lender will want to change the interest rate to then-current market conditions. At each annual option date, the borrower, GE, will agree to change the interest rate or will pay off the debt.

The economic substance of such lending is, we think, short-term debt, not long-term debt, because the lender can require the debt be paid, even on a whim. Those who set GAAP do not agree, however.

(86) GE's note 21 gives the details of its short-term borrowings. GE's note 25 gives the details of its long-term borrowings. This paragraph helps the analyst to understand GE's intermediate-term borrowings. From these data, the analyst can estimate cash requirements for debt retirements over the next several years.

(87) Refer to the third paragraph in the left-hand column on page 52. GE states that this pension plan is "unfunded." For its primary pension plan, GE funds pension liabilities as it recognizes them. Thus the ordinary pension-related entries are, first, to debit Pension Expense and to credit Pension Liability:

Pension Expense	X	
Pension Liability		X

and then to fund the liability with a debit to Pension Liability and a credit to Cash:

Pension Liability	Y	
Cash		Y

The actual funding need not be equal to the amount of pension expense recognized in the entry just preceding.

For this supplementary pension plan, GE makes the first entry, but does not fund the liability, so it does not make the second entry. Therefore GE includes an explicit pension liability in its balance sheet on page 29 among these other liabilities.

(88) Much of this item relates to bad debt expense and to warranty costs. GE uses the "allowance method" of recognizing bad debt expense and warranty expense for financial reporting. Neither bad debt expense nor estimated warranty expense recognized by the "allowance method" qualifies as a tax deduction.

We illustrate the accounting with warranty costs. As GE sells products carrying warranties, it makes the following entry recognizing the estimated liability for future repairs and replacements:

Note 22 Accounts Payable

December 31 (In millions)	1989	1988
GE		
Trade accounts	$2,606	$1,939
Collected for the account of others	195	180
Other (including associated companies)	100	17
	2,901	2,136
GEFS		
Accounts and drafts payable	4,144	4,132
Eliminations	(379)	(264)
	$6,666	$6,004

Note 23 GEFS Securities Sold but Not Yet Purchased, at Market

December 31 (In millions)	1989	1988
U.S. government and federal agency securities	$3,508	$1,560
State and municipal securities	4	9
Corporate stocks, bonds and foreign securities	578	519
	$4,090	$2,088

Note 24 GE All Other Current Costs and Expenses Accrued

At year-ends 1989 and 1988, this account included taxes accrued of $1,521 million and $1,568 million, respectively, and compensation and benefit accruals of $948 million and $982 million, respectively. Also included are amounts for product warranties, estimated costs on shipments billed to customers and a wide variety of other sundry items.

Note 25 Long-Term Borrowings

December 31 (In millions)	1989	1988
GE	$ 3,947	$ 4,330
GEFS	12,165	10,862
Eliminations	(2)	(110)
	$16,110	$15,082

Outstanding balances in long-term borrowings for GE at December 31, 1989 and 1988 are as follows.

December 31 (In millions)	Weighted average interest rate	Maturities	1989	1988
Notes	6.97%	1991-1992	$1,056	$1,163
Extendible notes (a)	7.69	1998-2006	600	800
Debentures/sinking fund debentures	8.43	1992-2016	513	545
Foreign currency notes (b)	8.14	1992-1993	900	900
Deep discount notes (c)	7.51	1993-1994	350	350
Industrial development/ pollution control bonds	6.17	1991-2019	236	262
Other	(d)		292	310
			$3,947	$4,330

(a) GE will reset interest rates at end of initial and each subsequent interest period. At each rate-reset date, notes are redeemable in whole or in part at GE's option or repayable at option of the holders at face value plus accrued interest. Current interest periods range from May 1, 1991 to April 8, 1993. Notes are included in the current portion of long-term debt when the interest-rate-reset date is within one year.

(b) In connection with a European Currency Unit 150 million note issue (7⅝% coupon rate) due in 1992, GE entered into a currency and interest-rate swap agreement under which GE assumes a fixed Japanese yen liability (22,262 million) for payment of principal in 1992 and pays interest in yen at a rate somewhat below the six-month yen LIBOR.

A Euro-yen 35 billion note issue due in 1993 is equal to US $194 million at a fixed exchange rate of yen 180.41 = US $1.00.

In connection with a US $500 million note issue (9⅛% coupon rate) due in 1993, GE entered into currency and interest-rate swap agreements under which GE assumes a fixed Dutch guilder liability (632 million) and a fixed German mark liability (373 million) for payment of principal in 1993. GE pays interest in the respective currencies at somewhat below the respective currency three-month LIBOR.

(c) Including amortization of original issue discount, the effective interest rates are: 4⅛% Euro-dollar notes (US $200 million) – 7.41%, 2¾% U.S. dollar notes ($150 million) – 7.66%.

(d) "Other" includes original issue premium and discounts and a variety of borrowings by affiliates and parent components with various interest rates and maturities. Through 1988, "other" also included an adjustment to bring RCA borrowings at acquisition date to fair market value. Such RCA borrowings have now all been retired.

Long-term borrowing maturities during the next five years, including the portion classified as current, are $150 million in 1990, $861 million in 1991, $442 million in 1992, $982 million in 1993 and $179 million in 1994. These amounts are after deducting debentures that have been reacquired for sinking-fund needs.

Note 26 GE All Other Liabilities

For GE except GEFS, this account includes noncurrent compensation and benefit accruals at year-ends 1989 and (87) 1988 of $1,511 million and $1,516 million, respectively. Other noncurrent liabilities include amounts for product warranties, deferred incentive compensation, deferred investment tax credit, deferred income and a wide variety of other sundry items.

Note 27 Deferred Income Taxes

The tax effects of principal temporary differences between the carrying amounts of assets and liabilities and their tax bases are summarized below.

December 31 (In millions)		1989	1988
GE except GEFS			
Provisions for expenses	(88)	$(1,785)	$(1,723)
Accumulated depreciation	(89)	929	852
Assets and liabilities related to pensions	(90)	409	331
Other — net		(189)	(101)
Net deferred tax asset	(91)	(636)	(641)
GEFS			
Financing leases		3,651	3,624
Tax transfer leases		332	335
Operating leases		331	177
Provision for losses		(392)	(377)
Other — net		257	255
Net deferred tax liability		4,179	4,014
Net deferred tax liability		$ 3,543	$ 3,373

Note 28 Minority Interest in Equity of Consolidated Affiliates

December 31 (In millions)	1989	1988
GE	$ 283	$ 228
GEFS	718	753
	$1,001	$ 981

Minority interest in equity of consolidated GEFS affiliates includes the issuance by GE Capital in 1988 of six thousand shares of $100 par value variable cumulative preferred stock for net proceeds of approximately $600 million. No additional preferred shares were issued in 1989. Dividend rates on this preferred stock during 1989 ranged from 6.42% to 7.85%.

Note 29 Share Owners' Equity

GE preferred stock up to 50,000,000 shares ($1.00 par value) is authorized, but no such shares have been issued. Authorized shares of common stock (par value $0.63) total 1,100,000,000.

Shares of GE common stock December 31 (In thousands)	1989	1988	1987
Issued	926,564	926,564	926,564
In treasury	(21,783)	(24,448)	(23,611)
Outstanding	904,781	902,116	902,953

GE share owners' equity is as follows.

GE share owners' equity (92) (In millions)	1989	1988	1987
Common stock issued			
Balance at January 1	$ 584	$ 584	$ 579
Adjustment for stock split	—	—	5
Balance at December 31	$ 584	$ 584	$ 584
Other capital			
Balance at January 1	$ 823	$ 878	$ 733
Adjustment for stock split	—	—	(5)
Foreign currency translation adjustments	(4)	(39)	145
Unrealized gains (losses) on securities held by insurance affiliates	5	18	(33)
Gains (losses) on treasury stock (93) dispositions	2	(34)	30
Other	—	—	8
Balance at December 31	$ 826	$ 823	$ 878
Retained earnings			
Balance at January 1	$17,950	$15,878	$14,172
Net earnings	3,939	3,386	2,915
Dividends declared	(1,537)	(1,314)	(1,209)
Balance at December 31	$20,352	$17,950	$15,878
Common stock held in treasury			
Balance at January 1	$ 891	$ 860	$ 375
Purchases — net	362	387	846
Dispositions			
Employee savings plans	(124)	(213)	(148)
Stock options and appreciation rights	(212)	(77)	(96)
Employee stock ownership plan	—	(11)	(39)
Dividend reinvestment and share purchase plan	(47)	(49)	(42)
Contribution to GE Pension Trust	—	—	(25)
Conversion of long-term debt	—	(1)	(24)
Incentive compensation plans	2	(5)	13
Balance at December 31	$ 872	$ 891	$ 860

In November 1989, GE's Board of Directors authorized the repurchase of up to $10 billion of Company common stock over a five-year period. This repurchase program is designed to be flexible. Shares will be acquired with

Estimated Warranty Expense (Provision)	X
Estimated Warranty Liability	X
Entry made in the period of sale for expected warranty costs.	

Later, when GE makes repairs and incurs warranty costs, the entry is:

Estimated Warranty Liability	Y
Assets Used and Liabilities Incurred	Y
To recognize cost of actual repairs and replacements.	

The repair and, therefore, the second entry often occur in a year subsequent to the year of sale. The cost of providing the warranty services does not become a tax deduction until GE actually makes the repair. This creates timing differences: GE subtracts an expense on the financial statements in the year of sale but deducts it on the tax return in a later year.

⑧⑨ Depreciation on the tax return exceeded the amount included in cost of goods sold and other expenses on the financial statements. Most companies have tax depreciation exceeding book depreciation because they use an accelerated method for taxes and the straight line for financial reporting. GE, however, uses an accelerated method (based on the sum of the years' digits) in its financial statements; see the Summary of Significant Accounting Policies on page 48. The excess of tax deductions for depreciation over book depreciation expense for GE arises from GE's using shorter depreciable lives for tax than for book calculations. See the Glossary at *asset depreciation range*.

    Note that the deferred tax balance increased [*decreased* — handwritten; *1992 $12 (829 - 841)*] during 1989 by $77 (= $929 - $852) million. If we assume no significant retirements of depreciable assets during 1989, we can approximate the excess of (tax depreciation deductions) over the (book depreciation expense) reported in the financial statements by using the $77 million timing difference for 1989. If income tax expense exceeds income taxes payable by $77 million because of depreciation timing differences and if the marginal income tax rate is 34 percent of pretax income, then depreciation on the tax return must have exceeded depreciation on the financial statements by $226 million, which we can deduce by solving for x where

$$.34x = \$77 \text{ million or}$$
$$x = \$77 \text{ million}/.34, \text{ or}$$
$$x = \$226 \text{ million}.$$

[handwritten: $.34x = -12$ million; $x = -12/.34$; $x = -35.3$ million]

Because GE retired depreciable assets, the difference is actually larger than $226 million.

⑨⓪ GE has had smaller financial income expenses for pensions than its income tax deductions. This results in a deferred tax liability.

⑨① Primarily because of the accounting for bad debts and warranties (explained in our comment 88), GE's cumulative income tax payments over all the time that has elapsed since it began accounting for deferred income taxes have exceeded cumulative income tax expense reported in the financial statements. This cumulative excess decreased in 1989. This has resulted in a "deferred tax debit" (whereas most companies have the reverse situation and a "deferred tax credit") of $636 million. [handwritten: 329]

⑨② APB *Opinion No. 12* (1966) requires the disclosure of all changes in owners' equity accounts.

⑨③ Firms may not recognize gain or loss on transactions in its own shares (called *treasury shares*). GE's accounting is correct, but the use of the terms *gain* and *loss* may mislead. When GE reissues previously acquired treasury shares, the adjustment to achieve equal debits and credits is not to a gain or loss account (to appear on the income statement), but to the account "Other capital." If GE acquires treasury shares for an outlay of $1,000 and then reissues them for $1,200, then the entries would be:

Common Stock Held in Treasury	1,000	
Cash		1,000

To record acquisition of treasury shares.

Cash	1,200	
Common Stock Held in Treasury		1,000
Other Capital		200

To record reissue of treasury shares for an amount greater than outlay to acquire them. If proceeds of reissue are $800, not $1,200, then the second entry debits the $200 to the "Other capital" account.

94. *ARB No. 43* (1953) requires the disclosure of the details of stock option plans and of the currently outstanding options.

95. At the end of 1989, the market price of a share of GE common stock was $64.50. The average price of the 20,091,000 options exercisable at the end of 1989 as $43.34. Thus, if individuals exercised all of their options, the present owners' equity would decline approximately $425 million [= ($64.50 - $43.34) x 20,091,000 shares] in contrast to the issue of new shares at the current market price. GAAP never recognizes this $425 million as compensation expense to the employees who receive the benefits.

96. GE's annual report includes five more pages of information about segments and unaudited quarterly results.

funds from a combination of borrowings and free cash flow. Should world economic conditions, a major acquisition or other circumstances warrant, the Company would modify the pace and dimension of the repurchase program to maintain the solidity of its financial position. As of December 31, 1989, 3,765 thousand shares having an aggregate cost of $236 million had been repurchased under the program and placed in treasury.

In April 1987, GE share owners authorized: (a) an increase in the number of authorized shares of common stock from 550,000,000 shares each with a par value of $1.25 to 1,100,000,000 shares each with a par value of $0.63; (b) the split of each previously issued common share, including shares held in treasury, into two shares of common stock each with a par value of $0.63; and (c) an increase in the number of authorized shares of preferred stock from 2,000,000 shares with a par value of $1.00 per share to 50,000,000 shares with a par value of $1.00 per share. All share data have been adjusted for this change.

The effects of translating to U.S. dollars the financial statements of foreign affiliates whose functional currency is the local currency are included in other capital. Cumulative foreign currency translation adjustments were $133 million, $137 million and $176 million of additions to other capital at December 31, 1989, 1988 and 1987, respectively.

⑭ Note 30 Other Stock-Related Information

Stock option plans, appreciation rights and performance units are described in the Company's current Proxy Statement. Requirements for stock option shares may be met within certain restrictions either from unissued or treasury shares. During 1989, options were granted to 3,800 employees and 15 nonemployee Directors. As of December 31, 1989, a total of 456 individuals were eligible to receive class-grant options, and all exempt salaried employees were eligible for special option grants. A total of 4,633 persons held options exercisable at the end of 1989 or in the future.

Stock option information		Average per share	
(Shares in thousands)	Shares subject to option	Option price	Market price
Balance at January 1, 1989	19,936	$36.41	$44.75
Options granted	5,038	57.19	57.19
Options exercised	(3,954)	28.28	55.64
Options surrendered on exercise of appreciation rights	(712)	30.77	56.37
Options terminated	(217)	44.45	—
Balance at December 31, 1989 ⑮	20,091	43.34	64.50

Outstanding options and rights expire and the award period for outstanding performance units ends on various dates from January 1, 1990 to December 15, 1999. Shares available for granting additional options at the end of 1989 were 6,473,950 (11,936,568 at the end of 1988).

Note 31 Commitments and Contingent Liabilities

At December 31, 1989, there were no known contingent liabilities (including guarantees, pending litigation, taxes and other claims) that, in the opinion of management, would be material in relation to General Electric Company and consolidated affiliates' financial position, nor were there any material commitments outside the normal course of business.

Note 32 Supplemental Cash Flows Information

"All other operating activities" in the Statement of Cash Flows consists principally of adjustments to current and noncurrent accruals of costs and expenses, amortization of premium and discount on debt, and adjustments to assets such as amortization of goodwill and intangibles.

Information about acquisitions and dispositions can be found in note 2. The Statement of Cash Flows excludes certain noncash transactions that had no significant effects on the investing or financing activities of GE or GEFS. The transfer of GE Americom from GE to GEFS at the end of 1989 increased GEFS' equity by $332 million.

Cash used in each of the last three years included:

(In millions)	1989	1988	1987
Interest (paid)			
GE	$ (793)	$ (640)	$ (577)
GEFS	(5,876)	(4,030)	(3,301)
	$(6,669)	$(4,670)	$(3,878)
Income taxes (paid) recovered (federal, foreign, state and local)			
GE	$(1,163)	$(1,284)	$(1,096)
GEFS	(168)	251	403
	$(1,331)	$(1,033)	$ (693)

"Net change in certain broker-dealer accounts" included:

(In millions)	1989	1988	1987
Marketable securities of broker-dealer	$(3,356)	$(1,009)	$ 1,826
Securities purchased under agreements to resell	(2,209)	(922)	72
Securities sold under agreements to repurchase	2,691	677	117
Securities sold but not yet purchased	2,002	681	(2,118)
	$ (872)	$ (573)	$ (103)

⑯

Balance Sheet for a Company Approaching Bankruptcy

On June 21, 1970, the Penn Central Company filed a bankruptcy petition for its major subsidiary, the Penn Central Transportation Company. On March 12, 1970, only three months before, Penn Central Transportation Company had issued its 1969 financial statements. The balance sheet and income statement from those statements appear here. They reinforce one important point: analysis of the shareholders' equity section of a balance sheet need not indicate impending insolvency or bankruptcy.

At the end of 1969, Penn Central Transportation Company had retained earnings of almost half a billion dollars which was a part of shareholders' equity of over $1.8 billion. Much of this equity, however, represented investments in track and roadbed, illiquid assets, for which there is no ready market. Penn Central could not dispose of these assets to raise funds. You can compute that at the end of 1968 and 1969, the Transportation Company had negative working capital; that is, current liabilities (as shown, plus debt due within one year) exceeded current assets. Working capital increased by about $18 million during 1969, but net quick assets—cash and receivables less current liabilities—decreased. The Company was in a less liquid position at the end of the year than at the start.

At the end of 1969, the Transportation Company had over $100 million of debt to repay during the following year. Although the Transportation Company had sufficient "net worth" to show almost half a billion dollars of retained earnings and almost two billion dollars of shareholders' equity, it did not have the funds to meet "only" a few hundred million dollars in current obligations. The company was approaching insolvency by the end of 1969, as you can see from these statements.

Like Penn Central Transportation Company, many bankrupt firms have positive net assets, or shareholder's equity, on the books at the time of bankruptcy.

Balance Sheet

Assets		December 31	1969	1968
Current Assets	Cash and temporary cash investments		$ 80,331,000	$ 46,915,000
	Accounts receivable and unbilled revenue ..		293,181,000	240,211,000
	Material and supplies, etc., at cost		104,303,000	88,692,000
	Total Current Assets		477,815,000	375,818,000
Noncurrent Assets	Investments and advances, at cost or less (notes 2 and 7).....................		1,139,038,000	1,217,796,000
	New Haven—net assets acquired, at cost (note 1)..........................		—	127,544,000
	Properties (notes 3, 6, 7 and 12)			
	Road, structures, etc................		2,066,769,000	1,904,536,000
	Revenue equipment (rolling stock)......		1,662,759,000	1,745,448,000
	Other		96,051,000	90,541,000
			3,825,579,000	3,740,525,000
	Less accumulated depreciation and losses upon merger		902,731,000	992,036,000
	Total Properties—Net		2,922,848,000	2,748,489,000
	Deferred charges and sundry assets		56,939,000	43,703,000
	Total Assets		$4,596,640,000	$4,513,350,000

Liabilities and Shareholder's Equity

			1969	1968
Current Liabilities*	Notes payable (none to subsidiaries in 1969; $19,420,000 in 1968)		$ 102,048,000	$ 87,420,000
	Accounts payable and accrued expenses		396,407,000	356,519,000
	Total Current Liabilities* (excluding debt due within one year)		498,455,000	443,939,000
Long-Term Debt	Due within one year..................		106,058,000	76,716,000
	Due after one year		1,585,585,000	1,407,610,000
	Total Long-Term Debt (note 7)		1,691,643,000	1,484,326,000
Other	Estimated liabilities incurred upon merger (note 6)..........................		101,935,000	119,346,000
	Casualty and other claims..............		90,667,000	81,803,000
	Amounts payable to subsidiary companies ..		167,711,000	122,582,000
	Other		240,857,000	231,015,000
	Total Other		601,170,000	554,746,000
Shareholder's Equity	Capital stock—$10 par value. Authorized 27,000,000 shares; issued 24,113,703 shares (1968—24,085,329) (note 8)		241,137,000	240,853,000
	Additional paid-in capital (note 8)........		1,068,730,000	1,068,257,000
	Retained earnings (note 13)		495,505,000	721,229,000
	Total Shareholder's Equity		1,805,372,000	2,030,339,000
	Total Liabilities and Shareholder's Equity		$4,596,640,000	$4,513,350,000

Statement of Earnings and Retained Earnings

Current Earnings	Year ended December 31	1969	1968
Income	Railway operating revenues	$1,651,978,000	$1,514,071,000
	Income from rental of properties, net	33,772,000	27,131,000
	Dividends and interest—consolidated subsidiaries	66,324,000	40,155,000
	Dividends and interest—other	2,661,000	15,451,000
	Net gain on sales of properties and investments	12,587,000	35,437,000
	Income under tax allocation agreements (note 5)	21,543,000	19,038,000
	Total Income	1,788,865,000	1,651,283,000
Costs and Expenses	Railway operating expenses, excluding items listed below	1,296,397,000	1,173,761,000
	Depreciation, including depreciation on leased lines (note 3)	91,279,000	94,135,000
	Taxes, except Federal income	144,059,000	125,602,000
	Equipment and other rents, net (note 13)	183,802,000	169,292,000
	Interest on debt	96,764,000	68,787,000
	Guaranteed dividends and interest— leased lines	26,173,000	26,315,000
	Miscellaneous, net	6,719,000	(1,454,000)
	Total Costs and Expenses	1,845,193,000	1,656,438,000l
Earnings (Loss)	From ordinary operations (note 13)	(56,328,000)	(5,155,000)
	Extraordinary item (loss on investment in long-haul passenger service facilities) (note 12) ..	(126,000,000)	—
Net Earnings (Loss)	*For the year (notes 12 and 13)*	(182,328,000)	(5,155,000)

Retained Earnings

		1969	1968
	From prior years:		
	As previously reported	730,047,000	788,220,000
	Adjustment (note 13)	(8,818,000)	(6,436,000)
		538,901,000	776,629,000
	Cash dividends	43,396,000	55,400,000
	Balance at end of year	$ 495,505,000	$ 721,229,000

Accounting Magic

Generally accepted accounting principles permit alternative treatments for certain accounting events. The treatment a company chooses affects the financial statements that the company issues. This section shows how alternative accounting treatments of identical events can lead to reported income figures that are perhaps surprisingly different from each other.[1]

The Scenario

On January 1, two companies started in business. The two companies are alike except for their accounting treatment of several events. Conservative Company chooses the accounting alternatives that will minimize its reported income while High Flyer Company chooses the alternatives that will maximize its reported income. Both companies choose, where permitted, accounting methods that will minimize income taxes. The following events occur during the year.

1. Both companies issue common stock to raise funds necessary to commence a merchandising business.
2. Both companies purchase $6,000,000 of equipment that they assume will have zero salvage value and useful life of 8 years.
3. Both companies make the following purchases of merchandise inventory:

Date	Units Purchased		Unit Price		Cost of Purchase
January 1	85,000	@	$60	=	$ 5,100,000
May 1	95,000	@	$63	=	5,985,000
September 1	100,000	@	$68	=	6,800,000
Total	280,000				$17,885,000

4. During the year, both companies sell 210,000 units at an average price of $100 each so that each realizes sales revenues of $21,000,000.
5. During the year, both companies have selling, general and administrative expenses, excluding officers' salaries, of $3,350,000.
6. At the end of the year, both companies "pay" bonuses of $150,000 to officers for jobs well done in addition to the $350,000 paid to them during the year in salaries. Conservative Company pays

---

[1] The idea and title for this example come from an article by Leonard Spacek, Business Success Requires an Understanding of Unsolved Problems of Accounting and Financial Reporting, Arthur Anderson Pamphlet (September 25, 1959), pp. 19-28. Since the time Spacek prepared his illustration, generally accepted accounting principles have changed, but several of the alternatives we illustrate he illustrated, too.

cash bonuses of $150,000 while High Flyer Company awards options for purchasing shares of common stock to its officers. Comparable options have market value of $150,000.

Accounting Alternatives

At the end of the year both companies prepare financial statements. Both must decide how to report the various events that occurred during the year. The following decisions made by each company are all generally acceptable.

Inventory Cost Flow Assumption. Both companies purchased during the year more goods than they sold. Each company must make an assumption about the cost of goods sold it will show on the income statement and, simultaneously, about the cost of ending inventory it will show on the balance sheet. Conservative Company makes a last-in, first-out (LIFO) cost flow assumption while High Flyer Company makes a first-in, first-out (FIFO) assumption.

Because the beginning inventory is zero, the cost of goods available for sale by each company equals the purchases of $17,885,000 during the year. Both companies have 70,000 units in ending inventory. Conservative Company, using LIFO, reports a cost of goods sold of $13,685,000 (= $17,885,000 - 70,000 x $60) while High Flyer Company reports a cost of goods sold of $13,125,000 (= $17,885,000 - 70,000 x $68).

Income tax regulations require a company to use LIFO in its financial statements if it uses LIFO for its tax return. High Flyer wants to report high income so does not use LIFO in its financial statements and, therefore, foregoes the savings in taxes from using LIFO on its tax returns.

Depreciation. Conservative Company depreciates its equipment using the double-declining-balance method on its financial statements while High Flyer Company uses the straight-line method. Conservative Company takes a full year of depreciation in the year it acquires equipment, while High Flyer Company uses a half-year convention under which it takes only one-half year of depreciation in the first year. (The modified accelerated cost recovery system used by both companies for income tax reporting effectively requires that both take one-half year of depreciation on their tax returns.) Conservative Company therefore reports depreciation expense of $1,500,000 (= 2 x 1/8 x $6,000,000) while High Flyer Company reports depreciation expense of $375,000 (= 1/8 x $6,000,000 x 1/2).

Officers' Bonuses. Conservative Company reports expense of $150,000 for the cash bonuses it pays while High Flyer Company reports no expense for the stock options it granted. Generally accepted accounting principles do not allow the firm to show the fair market value of qualified stock options granted to employees as an expense. (When the employees exercise the options, there will be an accounting transaction but the entry will record merely the cash the firm received when the employees exercise their options.)

Published Income Statements

Income Tax Calculation. We assume a combined federal and state income tax rate of 40 percent. Both companies show deductions for MACRS depreciation of equipment on the income tax return different from the amounts reported to shareholders. These are *timing differences*. That is, in subsequent years, the companies may report on their tax return amounts different in opposite directions from the amounts they report to shareholders. Consequently, each company reports deferred income taxes on its income statement and will show deferred tax liabilities on its balance sheet.

High Flyer Company reports smaller depreciation on the income statement than the amount of depreciation claimed on the tax return and will have deferred tax credits on its balance sheet. (Most published annual reports reflect this situation.) Conservative Company reports larger depreciation on the income statement than the amount it claims on the tax return and will have deferred tax debits on its balance sheet. (This case is rarely observed. The phenomenon arises here because there is only one item of equipment being depreciated and the first-year conventions for tax reporting and financial reporting differ.) The following equation holds for both companies:

Income Tax Expense	=	Income Tax Payable	+	Deferred Tax Credits	−	Deferred Tax Debits

Conservative Company:

$786	=	$906	+	$0	−	$120

High Flyer Company:

$1,520	=	$1,190	+	$330	−	$0

The income statements for both companies appear below. As a result of its conservative treatment of accounting alternatives, Conservative Company reports net income and earnings per share about half of High Flyer Company's. Both companies used generally accepted accounting principles and each would receive a "clean" opinion from its auditor.

Accounting Magic Comparative Income Statements
For the Year Ending December 31
(Amounts in Thousands Except Per Share Amounts)

	Conservative Company		High Flyer Company	
	Financial Statement	Tax Return	Financial Statement	Tax Return
Sales Revenues	$21,000	$21,000	$21,000	$21,000
Expenses				
Cost of Goods Sold	$13,685	$13,685	$13,125	$13,125
Depreciation on Equipment	1,500	1,200[a]	375	1,200a
Officers' Compensation:				
Salaries	350	350	350	350
Cash Bonuses	150	150	—	—
Stock Options	—	—	0	0
Other Selling, General and Administrative Expenses	3,350	3,350	3,350	3,350
Expenses Before Income Taxes	$19,035	$18,735	$17,200	$18,025
Income Before Taxes	$1,965	$2,265	$3,800	$2,975
Income Tax Expense[b]	786		1,520	
Net Income	$1,179		$2,280	
Earnings Per Share in Dollars (500,000 Shares Outstanding)	$2.36		$4.56	

[a]Amounts based on MACRS, 5-year class; 20-percent of cost is deducted in first year: .20 x $6,000 = $1,200).

[b]Computation of Income Tax Expense:

Income Before Taxes	$1,965	$2,265	$3,800	$2,975
Income Tax Expense on Current Income (at 40 percent)	$786		$1,520	
Income Tax Currently Payable		$906		$1,190
Income Taxes Deferred by Timing Difference for Depreciation:				
Dr. = .40 x ($1,200 − $1,500)	$(120)			
Cr. = .40 x ($1,200 − $375)			$330	

Comparisons of Fund Flows

Until the two companies paid their respective executive bonuses and income taxes, they were alike in all economically significant respects. Because of the difference in executives' bonuses—Conservative Company paid in cash, while High Flyer granted stock options with the same value—Conservative Company paid out $150,000 more cash than did High Flyer for this item. High Flyer Company, in order to report higher net income, had to pay income taxes $284,000 (= $1,190,000 - $906,000) larger than did Conservative Company. Thus, after tax payments, Conservative Company, in a real sense, is wealthier than is High Flyer. Overall, then, Conservative Company ends the year with $134,000 (= $284,000 - $150,000) more cash, or other liquid net assets, than does High Flyer.

You might find it instructive to construct statements of cash flows for each of the two companies. You will find that Conservative Company generates $134,000 (= $284,000 tax savings - $150,000 higher bonus) more cash, from operations than does High Flyer.

Managing Reported Earnings

The simple illustration for Conservative Company and High Flyer Company by no means exhausts the set of choices available to a firm to "manage" its earnings. Managing earnings refers to a process of taking deliberate steps within the constraints of generally accepted accounting principles to bring about a desired level of reported earnings. This section describes some of the techniques for managing earnings and offers arguments for and against an earnings management policy.

Techniques for managing earnings divide into three categories: (1) selection of accounting principles, (2) application of accounting principles, and (3) timing of asset acquisitions and dispositions. Some examples of actions in each of these categories are given next.

Selection of Accounting Principles

1. Revenue recognition—percentage of completion, completed contract, time of sale, installment.
2. Inventory cost-flow assumption—FIFO, LIFO, weighted average.
3. Depreciation method—straight-line, declining-balance, sum-of-the-years'-digits.
4. Leases—operating, capital.
5. Corporate acquisitions—purchase, pooling of interests.
6. Mineral resource activities—successful-efforts costing, full costing.

Application of Accounting Principles

1. Estimates of degree of completion of contracts on which the percentage-of-completion method is used.
2. Estimates of service lives and salvage values of depreciable assets.
3. Estimates of uncollectible rate on accounts receivable.
4. Estimate of cost of warranty plans.
5. Treatment of indirect costs as product costs versus period expenses.
6. Classification of common stock investments as Marketable Securities, a current asset, or as Investment in Securities, a noncurrent asset.
7. Selection of actuarial cost basis for pension plan.
8. Selection of interest rates for capitalized leases and for pension accounting.

Timing of Asset Acquisitions and Dispositions

1. Timing of discretionary expenditures for research and development, advertising, and maintenance costs, which become expenses in the period when the firm incurs costs.

2. Timing of the sale of property, plant, and equipment or of investments to accelerate or delay the recognition of a gain or loss.

3. Accelerating or delaying shipments of merchandise to customers at the end of a period.

These lists are not exhaustive. They indicate the variety of avenues available to management to manage earnings.

Arguments For and Against Managing Earnings

The arguments for and against managing earnings vary both as to their underlying logic and to the evidence cited to support the position. We present the arguments here in as unbiased a manner as possible so that readers can make up their own minds.

Capital Market Efficiency. The major argument against managing earnings is that capital markets are efficient. Market prices adjust quickly and *in an unbiased manner* to publicly available information. Earnings management therefore wastes valuable managerial time. An expanding number of theoretical and empirical studies provide support for the efficiency of capital markets.[2] For example, several studies have examined the effects of changes in accounting methods on stock prices. Changes in accounting methods with no real or economic effects (that is, those that do not affect cash flows) appear to have little effect on stock prices.[3] Using information from the financial statements and notes, capital market participants can distinguish changes with real effects from those that are merely "paper" changes. These participants react accordingly.

Proponents of earnings management acknowledge this recent work but counter with three observations. First, all the empirical work on market efficiency has looked at the aggregate market (for example, all stocks traded on the New York Stock Exchange). In many cases, the market has not been efficient at the individual-firm level (that is, in the pricing of securities for particular firms at a particular time). Proponents of this view point to examples where the market prices of particular firms' shares decreased dramatically after the effects of using specific accounting procedures after analysis of them appeared in the financial press.[4]

Second, the empirical work on market efficiency has focused for the most part on publicly-available information. There is little or no evidence to suggest that the market is able to access "inside" or non-public information. Information about the effects of changes in accounting methods is available in the financial statements and notes and has been studied empirically. However, information about management's efforts to manage earnings by way of the judicious application of accounting principles or the timing of asset

---

[2] See Eugene F. Fama, "Efficient Capital Markets: A review of Theory and Empirical Work," Journal of Finance (May 1970): 383-417. Nicholas J. Gonedes and Nicholas Dopuch, "Capital Market Equilibrium, Information-Production and Selecting Accounting Techniques: Theoretical Framework and Review of Empirical Work," *Studies on Financial Accounting Objectives: 1974,* Supplement to Vol. 12, *Journal of Accounting Research:* 48-129; and Robert S. Kaplan, "Information Content of Financial Accounting Numbers: A Survey of Empirical Evidence," in: *Symposium of Impact of Accounting Research in Financial Accounting and Disclosure on Accounting Practice, ed.* by T. Keller and R. Abdel-Khalik (Durham: Duke University Press, 1978). See also Thomas R. Dyckman and Dale Morse, *Efficient Capital Markets and Accounting: A Critical Analysis,* 2nd ed. (Englewood Cliffs, N.J.: Prentice-Hall, 1986).

[3] See, for example, Ray Ball, "Changes in Accounting Techniques and Stock Prices," *Empirical Research in Accounting: Selected Studies, 1972,* Supplement to Vol. *10, Journal of Accounting Research:* 1-38; Robert S. Kaplan and Richard Roll, "Investor Evaluation of Accounting Information: Some Empirical Evidence," *Journal of Business* (April 1972): 225-257; Shyam Sunder, "Relationship Between Accounting Changes and Stock Prices: Problems of Measurement and Some Empirical Evidence," *Empirical Research in Accounting: Selected Studies, 1973,* Supplement to Vol. I *1, Journal of Accounting Research: 1-45.*

[4] For several examples, see Abraham J. Briloff, *More Debits Than Credits* (New York: Harper & Row, 1976). For an analysis of these examples see George Foster, "Briloff and the Capital Market," *Journal of Accounting Research* (Spring 1979): 262-274.

acquisitions or dispositions usually does not appear separately in the financial statements. Consequently, scholars have not studied such efforts.

Third, proponents of earnings management note that most of the empirical work on capital market efficiency has focused on equity securities traded on the New York Stock Exchange. Scholars have not tested the efficiency of other capital markets (for example, the over-the-counter-market) as well as short-term credit and long-term debt markets.

Proponents of earnings management conclude that capital markets are not necessarily efficient in all cases. If, by managing earnings, the firm can take advantage of these inefficiencies and obtain capital at a lower cost than when they do not practice earnings management, then the shareholders of the firm are better off.

Opponents of earnings management might be willing to accept the notion that some degree of inefficiency exists in capital markets. They then argue that capital resources might get allocated in a less-than-socially-optimal way if, because of earnings management, certain firms are able to receive more resources than they otherwise would.

Management Incentives and Survival.   Over sufficiently long time periods, net income equals cash-in minus cash-out. Some corporate managers acknowledge that earnings management is not particularly beneficial in the long run. They point out, however, that the long run comprises a series of short-run periods during which shareholders make decisions whether to retain management. (See *agency theory* in the Glossary.) Shareholders, they argue, do not want to see wide, unexpected fluctuations in earnings from year to year. Earnings management is necessary to smooth out these fluctuations and create the impression that management has operations "under control."

Corporate managers also observe that all other firms practice earnings management so that their survival dictates that they do so as well. They further point out that scholars have not produced sufficient and convincing evidence for not managing earnings. Academic researchers point to an expanding number of studies that call into question the perceived benefits of earnings management. Reconciling the two viewpoints depends on the results of continuing research on the relation between accounting numbers and stock prices.

ACCOUNTING PRONOUNCEMENTS

The following list of accounting pronouncements contains most of the generally accepted accounting principles.

Committee on Accounting Procedure (1939-1959)

Accounting Research Bulletins (ARBs)

ARB No.

43. Restatement and Revision of Accounting Research Bulletins Nos. 1-42 1953
44. Declining-Balance Depreciation . . . . 1954, Revised 1958
45. Long-Term Construction-Type Contracts 1955
46. Discontinuance of Dating Earned Surplus 1956
47. Accounting for Costs of Pension Plans 1956
48. Business Combinations 1957
49. Earnings per Share 1958
50. Contingencies 1958
51. Consolidated Financial Statements 1959

Accounting Terminology Bulletins (ATBs)

ATB No.

1. Review and Résumé 1953
2. Proceeds, Revenue, Income, Profit, and Earnings 1955
3. Book Value 1956
4. Cost, Expense and Loss 1957

Accounting Principles Board (APB), (1959-1973)

APB Opinions

Opinion No.

1. New Depreciation Guidelines and Rules 1962
2. Accounting for the "Investment Credit" 1962
3. The Statement of Source and Application of Funds 1963
4. Accounting for the "Investment Credit" (Amending *No.2*) 1964

   5. Reporting of Leases in Financial Statements of Lessee 1964
   6. Status of Accounting Research Bulletins 1965
   7. Accounting for Leases in Financial Statements of Lessors 1966
   8. Accounting for the Cost of Pension Plans 1966
   9. Reporting the Results of Operations 1966
10. Omnibus Opinion—1966 1966
11. Accounting for Income Taxes 1967
12. Omnibus Opinion—1967 1967
13. Amending Paragraph 6 of APB *Opinion No.9*, Application to Commercial Banks 1969
14. Accounting for Convertible Debt and Debt Issued with Stock Purchase Warrants 1969
15. Earnings per Share 1969
16. Business Combinations 1970
17. Intangible Assets 1970
18. The Equity Method of Accounting for Investments in Common Stock 1971
19. Reporting Changes in Financial Position 1971
20. Accounting Changes 1971
21. Interest on Receivables and Payables 1971
22. Disclosure of Accounting Policies 1972
23. Accounting for Income Taxes—Special Areas 1972
24. Accounting for Income Taxes—Investments in Common Stock Accounted for by the
     Equity Method 1972
25. Accounting for Stock Issued to Employees 1972
26. Early Extinguishment of Debt 1972
27. Accounting for Lease Transactions by Manufacturer or Dealer Lessors 1972
28. Interim Financial Reporting 1973
29. Accounting for Nonmonetary Transactions 1973
30. Reporting the Results of Operations 1973
31. Disclosure of Lease Commitments by Lessees 1973

APB Statements

Statement No.
   1. Statement by the Accounting Principles Board 1962
   2. Disclosure of Supplemental Financial Information by Diversified Companies 1967
   3. Financial Statements Restated for General Price-Level Changes 1969
   4. Basic Concepts and Accounting Principles Underlying Financial Statements of Business
     Enterprises 1970

Financial Accounting Standards Board (FASB), (1973 to present)

Statements of Financial Accounting Standards

SFAS No.
   1. Disclosure of Foreign Currency Translation Information 1973
   2. Accounting for Research and Development Costs 1974
   3. Reporting Accounting Changes in Interim Financial Statements 1974
   4. Reporting Gains and Loses from Extinguishment of Debt 1975
   5. Accounting for Contingencies 1975
   6. Classification of Short-Term Obligations Expected to Be Refinanced 1975
   7. Accounting and Reporting by Development Stage Enterprises 1975

8. Accounting for the Translation of Foreign Currency Transactions and Foreign Currency Financial Statements 1975

9. Accounting for Income Taxes—Oil and Gas Producing Companies 1975

10. Extension of "Grandfather" Provisions for Business Combinations 1975

11. Accounting for Contingencies—Transition Method 1975

12. Accounting for Certain Marketable Securities 1975

13. Accounting for Leases . . . . 1976, Reissued 1980

14. Financial Reporting for Segments of a Business Enterprise 1976

15. Accounting by Debtors and Creditors for Troubled Debt Restructurings 1977

16. Prior Period Adjustments 1977

17. Accounting for Leases—Initial Indirect Costs 1977

18. Financial Reporting for Segments of a Business Enterprise - Interim Financial Statements . 1977

19. Financial Accounting and Reporting by Oil and Gas Producing Companies 1977

20. Accounting for Forward Exchange Contracts 1977

21. Suspension of the Reporting of Earnings Per Share and Segment Information by Nonpublic Enterprises 1978

22. Changes in the Provisions of Lease Agreements Resulting from Refundings of Tax-Exempt Debt 1978

23. Inception of the Lease 1978

24. Reporting Segment Information in Financial Statements That Are Presented in Another Enterprise's Financial Report 1978

25. Suspension of Certain Accounting Requirements for Oil and Gas Producing Companies . . . 1979

26. Profit Recognition on Sales-Type Leases of Real Estate 1979

27. Classification of Renewals or Extensions of Existing Sales-Type or Direct Financing Leases 1979

28. Accounting for Sales with Leasebacks 1979

29. Determining Contingent Rentals 1979

30. Disclosure of Information About Major Customers 1979

31. Accounting for Tax Benefits Related to U.K. Tax Legislation Concerning Stock Relief . . . 1979

32. Specialized Accounting and Reporting Principles and Practices in AICPA Statements of Position and Guides on Accounting and Auditing Matters 1979

33. Financial Reporting and Changing Prices 1979

34. Capitalization of Interest Cost 1979

35. Accounting and Reporting by Defined Benefit Pension Plans 1980

36. Disclosure of Pension Information 1980

37. Balance Sheet Classification of Deferred Income Taxes 1980

38. Accounting for Preacquisition Contingencies of Purchased Enterprises 1980

39. Financial Reporting and Changing Prices: Specialized Assets—Mining and Oil and Gas . . 1980

40. Financial Reporting and Changing Prices: Specialized Assets—Timberlands and Growing Timber 1980

41. Financial Reporting and Changing Prices: Specialized Assets—Income- Producing Real Estate . 1980

42. Determining Materiality for Capitalization of Interest Cost 1980

43. Accounting for Compensated Absences 1980

44. Accounting for Intangible Assets of Motor Carriers 1980

45. Accounting for Franchise Fee Revenue 1981

46. Financial Reporting and Changing Prices: Motion Picture Films 1981

47. Disclosure of Long-Term Obligations 1981

48. Revenue Recognition When Right of Return Exists 1981

49. Accounting for Product Financing Arrangements 1981

50. Financial Reporting in the Record and Music Industry 1981

51. Financial Reporting by Cable Television Companies 1981
52. Foreign Currency Translation 1981
53. Financial Reporting by Producers and Distributors of Motion Picture Films 1981
54. Financial Reporting and Changing Prices: Investment Companies 1982
55. Determining Whether a Convertible Security Is a Common Stock Equivalent 1982
56. Designation of AICPA Guide and Statement of Position (SOP) 81-1 on Contractor
    Accounting and SOP 81-2 Concerning Hospital-Related Organizations as Preferable
    for Purposes of Applying APB *Opinion 20* 1982
57. Related Party Disclosures 1982
58. Capitalization of Interest Cost in Financial Statements That Include Investments Ac-
    counted for by the Equity Method 1982
59. Deferral of the Effective Date of Certain Accounting Requirements for Pension Plans of
    State and Local Governmental Units 1982
60. Accounting and Reporting by Insurance Enterprises 1982
61. Accounting for Title Plant 1982
62. Capitalization of Interest Cost in Situations Involving Certain Tax-Exempt Borrowings
    and Certain Gifts and Grants 1982
63. Financial Reporting by Broadcasters 1982
64. Extinguishments of Debt Made to Satisfy Sinking-Fund Requirements 1982
65. Accounting for Certain Mortgage Banking Activities 1982
66. Accounting for Sales of Real Estate 1982
67. Accounting for Costs and Initial Rental Operations of Real Estate Projects 1982
68. Research and Development Arrangements 1982
69. Disclosures About Oil and Gas Producing Activities 1982
70. Financial Reporting and Changing Prices: Foreign Currency Translation 1982
71. Accounting for the Effects of Certain Types of Regulation 1982
72. Accounting for Certain Acquisitions of Banking or Thrift Institutions 1983
73. Reporting a Change in Accounting for Railroad Track Structures 1983
74. Accounting for Special Termination Benefits Paid to Employees 1983
75. Deferral of the Effective Date of Certain Accounting Requirements for Pension Plans of
    State and Local Governmental Units (Amendments of *SFAS No. 35*) 1983
76. Extinguishment of Debt 1983
77. Reporting by Transferors for Transfers of Receivables with Recourse 1983
78. Classification of Obligations That Are Callable by the Creditor 1983
79. Elimination of Certain Disclosures for Business Combinations by Nonpublic Enterprises . . 1984
80. Accounting for Futures Contracts 1984
81. Disclosure of Postretirement Health Care and Life Insurance Benefits 1984
82. Financial Reporting and Changing Prices: Elimination of Certain Disclosures (An amend-
    ment of FASB *Statement No. 33*) 1984
83. Designation of AICPA Guides and Statement of Position on Accounting by Brokers and
    Dealers in Securities, by Employee Benefit Plans, and by Banks as Preferable for Pur-
    poses of Applying APB *Opinion 20* (An Amendment of FASB *Statement No. 32* and
    APB *Opinion No. 30* and a rescission of FASB *Interpretation No.10*) 1985
84. Induced Conversions of Convertible Debt (an amendment of APB *Opinion No. 26*) 1985
85. Yield Test for Determining Whether a Convertible Security Is a Common Stock Equiva-
    lent (An amendment of APB *Opinion No. 15*) 1985
86. Accounting for the Costs of Computer Software to Be Sold, Leased, or Otherwise Marketed . . 1985
87. Employer's Accounting for Pensions 1985
88. Employer's Accounting for Settlements and Curtailments of Defined Benefit Pension
    Plans and for Termination Benefits 1985

89. Financial Reporting and Changing Prices 1986
90. Regulated Enterprises - Accounting for Abandonments and Disallowances of Plant Costs
    (An amendment of FASB *Statement No. 71*) 1986
91. Accounting for Nonrefundable Fees and Costs Associated with Originating or Acquiring
    Loans and Initial Direct Costs of Leases (an amendment of FASB *Statements No. 13,
    60, and 65* and a rescission of FASB *Statement No. 17*) 1986
92. Regulated Enterprises—Accounting for Phase-in Plans (an amendment of FASB *Statement
    No. 71*) 1987
93. Recognition of Depreciation by Not-for-Profit Organizations 1987
94. Consolidation of All Majority-owned Subsidiaries 1987
95. Statement of Cash Flows 1987
96. Accounting for Income Taxes 1987
97. Accounting and Reporting by Insurance Enterprises for Certain Long-Duration Contracts
    and for Realized Gains and Losses from the Sale of Investments 1987
98. Accounting for Leases: (1) Sale-Leaseback Transactions Involving Real Estate (2) Sales-
    Type Leases of Real Estate (3) Definition of the Lease Term (4) Initial Direct Costs of
    Direct Financing Leases 1988
99. Deferral of the Effective Date of Recognition of Depreciation by Not-for-Profit Organiza-
    tions 1988
100. Accounting for Income Taxes—Deferral of the Effective Date of FASB *Statement No. 96* . 1988
101. Regulated Enterprises—Accounting for the Discontinuation of Application of FASB *State-
    ment No. 71* 1988
102. Statement of Cash Flows—Exemption of Certain Enterprises and Classification of Cash
    Flows from Certain Securities Acquired for Resale 1989
103. Accounting for Income Taxes - Deferral of the Effective Date of FASB *Statement No. 96*
    (an amendment of FASB *Statement No. 96*) 1989
104. Statement of Cash Flows - Net Reporting of Certain Cash Receipts and Cash Payments
    and Classification of Cash Flows from Hedging Transactions (an amendment of FASB
    Statement No. 95) 1989
105. Disclosure of Information about Financial Instruments with Off-Balance-Sheet Risk and
    Financial Instruments with Concentrations of Credit Risk 1990

Statement of Financial Accounting Concepts

SFAC No.

1. Objectives of Financial Reporting by Business Enterprises 1978
2. Qualitative Characteristics of Accounting Information 1980
3. Elements of Financial Statements of Business Enterprises 1980
4. Objectives of Financial Reporting by Nonbusiness Organizations 1980
5. Recognition and Measurement in Financial Statement of Business Enterprises 1984
6. Elements of Financial Statements (a replacement of FASB *Concepts Statement No. 3*—in-
   corporating an amendment of FASB *Concepts Statement No. 2*) 1985